Unbelievably
Good Deals
That You Absolutely
Can't Get Unless
You're a
Parent

Unbelievably Good Deals

That You Absolutely Can't Get Unless You're a

Parent

CARY O. YAGER

CB

CONTEMPORARY BOOKS

Library of Congress Cataloging-in-Publication Data

Yager, Cary O.
    Unbelievably good deals that you absolutely can't get unless
you're a parent / Cary O. Yager
        p.   cm.
    Includes index.
    ISBN 0-8092-3205-7
        1. Parents—Services for—United States. 2. Children—
Services for—United States. 3. Family recreation—United States.
4. Children—Travel—United States. 5. Children's paraphernalia—
United States—Purchasing. 6. Deals—United States. I. Title.
HQ755.8.Y34   1997
362.82'8—dc21   97-19561
                                                     CIP

Cover design by Kim Bartko

15   14   13   12   11   10   9   8   7   6   5   4   3   2   1

*To Roy Olson, who taught me to
measure twice, saw once.
Or was it measure once, saw twice?
Thanks, Dad.*

Contents

Acknowledgments   ix

Introduction   xi

Part One: The Practical Parent   1

1. Corporate Programs   3
2. Family-Friendly Stores   11
3. Catalogs   17
4. Safety   27

Part Two: Fun, Fun, Fun   37

5. City-by-City Guide to Attractions Kids Love   39
6. Fifteen Other Attractions Kids Shouldn't Miss   109

Part Three: Traveling Family Style   121

7. Family-Friendly Resorts   123
8. Family Vacations   139
9. Establishments for Families on the Go   151
10. Trips for Kids Only   159
11. Trips for Grandparents and Their Grandchildren   163

Part Four: Resources for Parents and Kids   169

12. Books and Booklets   171
13. Magazines and Newsletters   195
14. The Internet   213
15. Support Organizations and Hot Lines for Parents   225

Index   241

Acknowledgments

This project would never have been completed without the help of my resourceful research assistant and baby-sitter, Carter Olson. Not only did she move to Chicago to help me finish this book, but she also made thousands of phone calls, pulled hundreds of pieces of data together, entertained my toddler, and never once complained about my hormonal mood swings owing to pregnancy or the lack of air-conditioning. For her competence and calming nature, I am extremely grateful.

Thanks also need to go to my husband, Ken; my son, Oley; and my baby-in-waiting for allowing me to totally disrupt their lives. Ken's unwavering support and sense of humor have made this project a positive experience for me. I would be lost without him.

My mother, with her kind soul and patience, deserves credit for taking the time for hundreds of procrastination phone calls. My father kept me going with his joke-of-the-week. Thank you also to Judy Olsen, Heidi Hookstadt, Gwen Oelerich, Lynnette Martin, and Joni Scarnato for their support.

Kathy Willhoite has been an exceedingly patient and understanding editor. I appreciate her putting up with me and advising me.

I also thank Jan and Sue and the teachers at Mother's Day Out here in Park Ridge for taking Oley in and cheering me on.

Introduction

When I became pregnant for the first time, I knew very little about babies. I didn't panic at first because I figured motherhood was in the natural order of things and I could handle it. After all, I'd already raised two puppies. I felt pretty comfortable about being able to feed, bathe, and nurture my baby. Then came the questions from well-meaning friends. Have you joined the Welcome Addition Club? Have you signed up for Gymboree? Did you get your free formula yet? Did you know that (fill in the blank) has a children's program? Have you read this month's *American Baby*? What was everyone talking about? I'd never heard of all these things. It was as if there was a secret society of parents out there who knew all about these great deals and programs for families and I wasn't a member. I decided to investigate and found hundreds of deals to make parenting just a little bit easier.

Parents need all the help they can get. I know there are lots of parents who don't even know this whole world of parental support exists. Information on safety, nutrition, childproofing, development, child rearing, and selecting toys and reading material is available for the asking. Families with special needs will find clearinghouses and organizations eager to help in any way they can. There are all kinds of fun places to play and see that cost very little. Hotels and resorts are finally realizing that if they offer parents a little more help, families are more likely to travel. According to the Travel Industry of America, parents took their children on more than 40 million business trips in 1995; that equals 15 percent of all business trips. Hotels are scrambling to make traveling easier on parents and children. As busy parents are now taking their children everywhere, companies are responding by providing sitters, family rest rooms, and activities for children. Parents can share and discuss their particular concerns in newsletters and magazines as well as on the

Internet. They can call hot lines to have immediate issues addressed by professionals. All they need is to know where to find it all. This book is here to make that easy for parents.

Deals come in all shapes and sizes. My first priority in putting this book together was deciding what the word *deal* meant. For readers' purposes, there are two types of deals. The first is a plain, old good deal in which the parent gets something for free or at very low cost. The second kind of deal is more abstract: a good deal is also a product or service with added value. For example, a family researching hotels for a summer vacation comes across two hotels that have all the amenities they are looking for and are comparable in price. One, however, offers a childproofing kit, an activity pack for children, babysitting services, and children's menus. This hotel is obviously the better deal. Most of the deals in this book fall into one of these two categories. A few other products and services are included because they are indispensable to parents.

This book does not cover every good deal available; that book would weigh about 75 pounds. I chose instead to give parents a representative sample of the deals being offered. Some very good programs and products are not included because they are more expensive and, consequently, not a bargain, per se. Another reason you may come across an item somewhere else that is not listed here is that many companies and organizations offer a wide variety of temporary promotions that come and go quickly. The items that you'll find in these pages are long-term good deals. Their prices may change a little, but they will still be good deals.

In selecting specific items of benefit to readers, I concentrated on four criteria: health, safety, education, and quality entertainment. These are the four criteria I follow when selecting products and services for my own children. There aren't any Power Rangers, toy guns, or "buy 10 boxes of cocoa-sugar cereal and get a decoder ring" offers here. The items I chose relate to the safety, health, and education of children. That doesn't mean that all the items are stiff and boring. There are all kinds of fun and exciting things for children to do that are educational. This book concentrates on activities that are active or stimulating or both. Parents are always looking for worthwhile ways to entertain their children that are inexpensive. In researching this book I found many fun, constructive activities for kids that are cheaper than movies, amusement parks, or Nintendo. This is not to say that kids shouldn't be allowed to go to the movies or a theme park—I am just suggesting supplementary activities that are inexpensive and educational.

I have aimed to make the entries as accurate and up-to-date as possible. Inevitably, between the time the book goes to the printer and the time it arrives in bookstores, some of the programs may have changed slightly or may no longer be offered. The prices and rates used are based on 1996 figures and can be expected to rise slightly.

Most of the businesses and organizations mentioned recognize that families come in all different shapes and sizes. In most cases, the programs and services apply to traditional two-parent families and to single-parent families. Many of the programs offered apply to grandparents and grandchildren as well as aunts, uncles, nieces, and nephews.

I hope parents will find the information as useful as I have. I have learned a lot since starting this project and have called or sent away for many of the items included in the book. I feel comfortable in knowing the material included is useful, practical, and helpful. My kids and I have benefited from my having worked on this project, and I know other families will too.

Unbelievably Good Deals

That You Absolutely Can't Get Unless You're a

Parent

PART ONE

The Practical Parent

Chapter One

Corporate Programs

 Many companies offer special programs to parents, most often to get them to try their products, sometimes because they believe in community outreach. Whatever the reason, parents can usually benefit. The corporations listed here have ongoing, long-term programs for parents, offering newsletters, coupons, services, and free formula. Tip: Many expectant mothers receive several cans of different kinds of formula; in most cases, the best course is to choose one brand and stick with it. However, instead of throwing away the unwanted formula, donate any unopened samples to a shelter or food drive.

Many other companies not listed here offer short-term promotions and coupons to parents. To learn if a company is running a special offer, call the company's consumer affairs office. To find the phone number, look on the product packaging or call toll-free information at (800) 555-1212.

Beech-Nut New Parents Pack

The Beech-Nut Nutrition Corporation will send expectant and new parents an introductory New Parents Pack. The pack contains a 30-page guide to feeding babies solid foods, with a chart to keep track of food reactions, a chart showing how much to feed babies at different stages, and a helpful list of do's and don'ts for feeding babies. Parents also receive product information, coupons, and a list of the 40 prerecorded messages available on the Helpline.

For information: Call the Beech-Nut Helpline at (800) 523-6633 to request a New Parents Pack.

Carnation Special Delivery Club

The Carnation Special Delivery Club offers expectant mothers a free *Mom-to-Be Planner*, nutrition information, and coupons for infant formula. The club will send parents "baby bulletins" throughout pregnancy and the first year. The mailings are filled with tips and advice on caring for babies and nutrition and include coupons for formula.

Carnation will also send coupons for their Follow-Up formulas.

For information: To enroll, call Carnation at (800) 328-7078.

Dutch Boy's "Easy-Does-It Painting Kids' Rooms"

All parents are faced with the "Can I redecorate my room?" dilemma at one point or another. Dutch Boy has the answer with ideas for innovative painting techniques that will turn any kid's room into a "cool" space. Dutch Boy will send parents a booklet on planning, preparing, and painting kids' rooms with fun and creative decorating ideas and a chart to figure out how much paint is needed for a particular space. Parents can call the Dutch Boy Paints' Consumer Helpline with any questions about Dutch Boy products or about painting in general.

For information: To order a booklet or to reach the Dutch Boy Paints' Consumer Helpline, call (800) 600-DBOY (600-3269).

Earth's Best Family Program

Earth's Best baby foods are made with organically grown products and do not contain chemical pesticides, preservatives, or fillers. The company is committed to doing good things for babies and for the environment. Parents who enroll in the Earth's Best Family Program receive a series of *The Earth's Best Family Times* newsletters, which cover a variety of topics, including introducing solid foods, games for newborns, and things parents and kids can do together to save the environment. The newsletters also contain coupons for Earth's Best products. Earth's Best operates an information line to answer consumers' questions and to receive feedback and suggestions on their products.

For information: To sign up for the Earth's Best Family Program, call (800) 442-4221.

Enfamil Family Beginnings

Mead Johnson Nutritionals has come up with, what I consider, the best new program for purchasing formula. Parents can call the Enfamil Family Beginnings toll-free number, order formula by the case over the phone, and have it shipped directly to their homes. Besides the convenience, this program is great for busy parents whose grocery store doesn't stock enough or stocks the wrong sizes of formula. Hard-to-find sizes are available, as well.

The Enfamil Family Beginnings program for new mothers is another way Mead Johnson is helping parents. In addition to mailings offering nutritional and other baby-related advice, new mothers receive a certificate for 10 percent savings at Motherhood Maternity Shops, recipe cards, baby flash cards, and a copy of *As Your Baby Grows*, a magazine with wonderful full-color photographs from Lennart Nilsson's book *A Child Is Born*, illustrating every step of fetal development. Parents are also enrolled in a "rewards" program that allows them to earn points toward gifts by purchasing Mead Johnson products. These rewards can really add up; parents who bottle-feed buy *a lot* of formula. A friend of mine received all kinds of freebies, from dish sets to books. Members will also receive retail checks for discounts on formula, a growth chart, and a holder for collecting formula labels.

For information: To enroll in the Enfamil Family Beginnings program, call (800) BABY-123 (222-9123).

Fisher-Price Family Registry

Members of the Fisher-Price Family Registry receive mailings on new products, special offers, and publications, including holiday shopping guides.

Any parent knows how easily toy parts mysteriously disappear. The bus driver vanishes in a quick flush; the pretend potato chips go down the disposal. In an effort to keep toys intact and in use, Fisher-Price publishes their *Bits & Pieces* catalog for parents who need to replace broken or lost parts.

For information: To enroll in the Fisher-Price Family Registry or to order the *Bits & Pieces* catalog, call consumer affairs at (800) 432-5437.

Healthtex Immunization Chart and Playwear Sizer Guide

Healthtex offers parents a pocket-size pull-chart outlining the immunization schedule for children from birth to 16 years of age as recommended by the American Academy of Pediatrics. The reverse side features sizing guides by height and weight for Healthtex playwear. The immunization chart is available in English and Spanish editions and is free of charge to parents.

For information: To receive an immunization schedule, send a self-addressed, stamped business-size envelope to Healthtex Immunization Chart (specify English or Spanish), PO Box 21488, Greensboro, NC 27420-1488. To find Healthtex playwear, call (800) 554-7637 for the location nearest you.

Heinz Baby Food Miracle Labels for Kids Program

The Heinz Baby Food Miracle Labels for Kids Program differs from other consumer programs in that the only benefit parents receive by participating is the knowledge that they are helping sick children at the Children's Miracle Network hospitals around

Top 10 Baby Products Under $10
(according to an informal poll of experienced mothers)

1. Playtex Spill-Proof cup
2. Dishwasher basket for nipples, bottle tops, etc.
3. Soft-bite spoons
4. Bathwater thermometer
5. Plastic bibs with pouches
6. No-Choke Test Tube
7. Outlet plug covers
8. Board books
9. Onesies
10. Fisher-Price Corn Popper

the country. For every Heinz Baby Food label returned, Heinz will donate up to 6 cents to a Children's Miracle Network hospital. Since the program began in 1979, more than $5 million has been donated to participating hospitals.

For information: To find out more about the Heinz Baby Food Miracle Labels for Kids Program, call (800) USA-BABY (872-2229).

Huggies

Huggies has periodic promotions that you can find out about by calling their consumer services department. They often will send out coupons or have proof-of-purchase special offers.

For information: Call Huggies consumer services at (800) 544-1847.

www. huggies.com

KidVantage Program from Sears, Roebuck and Co.

To help families with the sometimes overwhelming clothing budget, Sears offers the KidVantage program. Through its WearOut Warranty, Sears pledges that it will replace—at no cost—children's clothing purchased at Sears if it wears out while the child is still in the same size. The policy applies to more than 70 national brands available in the stores, including OshKosh, Levi's, Hush Puppies, Toughskins, and Winnie-the-Pooh. Sizes from newborn to 20 in boys and newborn to 16 in girls are covered.

Frequent shoppers are also rewarded. For every $100 spent on children's clothing at Sears, parents will receive a coupon for 15 percent off their next purchase, and for every $50 spent, parents receive a coupon for 10 percent off their next purchase. Customers joining the program will receive a KidVantage card where their purchases will be recorded.

For information: KidVantage cards are available at all Kids & More service counters in Sears stores.

OshKosh B'Gosh Genuine Parents Club

The OshKosh B'Gosh Genuine Parents Club began as a way to provide useful advice and valuable offers to loyal customers. Upon enrollment, the club sends parents a welcome letter and gift, such as a six-month subscription to *Parents* magazine. The club follows up by sending out periodic newsletters packed with fashion updates, consumer news, parenting tips and trivia, contests, and activities for kids. Coupons and promotional offers are frequently included in the newsletters.

For information: To enroll, call (800) AT-BGOSH (282-4674).

Stride Rite Progression Fit System

Stride Rite has developed a new line of infant shoe wear based on the Stride Rite Progression Fit System, which takes size and walking ability into account in the design and fit of their shoes. The shoes come in stage one and stage two sizes for early and advanced walkers, respectively. These new shoe sizes make room for curled-up toes, have smooth seams for comfort, and provide extra shock absorption. The experienced shoe fitters at Stride Rite will help parents find the right shoe for their child.

For information: Visit any Stride Rite store in your area.

Triaminic Parents Club

Parents who join the Triaminic Parents Club will receive a free subscription to the Triaminic Parents Club magazine, filled with advice from pediatricians, resources for products and information, articles featuring seasonal topics, coupons for Triaminic products, and special deals on products (such as Schoolhouse Rock videos, bicycle helmets, and books).

For information: Call Triaminic at (201) 575-5115.

The Welcome Addition Club

The Welcome Addition Club is sponsored by Similac Infant Formulas. As members, parents receive savings on infant formula and *The Welcome Addition,* a newsletter filled with parenting tips, reviews of books and videos, resources, and news on nutrition, parenting concerns, baby care, and new products. The newsletter contains special checks for $1 or $2 off a can of formula. Because these certificates are checks not coupons, they can be used anywhere, including drug stores or stores like Target, Walmart, and Baby Superstore, not just grocery stores. Parents also receive a starter supply of infant formula when they join, usually an entire case.

For information: To enroll, call The Welcome Addition Club at (800) BABYLINE (222-9546).

Chapter Two

Family-Friendly Stores

 A whole new breed of stores has cropped up to give parents the merchandise and services they need. Here in the family-friendly '90s, parents will find stores that have rest rooms with changing tables in both the men's and the women's lounges, play areas, shopping carts with attached infant seats, and candy-free checkout aisles. Toy stores, bookstores, and educational-games stores offer programs and activities for kids and families. Alternatives to traditional toy stores are also cropping up. Parents can find educational, nonviolent games and toys at a new breed of specialty stores, museum shops, and cable TV stores. Prices at these specialty stores tend to be higher than at toy superstores, but for parents who are looking for quality products encouraging creativity and learning, the variety is there.

The stores listed in this chapter are family-friendly stores offering discounted prices on quality merchandise, amenities to make shopping with children easier, or services that give parents a helping hand.

Baby Superstore

Baby Superstore is a new-parent's dream. I outfitted my first baby completely from this store. Stuck at home on bed rest, I sent my husband alone to Baby Superstore with a lengthy list. With the aid of the helpful staff, he returned with furniture, car seat, stroller, high chair, portable crib, toys, layette, bathtub, diapers, bottles, books, thank-you notes, bedding, and all those little baby accessories. It is the epitome of one-stop shopping. The prices are low, the selection is tremendous, and the staff is very helpful. The only problem with Baby Superstore is that there aren't enough of them.

For information: To find the location of a Baby Superstore in your area, call (864) 968-9292.

Barnes & Noble

The more than 360 Barnes & Noble stores across the country are wonderful places for kids. Not only does Barnes & Noble carry a large selection of children's and parenting books, but each store also offers a variety of activities for children, including storytelling hours that may feature Madeline or Clifford the Red Dog in person, arts and crafts, and American Girls and Goosebumps reading clubs. All events are free and open to the public. To find out about upcoming events, customers can ask for a copy of the store's monthly calendar of events.

For information: To find a Barnes & Noble in your area, check your local yellow pages.

Gymboree

Gymboree carries quality clothes for infants and children, accessories, and a few toys and bath items. Their well-made clothes are manufactured with both children and parents in mind. Many of the clothes "grow" with kids: the legs and arms have cuffs that can be rolled down to extend wearing time. Gymboree clothes are not cheap, but the stores have fabulous sales.

Gymboree also offers a gift service. By calling their toll-free number customers can choose from apparel sets for new babies. Gymboree will include a personal message, wrap the gift, and

Second-Hand Stores

One of the best ways to save money while making the seemingly endless purchases of baby and child gear is a second-hand store or consignment shop that specializes in children's products. These stores are stocked with clothes, toys, strollers, bedding, books, high chairs, furniture, car seats, and all kinds of baby equipment. Many of the items are like new; some *are* new, with the tags still attached. You can find some fabulous bargains on quality products.

As every parent knows, kids often grow out of clothes before they've had a chance to wear them more than a couple of times. Sometimes they grow out of clothes before they have a chance to wear them even once. Most parents at some point have bought their kids a toy that they thought was the most terrific toy ever, only to have the child give it a quick once over and then toss it aside forever. These almost-new items can be found at second-hand stores.

The key to getting good deals at second-hand stores is to stop by frequently and to develop a relationship with the owner. New merchandise is continually being dropped off and the quality items are not on the shelves for long. If you are on good terms with the owner, you may get a call when that particular item you've been looking for shows up at the store.

Not only are children's second-hand and consignment shops a good place to save money; they are a good place to make money by dropping off the children's goods you no longer need. Most stores pay you for your merchandise.

send it. Busy moms will find this service to be a very convenient way to send new-baby presents. Prices range from $32 to $95 for the gift sets. If the new baby has a sibling, Gymboree will include a complimentary gift just for him or her.

For information: Call Gymboree at (800) 4-GYMBOREE (449-6267) for gift service or to locate a store in your area.

Noodle Kidoodle

Noodle Kidoodle is a busy toy store filled with good deals on books, videos, software, puzzles, games, arts and crafts, electronics, and construction kits. Parents will find toys for pretending, learning about science and nature, and stimulating infants and preschoolers. With everyday guaranteed discounts, parents receive 20 percent off list price for audio- and videotapes, 10 percent off list price for books, and 15 to 50 percent off for computer software. While in the store, keep an eye out for Noodle Knockouts—special savings on particular items. Noodle Kidoodle offers free gift wrapping, special orders, gift certificates, and shipping anywhere in the United States. All stores have rest rooms equipped with changing tables.

For information: Call Noodle Kidoodle at (516) 293-5300 to locate a store in your area.

Once Upon a Child

Once Upon a Child is a national chain of stores that sells, buys, trades, and consigns nearly new goods at prices generally below retail. Baby equipment and accessories are available at great prices. The stores carry new and used clothes for children and infants, toys, furniture, and assorted baby gear. The chain also operates Play It Again Sports, which specializes in nearly new kids' sporting goods.

For information: To find the store location nearest you, call (800) 433-2540.

Target

Target is one of my all-time favorite stores. It offers a tremendous selection of baby equipment and kids' clothing at great prices. Many of its baby clothes are 100 percent cotton, which can be tough to find at such low prices. The children's clothing uses up-to-date colors, styles, and materials and is of respectable quality. I buy my kids their basic wardrobes at Target and fill in the gaps with clothes from more expensive stores. Target is also a great place for children's coats and shoes as well as anything else you might need for your home or family, including maternity clothes and seasonal decorations.

Target also offers the Lullaby Club, where parents-to-be can register for baby gifts.

For information: Call (800) 800-8800 to find the location of a store in your area.

Toys "R" Us

Toys "R" Us has every toy you can imagine under one roof at great prices. In addition to their everyday low prices, they publish coupon books several times a year and have good sales. Toys "R" Us does all kinds of other promotional campaigns as well. In the past they've produced the "Hot Spots for Kids Savings Book" with coupons for airline tickets, rental cars, and a variety of restaurants and attractions; "Safety Facts," a compilation of consumer-product safety alerts from the U.S. Consumer Product Safety Commission; and a toy guide for "differently-abled" kids.

Toys "R" Us has a baby registry for new parents. Parents can choose from a huge selection of baby furniture, strollers, infant seats, car seats, play yards, high chairs, exercisers, carriers, swings, bedding, bibs, bottles, bath accessories, layette items, safety products, feeding accessories, toiletries, diapers, and infant toys.

For information: To find a Toys "R" Us in your area, call (800) 869-7787.

Zany Brainy

Zany Brainy is a toy store with a conscience. Inside their doors, parents will find toys, books, games, computer software, videos, and crafts that are educational, gender neutral, and nonviolent. There are also areas where kids can try products before they buy them. The stores also host activities for children.

For information: To find the Zany Brainy nearest you, call (610) 896-1500.

Chapter Three

Catalogs

Busy moms and dads will appreciate the convenience of catalogs for purchasing children's clothing, accessories, toys, and books. Parents won't find better prices than they would in stores, but they will find unusual or hard-to-find items and enjoy the convenience of not having to travel to three stores to track them down. For some parents, the time-saving convenience is worth a few extra pennies. Another benefit to catalog shopping is that, in some cases, depending on the location of retail stores, buyers don't have to pay sales tax.

After the Stork

After the Stork offers clothing for the whole family, from size 6 months to adult. Inside the pages of this catalog, parents will find colorful play, casual, and dress clothes, mother/daughter and father/son sets, shoes, outerwear, and accessories. After the Stork is committed to safety and has removed drawstrings from all their clothing. The catalog also sells SunSkins sun-protective clothing and reflective tape for nighttime safety. Parents with a creative flair can purchase plain cotton separates in 10 colors along with fabric paints with which to decorate them. After the Stork delivers merchandise within 2 to 5 business days.

For information: Call After the Stork at (800) 441-4775. Hearing-impaired people can call the TDD/TTY line, (800) 505-1095.

Baby Clothes Wholesale

For inexpensive, brightly colored clothes for newborns through boys' size 7 and girls' size 6x, order from the Baby Clothes Wholesale catalog. Most items are less than $15. You'll find mainly casual and play clothes, with a selection of infant sleepers and accessories.

For information: Call Baby Clothes Wholesale at (800) 568-1930 or (800) 568-1940 for a catalog.

Back to Basics Toys

The owners of Back to Basics Toys started the company to offer parents alternatives to the violent, poorly made, and cartoon-based toys appearing on toy-store shelves. Their goal is to offer parents high-quality, safe, nonviolent toys that encourage creativity, learning, and physical development. Back to Basics Toys has earned the Parents' Choice Seal of Approval and a Top-Rated Catalog Award from the Oppenheim Toy Portfolio.

The catalog offers many beautifully crafted wooden toys, puzzles, art kits, tops, wooden train sets, dolls, musical instruments, large toys, outdoor toys, and perennial favorites (including Chinese checkers, Colorforms, tepees, and pogo sticks). Every item comes with a "Product Information Guide" that provides suggestions for using the toy, contacts for obtaining extra parts and accessories, and lists of children's books that compliment the product. The name and phone number of the manufacturer are also included so parents can contact the manufacturer directly if the need ever arises.

For information: To order a catalog, call Back to Basics at (800) 356-5360.

Birthday Express: The Children's Party

Parents will find everything they need for children's parties in the Birthday Express catalog. Ordering all the plates, cups, forks, spoons, napkins, centerpieces, candles, table covers, crepe paper, streamers, balloons, favors, invitations, activities, and wrapping paper needed for a festive occasion is a snap. The party supplies are grouped together by theme. Choose from tropical fish, magicians, ballerinas, pirates, jungles, firehouses, superheroes, and favorite characters from movies and TV, be it Barney, Pocahontas, Barbie, Winnie-the-Pooh, or Thomas the Train. Each party theme is available in a deluxe or basic pack for eight children. Prices range from $19.95 to $35.95 a pack, with a $1.95 charge for each additional child.

For information: Call Birthday Express at (800) 424-7843.

ChildsWork/ChildsPlay

ChildsWork/ChildsPlay is a catalog of games and books that relate to the mental health of children. The catalog, from the Center of Applied Psychology, offers tools that help children work through problems with play. The products are geared mainly to professionals, but there are some great items for parents, including books such as *A Parent's Survival Guide to Childhood Depression, The Very Angry Day That Amy Didn't Have, Anybody Can Bake a Cake: A Motivational Workbook for Kids, My Dad Is Getting Married Again,* and *The Problem-Solving Workbook.* There are also board games to play with children, such as Lifestories, Mind Your Manners, and My Two Homes. The products are designed to teach self-esteem, recognizing and accepting emotions, and dealing with specific, difficult situations, such as divorce, abuse, sibling rivalry, and peer pressure.

For information: Call ChildsWork/ChildsPlay at (800) 962-1141 to order a catalog.

Chinaberry

Chinaberry is a catalog of books for the entire family. The editors value the family and select products to encourage loving relationships and responsible parenting. The catalog contains detailed descriptions of products, tips for encouraging children to read, and four levels for determining the appropriateness of the material for each child. A wide variety of carefully selected books is available. In addition, parents can purchase finger puppets, games, activity books, craft kits, audiotapes, Odds Bodkin story tapes, and aromatherapy pillow mists. Also offered is a selection of fiction and parenting books just for adults.

For information: Call Chinaberry at (800) 776-2242 to order a catalog.

Constructive Playthings

Constructive Playthings is a winner of the Oppenheim Toy Portfolio Top-Rated Catalog Award. In this catalog, parents will find a large variety of toys and products to stimulate active minds and hands. Constructive Playthings carries games, puzzles, books, infant toys, art supplies, music makers, building sets, puppets, and toys for pretending, along with a puppet theater, a tepee, and gifts for teachers.

For information: Call Constructive Playthings at (800) 832-0572 for a catalog.

Cuisenaire

Cuisenaire is a catalog filled with fun ways to learn math and science for kids from kindergarten to ninth grade. Parents can purchase high-quality educational products for home use to complement and supplement what their children are learning in school. For younger children, check the Explorations Kits, Inchworms, blocks, and Cuisenaire Rods, which encourage building as well as learning color/size relationships. For older kids, there are dominoes, Unifix, measurement kits, microscopes, and weather kits. In this catalog, parents will find an array of materials and products to teach kids about basic math concepts, decimals, fractions, algebra, probability, geometry, problem solving, measurements, solar energy, earth science, life science, physical science, and design technology.

For information: Call Cuisenaire at (800) 237-0338 to order a catalog.

Hand in Hand

Hand in Hand offers some unusual and interesting products parents won't find in their local toy superstore, including wicker and wrought-iron children's furniture, the Monterey Bay Aquarium collection of whales, a Battenberg lace parasol, and a leather tool belt for kids. Hand in Hand carries an inviting variety of toys, clothes, furniture, decorations, videos, books, strollers, safety products, feeding accessories, art supplies, musical instruments, and outdoor toys.

If you spot an item at a cheaper price in a current mail-order catalog, Hand in Hand will match the lower price.

For information: Call Hand in Hand at (800) 872-9745 to receive a catalog.

HearthSong

HearthSong strives to offer parents toys, books, and craft kits that have lasting value and that stimulate active minds and bodies. HearthSong has received the Parents' Choice Seal of Approval for six years in a row. The catalog is filled with quality books, dolls, games, puzzles, and special items, such as Robin Hood's Castle and a stable and horse set. There is a wide selection of craft kits: kids can roll candles, tumble rocks for jewelry, create perfumes and bath oils, press flowers, cast soap, model beeswax, sew bead jewelry, weave African designs, quilt, emboss metal, grow crystals, hook rugs, make balloon animals, and decorate chocolates.

For information: To order a catalog, call HearthSong at (800) 325-2502.

Lands' End Kids' Catalog

Lands' End produces quality clothes for kids, from infants to girls' size 16 and boys' size 20. Like its adult counterpart, the Lands' End Kids' catalog offers mainly casual play clothes and outerwear (coats, jackets, rainwear, and snowsuits). Lands' End also sell shoes, bathing suits, accessories, and bedding. Its dia-

10 Activities for Children Using Old Catalogs

1. Cut out pictures and paste them to construction paper to illustrate a story that the child has read or written.

2. Create collages.

3. Make wastebaskets by gluing cut-out pictures to round ice-cream containers.

4. Take a stack of old catalogs to the recycling center to teach kids about responsibility toward the environment.

5. Make homemade greeting cards by pasting cut-out pictures onto folded construction paper or card stock.

6. Make flash cards using three- by five-inch cards and gluing cut-out pictures to them. You can use the cards to teach younger children about colors, shapes, numbers, and letters. Older children can use the cards to build their vocabularies.

7. Create stories by cutting out words and arranging them into sentences.

8. Have your children pick out an inexpensive toy or outfit, help them order it over the phone, and, when it arrives, take them to a local church or shelter to donate the item to someone less fortunate.

9. If you are mailing a package or box to someone, let your children ball up individual pages of catalogs for use as packing material.

10. Play store by using play money and cut-out pictures of actual products as the merchandise.

per bags are unbeatable—practical, roomy, light, and not so cute that fathers won't carry them.

Parents who aren't sure of what size to order for a child can request assistance from a Specialty Shopper, who will help select the right size. Parents can also request a "Book of Caring," a pamphlet describing how to keep clothes looking their best. Lands' End delivers its merchandise in about 3 days via UPS, with an extra charge for express service.

For information: Call (800) 356-4444 to order a catalog. Hearing-impaired people can call the TDD line at (800) 541-3459.

Learn & Play

Learn & Play is a catalog filled with fun and creative products for kids. Kids will love the craft kits, games, rubber-stamp sets, trains, books, workbooks, kitchen toys, electronic games, costumes, and outdoor toys. The catalog offers a wide variety of stimulating and entertaining products.

For information: To order a catalog, call Learn & Play at (800) 247-6106.

One Step Ahead

Every parent should have a copy of the One Step Ahead catalog. Filled with products that inexperienced (and even some experienced) parents are unaware of but would find most useful, this catalog is aimed at making parenting one step easier. It's packed with quality toys for infants and small children, bedding, nursery accessories, organizers, feeding accessories, safety products, infant accessories, bath and health supplies, maternity and nursing accessories, auto-safety products, strollers and carriers, and booties and shoes. You'll also find innovative products, including a beeper that goes off if a child strays more than 15 feet away from his or her parent and a side-facing car bed that lets your infant lie flat. The catalog also contains a number of small, very practical items, such as stroller cup holders, neck protectors for car seats, potty-training aids, and childproofing equipment.

For information: To order a catalog, call One Step Ahead at (800) 274-8440.

Oriental Trading Company, Inc.

For inexpensive party supplies, party favors, stickers, and costumes, call for a copy of the Oriental Trading Company's catalog. It offers an astonishing array of novelties, including personalized pencils, stickers, toys, art supplies, stuffed animals, hats, decorations, hula skirts, feather masks, luminaries, and piñatas to use as party favors, prizes, and entertainment. All the accessories for theme parties are also available.

For information: Call (800) 228-2269 for a catalog.

Perfectly Safe

Every item in the Perfectly Safe catalog has been tested and evaluated for safety and quality by 31 advisory families. The catalog contains scores of products to help keep families safe. There are safety products for kitchens, windows, doors, furniture, electrical systems, nurseries, bathrooms, cars, and for outdoor use. Perfectly Safe has even developed some of its own products in response to requests from customers, including the Kid Switch to bring light switches down to a child's level and a Stove Top Guard to keep pots from falling or being knocked off the stove.

Perfectly Safe ships most orders within 24 hours and uses only recycled or environmentally safe packaging.

For information: To receive a catalog, call Perfectly Safe at (800) 837-KIDS (837-5437).

The Right Start

The Right Start is the gadget-loving parent's dream. Parents will be amazed at all the practical products for babies and kids, including nursery items, bedding, swings, strollers, safety products, diaper bags, feeding accessories, carriers, toys, closet organizers, bath accessories, and a kid-size recliner to boot. Many hard-to-find items are available, including a fanny pack/baby seat, seat belt adjusters, pool alarms, and portable strap seats for movie theaters.

The Right Start has a baby registry and the Silver Rattle Club. Annual membership to the club is $50. Members receive a 20 percent discount on all purchases from the catalog or at any Right Start retail store and special promotions for vacations, entertainment, and products. This club really benefits only frequent shoppers.

For information: Call The Right Start at (800) LITTLE-1 (548-8531) for a catalog.

Toys to Grow On

Toys to Grow On is packed with toys that encourage children to create, pretend, learn, and build. These are toys that will make children feel good about themselves. Kids can play dress-up, hunt for treasure, read books, write their own book, visit a treasure island in their own bathtub, build a town, create a city for bugs, experiment with kitchen science, play school, fight fires, whip up snow cones, and design their own piñatas. Kids will have a ball pretending and imagining all the wonderful things they can be.

For information: To order a catalog, call Toys to Grow On at (800) 542-8338.

Chapter Four

Safety

Safety is a primary concern of all parents. From the moment of their child's conception, parents start a journey of worry that never really ends. Will my baby be OK? Will he stick his finger in that light socket? What if she finds the bottle of aspirin I left on the top shelf of the kitchen cabinet? What if it rains on his way home from school and he loses his umbrella? How high a fever is too high? What if the other kids are drinking at this party? Please, just let her get home safely. The anxieties never go away, but parents can arm themselves with accurate information to help them keep their kids safe and to help them as well when something does go wrong.

The organizations in this chapter offer free or inexpensive materials to educate parents and kids on safety issues.

Bucklebear Club

Join Bucklebear® and the Center for Injury Prevention in teaching children about safety. The Center for Injury Prevention helps local communities protect children by providing parents with educational materials about injury prevention and information on finding equipment and supplies. The Bucklebear Club motivates kids to practice injury prevention by encouraging them to buckle up their seat belts and to follow other safety advice. Members receive a kit that includes a Bucklebear T-shirt, a Bucklebear clicker, a reflective zipper pull, a personalized letter to each child, a birthday card from Bucklebear, and a Riding with Bucklebear coloring book. The kit costs $19.95 plus $5 for shipping and handling.

For information: Call (800) 344-7580 or write to Center for Injury Prevention, 1007 Ellis St., Stevens Point, WI 54481. You can contact their website at http://www.bucklebear.com.

Burn Kit

For about $5 (the price changes depending on the materials included), parents can receive a burn kit from the Alisa Ann Ruch Burn Foundation. Alisa Ann Ruch was a lovely 8-year-old girl who died tragically in a very preventable burn accident. In her honor, the foundation strives to provide burn survivors with much-needed assistance and to educate the public on methods of fire and burn prevention. The foundation teamed up with the creators of the *Baby Blues* cartoons to produce the kit, which uses the popular characters from the comic strip to teach parents and children about burn prevention. The kit includes such items as a bathwater thermometer, a refrigerator magnet, and tips on preventing fires, preventing burns and scalds, and the treatment of burns, including emergency care of hot liquid burns. Because the foundation is constantly improving its materials, future kits may include different items.

For information: Call (800) 242-BURN (242-2876) or (818) 883-7700 or write to Alisa Ann Ruch Burn Foundation, 20944 Sherman Way, Ste. 115, Canoga Park, CA 91303.

Child Safety Tips

Covering topics from allergic reactions to water safety, this concise, informative booklet lists in bullet-point format what to do when a problem occurs. The booklet also provides basic safety tips on a number of topics. It's easy to use and great to keep on

hand for emergencies, major or minor. The booklet was produced by the Scottish Rite Children's Medical Center in Atlanta,
known for its dedication to children.

For information: Call Scottish Rite Children's Medical Center at
(404) 250-2140 to request a copy of the booklet.

Egleston Children's Hospital

Egleston Children's Hospital provides parents with a variety of
helpful safety materials covering such topics as childproofing,
accident prevention, fire and burn prevention, car safety, water
safety, first aid, and playground safety. The materials are easy to
understand and well illustrated and offer practical solutions and
advice. Parents can receive booklets, posters, activity books, and
a subscription to the *The Small Street Journal*, a newsletter covering seasonal safety topics, complete with an activity sheet for
children. I highly recommend these excellent materials for every
parent.

For information: Send a letter or postcard requesting child
safety materials to Child Advocacy Department, Egleston Children's Hospital, 1405 Clifton Road, NE, Atlanta, GA 30322. Do
not send a self-addressed, stamped envelope.

Family Talk About Drinking

Anheuser-Busch has put together a very informative program on
talking to children about drinking. Every family should participate in this program. Nationally recognized authorities in the
fields of child counseling, family therapy, and alcohol research
have developed this comprehensive video and set of guidebooks
to encourage honest, open communication between parents and
children about drinking. The video presents different scenarios
involving drinking that are likely to arise in the course of a
child's school years. Topics covered include responding to children who ask their parents if they are going to let an obviously
tipsy Uncle Jack drive home, and why does Mommy drink wine
if alcohol is a drug. The program offers suggestions on what to
do if a parent catches a child drinking and on teaching kids to

CPR Prompt Home Learning System

The CPR Prompt Home Learning System is an absolute must for any parent who hasn't been able to find the time to take a CPR and choking first-aid class. This system, approved by the American Heart Association, enables parents to learn and practice CPR and choking first aid in their own homes, at their convenience. The kit includes a 30-minute training video, a learning guide, and two practice mannequins—an infant-size and an adult-size. The mannequins offer feedback so that you know when you are performing the techniques correctly. The CPR Prompt Home Learning System is $59.95 and can be ordered from the One Step Ahead catalog.

For information: Call One Step Ahead at (800) 274-8440.

handle peer pressure. The guidebooks complement the video by outlining salient points and describing more scenarios and how to handle them. The program stresses that it's never too early to talk about drinking and the importance of good parenting in combating the very real dangers of alcohol. I strongly recommend that every family call for a set of materials.

For information: To receive the free video and guidebook, call (800) 359-TALK (359-8255).

Hidden Hazards in Your Home

William Shatner hosts this 10-minute video on the dangers of gasoline and tap water. Sponsored by the National SAFE KIDS Campaign and the Gas Appliance Manufacturers Association, the video offers practical advice on minimizing the dangers of these two substances. Along with the free video, parents receive a booklet summarizing the tips in the video and a postcard to send in to receive more safety materials. The entire family will benefit from the Home Activity Guide, which points out flammable liquids around the house, and the Vapora Stickers, which can be used to identify these liquids. Kids ages 5 to 9 will learn about the dangers of flammable liquids in the *Step Up to Safety with Sparky®* activity book, while the "Daredevil vs. Vapora" Marvel comic book teaches kids 10 and older the dangers of gasoline by pitting the superhero Daredevil® against the evil Vapora.

The materials are all free and can be received by contacting the Gas Appliance Manufacturers Association (GAMA).

For information: Call (800) GAMA-811 (426-2811) or write to GAMA, 4 W. Nebraska St., Frankfort, IL 60423-9925.

Pediatric Primer

Dr. Charles Ginsburg, chief of staff of the Children's Medical Center of Dallas, has assembled a collection of his short articles on child safety and other issues. This book presents practical advice on all the topics that keep parents up at night: colicky babies, ear infections, fevers, hearing problems, bed-wetting, picky eaters, school avoidance, tantrums, and toilet training. Illustrated with photographs, this helpful guide will ease many parents' minds. It is free to anyone sending in a written request.

In addition to the *Pediatric Primer,* the Children's Medical Center of Dallas publishes a quarterly newsletter, *Your Child's Health,* that is distributed free of charge to area parents. Topics in past newsletters included easing family stress, dealing with bullies, choosing suitable toys, and teaching kids to cook.

If you happen to live in or are visiting the Dallas area, be sure to visit the hospital and check out the Trainscape. With more than 1,000 feet of tracks to chug along, the eight whistling model trains make hospital visits a little less scary. The Trainscape is open to the public. Taking children to see the trains is a great way to introduce them to the hospital should they ever have to return. The display includes 16-foot mountains, miniature mining towns, and an 8-foot replica of the Dallas skyline.

For information: To request a copy of the *Pediatric Primer* or *Your Child's Health*, send a written request to Public Relations Department, Children's Medical Center of Dallas, 1935 Motor St., Dallas, TX 75235-7794.

Practical Advice for Parents, Practical Advice for Parents of Teens

Children's Hospital of Wisconsin offers two books for parents. *Practical Advice for Parents* was written by the experts at Children's Hospital to address parents' concerns about growth and development, nutrition, immunizations, poison prevention, toy safety, injury prevention, caring for a sick child, and common childhood diseases. The 102-page book covers the years from birth to age 12. The book costs $2.

Practical Advice for Parents of Teens, also created by the experts at Children's Hospital, offers advice to parents of teenagers. Topics include sex, pregnancy, AIDS, alcohol, tobacco, violence, nutrition, diseases, injury prevention, and growth and development. This book is also $2.

For information: To order either book, send $2 per copy to Public Relations Department, Children's Hospital of Wisconsin, PO Box 1997, Milwaukee, WI 53201.

Safe Sitter

Parents with older children who are of baby-sitting age will want them to take the Safe Sitter course. Not only will a child be more confident when watching other children, but parents will feel more confident knowing that the sitter is familiar with how to handle emergencies as they come up.

The Safe Sitter program was born out of a preventable tragedy when the child of one of Dr. Patricia Keener's colleagues choked to death while being cared for by an adult sitter who did

The Fire House

A trip to the fire station is a real treat for children. Not only is it fun and exciting to sit in a fire truck and try on fire-fighting equipment; kids learn important lessons about safety and fire prevention as well. For me, the most valuable part of a trip to the firehouse is that my kids learn not to hide from firefighters. A fire is a frightening and disorienting experience and children need to learn that the scary creature in the gas mask is there to help, not hurt, them. By making children more comfortable with fire engines, sirens, flashing lights, and firefighters, you increase the odds that they will come out of a fire unscathed.

Many fire stations, like the one near my home in Park Ridge, Illinois, have annual open houses. The open houses are usually in the fall, before people turn on their Christmas lights and heaters. During the open house, firefighters put on demonstrations about fire safety and prevention. Safety materials geared toward both parents and children are distributed along with fire hats and balloons. Some stations even have a house that simulates fire conditions, and children can practice escaping a house fire. Not only do kids learn valuable and possibly life-saving information during these visits; they have a ball, too. And it's free!

Call your local fire station to arrange a visit or find out if they have an open house.

not know how to save a choking infant. In response to the tragedy, Dr. Keener, an Indianapolis pediatrician, began a program to teach 11- to 13-year-olds how to be "medically responsible, creative, and attentive baby-sitters." The program now reaches preteens at nearly 700 teaching sites in all 50 states. The course takes 2 days to complete and is followed by a written and practical test. The hands-on curriculum includes choking and rescue breathing, accident management, safety for the sitter, child development, and the business of baby-sitting. After the course, each student should be able to help an infant who decides that the shiny penny on the floor must be tasty, deal with a 2-year-old's temper tantrums, handle an electrical power failure, and cope with drunk parents who want to drive him or her home.

Contact Safe Sitter to find out when classes will be held at a facility near you. Fees for the classes vary by facility.

For information: Call (800) 255-4089 or (317) 355-4888 or write to Safe Sitter, 1500 N. Ritter Ave., Indianapolis, IN 46219.

Safety Pamphlets

Children's Hospital in Columbus, Ohio, offers several easy-to-read pamphlets that provide parents with basic safety information. Topics currently available include baby walkers, bicycles, summer, sun, water, winter, and toy safety. The topics may change from time to time.

The hospital also hosts several educational programs attended by people from all over the country. Topics of particular interest to many parents are Baby-Sitting Children with Disabilities, Cyclic Vomiting Syndrome Workshop, and Celiac Disease Workshop. A biannual calendar listing these workshops and other educational programs is available.

For information: Write to Community Education, Children's Hospital, 700 Children's Dr., Columbus, OH 43205-2696.

Scruff℠ Beats the Scary Streets Comic-Activity Book

Let your kids help McGruff®, the crime dog, and his nephew Scruff "take a bite out of crime." This colorful activity book teaches kids important safety tips in a fun and memorable way. Kids are asked to draw pictures of places they can go to get help, read a story about how to handle confrontations, identify and cross out the dangerous items in a picture, play the "What If" game to find the right response to different difficult situations, and solve a crossword puzzle with safety tips as clues. Throughout the booklet, kids will learn how to respond to threats in a safe manner. The booklet is free and comes in both English and Spanish editions.

For information: Write to National Crime Prevention Council, 1700 K St. NW, Second Floor, Washington, DC 20006-3817.

The Small Street Journal

Egleston Children's Health Care System is dedicated to family health and safety. They issue quarterly newsletters called *The Small Street Journal* filled with health and safety tips for each season. The newsletter has published such articles as "Crib Notes," "Jump into Summer Water Safety," "Safe Habits, Save Lives," "Keep Head Injuries in Mind," "Spring Clean with an Eye Out for Safety," and "Sports for Kids: Playing It Safe." Each newsletter comes with a "Small Street Beat for Kids" activity sheet.

Egleston also offers the "What's Dangerous on Danger Drive?" poster to aid kids (and parents) in spotting everyday hazards. The *Parents' Guide to Child Safety* is also available. This booklet covers car, water, and street safety; fire, burn, choking, and poison prevention; and playground and home-alone safety. *The Safety Kids with Safetysaurus Sam: Safe at Home* is an activity book for kids that makes learning the basic rules of safety fun.

For information: To request materials, write to Child Safety Materials, Egleston Children's Health Care System, Child Advocacy Center, 1405 Clifton Rd. NE, Atlanta, GA 30322.

PART TWO

Fun, Fun, Fun

Chapter Five

City-by-City Guide to Attractions Kids Love

 Every family I know is looking for ways to entertain their children without breaking the bank. I have selected 20 cities around the country to show parents what kinds of inexpensive activities are available. This is by no means an exhaustive guide—many locales in fact have entire books on the subject of what to do with your kids in their town. I have chosen quality entertainment at reasonable costs. Most of the activities listed in this chapter have special discounts or free admission for children or offer special features just for kids. Occasionally you will come across an item that is not necessarily a good deal for parents only but is a good deal nonetheless.

Remember that it's always smart to call to check times and fees before you head out.

Atlanta, Georgia

Center for Puppetry Arts

The Center for Puppetry Arts displays puppets from around the world in the world's largest private collections. More than 200 puppets from various time periods, styles, and cultures are represented. Preschoolers and grade-schoolers are most likely to enjoy the interactive exhibits, including a trash can that turns into a giant 9-foot phoenix right before their eyes. The center conducts workshops on puppet making and creating puppet shows. The center also presents puppet shows for families, featuring artists from around the world and adaptations of classic children's stories.

Admission to the museum is $5 for adults and $4 for children ages 2 to 13, students, and seniors. Hours are Monday through Saturday 9 A.M. to 5 P.M. Puppet show tickets are $6.50 for adults and $5.50 for children ages 2 to 13. Shows are held throughout the week; call for show times.

For information: Call the Center for Puppetry Arts Museum at (404) 873-3391. The museum is located at 1404 Spring St. NW.

Fernbank Museum of Natural History

The Fernbank Museum is the largest natural history museum in the South. It includes a fantastic dinosaur exhibit that children love, as well as exhibits on the evolution of Georgia and the universe. Kids will also enjoy the IMAX theater shows. The Children's Discovery Rooms bring the fundamental concepts of nature to life through the Fantasy Forest and the Coca-Cola Georgia Adventure.

Admission is $9.50 for adults, $8 for students and seniors, and $7 for kids 3 to 12. Children 2 and under are admitted free. The museum is open Monday through Saturday 10 A.M. to 5 P.M. and Sunday noon to 5 P.M.

For information: Call the Fernbank Museum at (404) 370-0960. The museum is located at 767 Clifton Rd. NE, in Decatur.

Fernbank Science Center

The Fernbank Science Center is located a short distance from the Fernbank Museum and features one of the nation's largest planetariums, an observatory open for viewing Thursday and Friday evenings, and a paved trail through 65 acres of forest.

Inside the center, kids will enjoy the taxidermy exhibits featuring wildlife in its natural environment, dinosaur exhibits, and an *Apollo 6* command module. The Fernbank Greenhouse is open Sunday afternoon 1 P.M. to 5 P.M. Each visitor receives a free plant of whatever is in season, from tomatoes to dogwoods. The planetarium boasts a 70-foot-diameter projector dome, a Zeiss Mark V projector, and 500 seats, making it the largest in the Southeast. With special shows for children, the planetarium is a big hit with parents and kids alike.

Admission to the Science Center is free. Planetarium shows are $2 for adults and $1 for students. Children must be at least 5 years old to be admitted to regular shows. Children under 5 can attend children's shows. Seniors are admitted free. The center is open Monday 8:30 A.M. to 5 P.M., Tuesday through Friday 8:30 A.M. to 10 P.M., Saturday 10 A.M. to 5 P.M., and Sunday 1 P.M. to 5 P.M. Call for times of planetarium shows.

For information: Call the Fernbank Science Center at (404) 378-4311. The center is located at 156 Heaton Park Dr. NE, in Decatur.

Kennesaw Civil War Museum

The Kennesaw Civil War Museum is a must-see for train lovers. Kids love The General, a steam locomotive from the Civil War. The train has a lot of history attached to it and is dear to the hearts of Atlanta's natives. The General was stolen on April 12, 1862, in what is known as Andrew's Raid, and was eventually recovered. It inspired the Disney movie *The Great Locomotive Chase.*

Admission is $3 for adults, $2 for seniors, and $1.50 for children ages 7 to 15. Kids 6 and under are admitted free. From March 16 to October 14, the museum is open Monday through Saturday 9:30 A.M. to 5:30 P.M. and Sunday noon to 5:30 P.M. From October 15 to March 15, hours are 10 A.M. to 4 P.M. Monday through Saturday and noon to 4 P.M. Sunday. The museum is closed Easter, Thanksgiving, Christmas, and New Year's Day.

For information: Call (800) 742-6897. The museum is located at 2829 Cherokee St. in Kennesaw.

SCITREK

SCITREK is a hands-on playground featuring more than a hundred interactive exhibits. Kids will explore, manipulate, imagine, and touch their way through exhibits in such categories as electricity and magnetism, light and perception, and mechanics and simple machines. Kids under 4 feet tall will love "Kidspace," a special place just for the littler ones, ages 2 to 7. A favorite of all children is the Van de Graaf generator, which literally makes your hair stand on end.

Admission is $7.50 for adults and $5 for kids ages 3 to 17, students, and seniors. Children under 3 years of age are admitted free; and the museum is free to all 4 P.M. to 5 P.M. daily. On Monday through Saturday, SCITREK is open 10 A.M. to 5 P.M. and Sunday noon to 5 P.M. On the second Tuesday of each month, hours are extended to 8 P.M. The museum is closed on Easter, Thanksgiving, Christmas, and New Year's Day.

For information: Call SCITREK at (404) 522-5500. The museum is located at 395 Piedmont Ave.

Stone Mountain Park

Stone Mountain Park is a 3,200-acre complex 17 miles west of Atlanta proper. Civil War fans will enjoy the tremendous, Mount Rushmore-style carving of Confederate war heroes Jefferson Davis, Stonewall Jackson, and Robert E. Lee on horseback on the side of Stone Mountain, the largest exposed mass of granite in the world. For those who need more action than viewing allows, there are steam train rides, hiking trails, riverboat rides, canoeing, fishing, camping, two 18-hole golf courses, miniature golf, a 20-building antebellum plantation, and Toddler's Cove (a playground for tots). The park holds events and festivals throughout the year, including a popular laser show during the summer.

Admission to the park is $6 per car; a $20 annual pass is also available. Individual attractions are priced separately. Major attractions are $3.50 for adults, $3 for seniors, and $2.50 for children over age 2. Children 2 and under are admitted free. If you are planning to spend the day, you can purchase multiple-attraction tickets at a discount. The park is open 6 A.M. to midnight daily. Call for hours of individual attractions.

For information: Call Stone Mountain Park at (770) 498-5702, or (770) 498-5690 for recorded information.

World of Coca-Cola

Fans of Coca-Cola will enjoy more than a thousand items of soft-drink memorabilia. This popular attraction also features a 1930s soda fountain, loop-the-loop vending machines that offer free drinks, old radio and television commercials, and a soda fountain of the future. A self-guided tour is offered every half hour. The lines are pretty long in the summer, so plan accordingly.

Admission to the World of Coca-Cola is $4.50 for adults, $3.50 for seniors, and $2.75 for children 6 to 12. Children 5 and under are admitted free. The facility is open Monday through Saturday 10 A.M. to 8:30 P.M. and Sunday noon to 5 P.M. The World of Coca-Cola is closed Easter, Thanksgiving, Christmas, and New Year's Day.

For information: Call the World of Coca-Cola at (404) 676-5151. The museum is located at 55 Martin Luther King Jr. Dr.

Zoo Atlanta

Zoo Atlanta went from being one of the worst zoos in the United States to what is now considered one of the 10 best. Willie B., a gorilla, is definitely the star of this zoo. You can find him in the Yerkes Primate Center. The Masi Mara exhibit of the savannas of East Africa is also a favorite here. The elephant shows and birds of prey shows are a lot of fun for kids. A petting zoo keeps smaller children amused. The zoo also sponsors "Night Crawlers," in which families can spend the night at the zoo, participating in flashlight tours, animal encounters, and night hikes.

Admission is $9 for adults, $6.50 for seniors, and $5.50 for children ages 3 to 11. Children 2 and under are admitted free. The zoo is open Monday through Friday 9:30 A.M. to 4:30 P.M.

and weekends 9:30 A.M. to 5:30 P.M. Strollers are available for rental. Nursing mothers can feed their babies at the nursing stations.

For information: Call Zoo Atlanta at (404) 624-5600. The zoo is located at 800 Cherokee Ave. SE in Grant Park.

Baltimore, Maryland

Baltimore Zoo

The Baltimore Zoo is a great zoo with a popular African Watering Hole exhibit, where animals gather around the water as they would in the wild. There is also a good children's zoo for those who need to reach out and touch. The newly renovated reptile house is a hit with the small set.

Admission is $7.50 for adults and $4 for kids ages 2 to 15 and seniors. Children under 2 are admitted free. The zoo is open 10 A.M. to 4 P.M. Monday through Friday and 10 A.M. to 5:30 P.M. on weekends, with shorter hours in the winter.

For information: Call the Baltimore Zoo at (410) 366-LION. The zoo is located in Druid Hill Park.

Maryland Science Center and Planetarium

The Maryland Science Center and Planetarium offers hundreds of hands-on activities for curious minds and busy hands. In addition, there are live demonstrations and interactive displays, including a simulated space station control center that is a big hit with kids. The facility also features sky shows in the planetarium and a 390-seat IMAX theater.

Admission is $9 for adults and $7 for children ages 4 to 17. Children 3 and under are admitted free. The museum is open 10 A.M. to 5 P.M. Monday through Friday and 10 A.M. to 6 P.M. on weekends.

For information: Call the Maryland Science Center and Planetarium at (410) 685-5225. The museum is located at 601 Light St.

50 Free Things to Do with Your Kids

1. Visit a fountain.
2. Go fishing in your bathtub.
3. Make a construction-paper garden to decorate the bottom of your refrigerator.
4. Be a marching band with homemade instruments: popcorn kernel Tupperware shakers, plastic mixing bowl drums, pot lid cymbals.
5. Bake and decorate cookies.
6. Finger paint with tinted shaving cream (tint with food coloring).
7. Play hide-and-seek.
8. Visit a pet store.
9. Plan a nature treasure hunt and collect leaves, rocks, etc.
10. Go to the park.
11. Play grocery store with items in your cupboard and pretend money.
12. Attend a storytelling hour at the library or a local bookstore.
13. Make a train for stuffed animals by decorating shoe boxes and tying them together.
14. Watch a sunrise or sunset together.
15. Play dress-up.
16. Decorate milk cartons that have been washed and dried.
17. Visit Mommy's or Daddy's office.
18. Sing and dance in the living room.
19. Make up silly songs and write down the words to giggle over later.
20. Rouse kids after they go to bed for a pajama run to the ice-cream parlor.
21. Take a stroll at night.
22. Have a tea party, and invite an elderly neighbor or some friends.

23. Have a family breakfast in bed.
24. Create your own board game.
25. Take a trip to the nursery to look at flowers and trees.
26. Make snow angels and snowmen after a big snow.
27. Rake leaves.
28. Give the toys a bath.
29. Do a rain dance.
30. Help your children write a family newsletter.
31. Go to the airport to watch the planes take off.
32. Look through picture albums.
33. Feed the ducks at a local pond.
34. Let your children create the menu for a meal and then cook it together.
35. Camp out in the living room with sleeping bags and flashlights.
36. Visit a fire station.
37. Have a book-a-thon—read as many books as you can.
38. Make a fort.
39. Create some macaroni art.
40. Try some at-home science, such as learning about volume by filling up measuring cups and other containers.
41. Make some mud pies.
42. Put on a play.
43. Have a wagon and bicycle parade.
44. Run through the sprinkler on a hot day.
45. Wash the car.
46. Rearrange your child's room, letting him or her take charge.
47. Tape old wrapping paper to the wall (blank side out) and let your graffiti artists go to town.
48. Explore the attic.
49. Give the dog a bath.
50. Tell each other stories.

National Aquarium

If your children can't get enough of stingrays, piranhas, electric eels, and poison-dart frogs, you must visit the National Aquarium in Baltimore. Outside the aquarium, you will be entertained by the frisky harbor and gray seals in the outdoor seal pool. One seal, in particular, is a favorite: he's a 750-pound, 21-year-old gray seal who has called the seal pool home since 1981. Upon entering the facility, children are enchanted by the floor-to-ceiling "bubble tubes" and the largest collection of stingrays in the world. Kids can visit tropical rain forests, delight in dolphin shows, and tackle the Exploration Station—a high-tech, hands-on learning environment where they can sing whale songs, try to "catch" a squid, and enjoy life from a whale's perspective. View 11 species of jellyfish in the new, eerie Jellies: Phantoms of the Deep exhibit or the Atlantic Coral Reef, a 335,000-gallon replica of a tropical reef, teeming with brightly colored fish. Being on hand at feeding times is an extra treat; check the schedule in the lobby.

The National Aquarium is open 10 A.M. to 5 P.M. Saturday through Thursday and 10 A.M. to 8 P.M. Friday, with longer hours in July and August. Admission is $11.50 for adults and $7.50 for children ages 3 to 11. Children under 3 are admitted free. After 5 P.M. on Fridays, September through March, admission is only $5. Family memberships are about $60 per year and entitle families to free admission for two adults and all children under 21, express entry through the members-only entrance, a subscription to *Watermarks,* discounts at the gift shop and on educational programs, and tickets to special events. Educational programs for families include behind-the-scenes tours, family sleepovers, story hours, breakfast with the dolphins, and classes on seaweed art and jellyfish.

For information: Call the National Aquarium general information line at (410) 576-3800. Hearing-impaired people can call the TDD/TTY line, (410) 625-0720. The aquarium is located at Pier 3, 501 E. Pratt St.

Boston, Massachusetts

Boston by Little Feet

The Boston by Foot tour company offers a special tour of the city for kids ages 6 to 12. Families meet on Congress Street at the statue of Samuel Adams in front of Faneuil Hall. The one-hour walking tour of downtown Boston is full of games, activities, and fun facts for kids. The tour includes new and historic buildings and emphasizes the history and architecture of Boston. Kids receive a free Explorer's Map and Guide.

The tours are $5 per person. Kids must be accompanied by an adult. Tours begin at 10 A.M. on Saturdays and Mondays and 2 P.M. on Sundays, May through October. Reservations are advised for holidays and peak weekends.

For information: Call (617) 367-2345 or write to Boston by Foot, 77 N. Washington St., Boston, MA 02114.

Boston Children's Theatre

The Boston Children's Theatre stages live productions of classic children's books, performed by children. Past productions have included *The Lion, the Witch, and the Wardrobe; Snow White; Narnia;* and *Music Man.*

Tickets are $10 to $12 per person. Call the theater for shows, times, and dates.

For information: Call (617) 424-6634 or write to Boston Children's Theatre, 647 Boylston St., Boston, MA 02116.

Boston Common/Boston Public Garden

Boston Common and Boston Public Garden are two parks located across the street from each other. They are great places for kids who are tired of touring to let off a little steam and run around. Established in 1634, Boston Common is the nation's oldest park. It features a frog pond where kids can wade on hot summer days. The park is bordered by Beacon, Park, Tremont, Boylston, and Charles Streets.

Boston Public Garden, bordered by Arlington, Boylston, Beacon, and Charles Streets, is famous for its swan boat rides on the lagoon. These peddle-powered boats first appeared in 1877 and have been a big favorite of Boston's kids ever since. The 12-minute rides are $1.25 for adults and $.75 for kids. Visit the parks during the day because they are not patrolled well at night.

For information: Call the Boston Parks and Recreation Department at (617) 635-4505.

Boston Public Library

The Boston Public Library hosts a variety of programs for children, including movies, workshops, story hours, puppet shows, magic shows, and concerts. There is a Lapsit program for 12- to 36-month-olds, a preschooler program, and after-school group fun programs, as well as children's book discussion clubs, family concerts, and special family programs and performances.

The library is open 9 A.M. to 9 P.M. Monday through Thursday and 9 A.M. to 5 P.M. Friday and Saturday.

For information: Call the Boston Public Library at (617) 536-5400.

Children's Book Shop

For kids on the lookout for reading material, the Children's Book Shop has a selection of about 20,000 titles for kids from one to 14, including a wonderful selection of young-adult fiction. A few racks of books for adults will keep parents busy while their children browse. The shop offers an 8-week story hour program in the summer and author and illustrator appearances throughout the year.

The Children's Book Shop is open 10 A.M. to 5:30 P.M. Monday, Tuesday, Wednesday, and Friday; 10 A.M. to 8 P.M. Thursday; and 1 P.M. to 5 P.M. Sunday.

For information: Call (617) 734-7323. The bookstore is located at 238 Washington St. in Brookline.

Children's Museum

The Children's Museum of Boston, formerly an old woolens warehouse, is four stories of educational fun and is considered to be one of the best children's museums in the Northeast. Kids will love the new Boats Afloat exhibit, where they can play with boats of every shape and size in a 28-foot, 800-gallon model of Boston's Fort Point Channel. Kids can don foul-weather gear, hop aboard the "Minnow," pull up the anchor, and navigate a course on high-tech Ratheon and U.S. Coast Guard equipment. Other exhibits include a giant, two-story climbing structure, a giant's desktop, the Kidstage, Teen Tokyo, a century-old Japanese house, the Hall of Toys, the Dress-Up Shop, and a Latino market. A big hit with the kids is the assembly-line exhibit where children learn how factories operate. Parents can learn a few things of their own in the Parent's Resource Room.

The museum also sponsors special activities just for kids. Parents of preschoolers can ask for a booklet (available from the information desk) on exploring the museum with the under-5 set, including a special section for children under 2. Kids can see a show at the Kidstage, experiment with science in Saturday-morning workshops, join the Cavalcade Parade, make crafts, and cook up some treats. Friday night is family night: you can visit the museum Friday from 5 P.M. to 9 P.M. for a special $1 admission fee.

Regular admission is $7 for adults, $6 for children ages 2 to 15, and $2 for 1-year-olds. Children under the age of 1 are free. The museum is open 10 A.M. to 5 P.M. Tuesday through Sunday, except Friday when the museum is open until 9 P.M. The museum is also open on Monday holidays and during Boston school vacation weeks. Most rest rooms have baby changing tables, and disposable diapers are available for $.50 at the welcome desk. Stroller parking is located in the second-floor lobby; backpacks are available for toting around little ones.

For information: Call (617) 426-8855 or (617) 426-6500. Hearing-impaired people can call the TTY line at (617) 426-5466. The museum is located at 300 Congress St.

Computer Museum

Even technophobes will enjoy the Computer Museum with its interactive exhibits and fun activities. Visitors can log on to the Internet, try out a PC, color a map of the United States with verbal commands, play the piano with orchestral accompaniment, and alter the contours of their faces on-screen. Visitor Assistants in blue vests are there to help in any way they can. It's a friendly environment for learning about computers.

The museum produces a flyer listing the exhibits that kids will enjoy. Kids can operate Lego robots, measure their height with a talking computer, make their own postcard, walk through a two-story giant computer, animate their own cartoon, draw pictures on the wall, listen to a story read by a computer, and drive on a virtual-reality racetrack.

Admission is $7 for adults and $5 for students and seniors. Sunday afternoons from 3 P.M. to 5 P.M., admission is half price. The museum is open 10 A.M. to 5 P.M. Tuesday through Sunday. Children under 4 are admitted free.

For information: Call the Computer Museum at (617) 423-6758.

Discovery Museums

The Discovery Museums are two museums for children, located in the suburb of Acton. Kids are greeted by Bessie, a green dinosaur out in front. The Children's Museum resides in a converted Victorian house and looks like a giant playhouse. With exhibits designed for children ages 1 to 6, the facility offers lots of hands-on fun and room for imaginations to run wild. Favorites include the closet door that opens to a whale video, a room-size chain reaction track, the Discovery Ship, and a room full of Duplo building blocks. The Science Museum, for kids 6 and older, is a modern, hands-on museum filled with educational and fun exhibits, including Whisper Dishes, an inventor's workshop, a walk-through tornado, and the Liquid Crystal Wall.

Admission to one museum is $6 per person; admission to both is $9 per person. Both museums are open 9 A.M. to 4:30 P.M. Tuesday through Sunday during the summer. During the school year the museums are open 1 P.M. to 4:30 P.M. on Tuesday, Thursday, and Friday; 9 A.M. to 6 P.M. on Wednesday; and 9 A.M. to 4:30 P.M. on weekends.

For information: Call (508) 264-4201. The museums are located at 177 Main St. in Acton.

Franklin Park Zoo

The 72-acre Franklin Park Zoo features a wonderful rain forest exhibit with gorillas, baboons, hippos, and crocodiles in a huge, climate-controlled, hangarlike structure. Birds fly freely inside this magical place. There is also a children's zoo for petting domesticated animals.

Admission is $5.50 for adults, $4 for college students and seniors, and $3 for children ages 4 to 12. Children under the age of 4 are admitted free. The zoo is open Monday through Friday 9 A.M. to 5 P.M. and on weekends and holidays 9:30 A.M. to 5:30 P.M.

For information: Call Franklin Park Zoo at (617) 442-2002. The zoo is located at 1 Franklin Park Rd.

Museum of Science

With more than 400 interactive exhibits, the Museum of Science is considered to be the best science museum in the Northeast. Located on the Charles River in Science Park, it offers hands-on learning fun, along with sky shows at the planetarium and an Omni Theater. Kids love the Human Body Discovery Space, the Theater of Electricity, and the Sound Stairs, which play a different note with each step you take. The holograms are also a big hit. For preschoolers, the Discovery Center lets little ones touch and hold bones, shells, and rocks.

Admission is $8 for adults and $6 for children ages 3 to 14 and seniors. Tots under 3 are admitted free. The museum is open Monday through Thursday and weekends 9 A.M. to 5 P.M.

and on Friday 9 A.M. to 9 P.M. Wednesday afternoons are free for everyone. Summer hours are 9 A.M. to 7 P.M. daily.

For information: Call the Museum of Science at (617) 723-2500. The museum is located in Science Park.

New England Aquarium

The New England Aquarium exhibits more than 12,000 fishes, birds, and mammals at this stunning facility in Boston. The centerpiece of the aquarium is the awesome 187,000-gallon Ocean Tank, one of the world's largest cylindrical saltwater tanks. You can view turtles, sharks, moray eels, and tropical fish from every angle. Other features include the popular penguin colony, a re-created shoreline where you can study the tides, and sea lion shows on the Discovery, a floating pavilion adjacent to the aquarium. For kids, the "Thinking Gallery" is filled with computer games, video presentations, and a giant fish puzzle that kids will love.

The aquarium offers an annual family membership for about $60. The membership includes unlimited admission for two adults and their children (ages 18 and under) or two members and two guests. You also receive a subscription to the *Aqualog;* invitations to special events; and discounts for educational programs, the gift shop, parking, and renting the facility for special events. Members are invited to take part in a variety of programs, including family sleepovers, behind-the-scenes tours, preschool story hours, microscopic journeys for students in grades six to eight, and all kinds of classes for kindergarteners and up.

Admission is $8.50 for visitors 12 and over, $7.50 for seniors, and $4.50 for kids ages 3 to 11. Children 2 and under are admitted free. The aquarium is open 9 A.M. to 5 P.M. Monday, Tuesday, Wednesday, and Friday; 9 A.M. to 8 P.M. Thursday; and 9 A.M. to 6 P.M. Saturday, Sunday, and holidays. From July 1 to Labor Day, the aquarium operates on longer summer hours.

For information: Call (617) 973-5200. Hearing-impaired people can call the TDD line, (617) 973-0223. The aquarium is located at Boston's Central Wharf.

Chicago, Illinois

Adler Planetarium

The Adler Planetarium offers two sky shows: one for adults and one designed for children 5 and under. New shows are featured every 6 months. The planetarium also has exhibits, including an antique instrument collection, a real moon rock, and a variety of hands-on areas for kids. Kids can find out how much they would weigh on Mars, see an actual meteorite, and use astronomy tools to find a new star.

Admission to the buildings and general exhibits is $3 for adults and $2 for children ages 4 to 17 and seniors. The children's sky show is $4 per person. The regular sky show (for visitors 6 and older) is $5 for adults and $4 for kids ages 4 to 17 and seniors. On Tuesday, admission is free for all. The children's shows are Saturday and Sunday at 10 A.M. and last for 30 minutes. The one-hour regular shows are Monday through Thursday at 2 P.M., Friday at 2 P.M. and 8 P.M., and Saturday and Sunday at 11 A.M., 1 P.M., 2 P.M., 3 P.M., and 4 P.M. The facility is open daily 9 A.M. to 5:00 P.M. Friday the facility stays open until 9 P.M.

For information: Call (312) 922-STAR (922-7827). The planetarium is located at 1300 S. Lake Shore Dr.

Art Institute of Chicago

The Art Institute of Chicago meets the needs of families looking for fun, educational activities. The permanent collection includes two exhibits that kids really enjoy. The George F. Harding Arms and Armour Collection houses more than 2,000 swords, daggers, guns, maces, pieces of equestrian armor, and full suits of armor from the fifteenth through the nineteenth centuries. The Thorne Miniature Rooms exhibit features 68 complete miniature rooms replicating the art, decor, and architecture of different time periods from the late sixteenth century to the 1930s.

The museum hosts a number of programs specifically for families. Family Gallery Walks, for families with children ages 9 and up, are led by guides and organized around central themes. Artist Demonstrations give kids a chance to watch professional artists at work. Gallery Games, which can be picked up at the information desk inside the Kraft Education Center, encourage family discussions and suggest activities to do at home. In the Family Room, you can take a break from viewing the gallery to sit down and relax while your kids look through picture books and put together puzzles.

The Kraft Education Center allows kids to learn about art in a friendly environment. The center features rotating exhibitions by children's book illustrators. Telling Images: Stories in Art features six exhibits that introduce children to the stories in art. One features an elephant tusk with five stories carved into it. Kids can press a button to hear the stories out loud. Interactive displays, computer games, and storytelling are all part of the fun.

The museum is open 10:30 A.M. to 4:30 P.M. Monday, Wednesday, Thursday, and Friday; 10:30 A.M. to 8 P.M. Tuesday; 10 A.M. to 5 P.M. Saturday; and noon to 5 P.M. Sunday and holidays. Suggested admission is $7 for adults and $3.50 for children and students with ID. Children under the age of 6 are admitted free. Tuesdays are free for everyone. Family programs are scheduled for weekends during the school year and all week long during the summer.

For information: For general information about the museum, call (312) 443-3600. For family programs, call the Department of Museum Education at the Art Institute at (312) 443-3689 or write to Family Programs, Department of Museum Education, The Art Institute, 111 S. Michigan Ave., Chicago, IL 60603-6110.

Brookfield Zoo

The Brookfield Zoo is 200 acres of naturalistic settings filled with animals and birds. Tropic World, the tropical rain forest exhibit, is on the must-see list. The kids will enjoy touching the animals in the separate Children's Zoo. The Australia House and Habitat Africa are also big hits with kids. For children who need to scramble around, there is a nice playground area.

Admission to the zoo is $5 for visitors ages 12 to 64 and $2.50 for children ages 3 to 11 and seniors. Children under 3 are admitted free. Tuesday and Thursday are reduced-admission days; tickets are $3.50 for adults and $1.50 for kids and seniors. Parking is $4. There are additional fees for the Motor Safari open-air tram, the Children's Zoo, and the Dolphin Show. The zoo is open 10 A.M. to 4:30 P.M. Monday through Friday and 10 A.M. to 5:30 P.M. on weekends. Strollers and wagons can be rented.

For information: Call (708) 485-0263. The zoo is located at First Ave. and 31st St. in Brookfield.

Chicago Academy of Sciences

The Chicago Academy of Sciences is full of hands-on exhibits to teach and inspire, including life-size dioramas and animal tracks. The academy specializes in the history of the Great Lakes region. In addition to exhibits, take advantage of a variety of lectures and workshops. The museum has created the Children's Gallery just for kids filled with fossils and live animals. The gallery is open 10 A.M. to 3 P.M. daily.

Admission to the museum is $3 for adults, $2 for children ages 3 to 17 and seniors. Children under age 3 are admitted free. Monday is free-admission day at the museum, which is open 9:30 A.M. to 4:30 P.M. Monday through Friday, 10 A.M. to 6 P.M. on Saturday, and noon to 6 P.M. on Sunday. The museum is closed on Christmas.

For information: Call the Chicago Academy of Sciences at (773) 549-0606, or (773) 871-2668 for special events. It is located at 435 E. Illinois St. at North Pier.

Chicago Children's Museum

The museum is located on Chicago's Navy Pier, jutting out into Lake Michigan and offering a view of the city's skyline. Navy

Pier is a festive area featuring parks, gardens, restaurants, and attractions, including a giant Ferris wheel and a carousel. The museum, which was renovated in 1995, has many innovative, interactive exhibits that children can't get enough of. Kids can climb up 35 feet of rigging on the Climbing Schooner to the crow's nest and then slide down a ladder to the lower deck. In the Inventing Lab, kids can build their own alarm clocks, computer software programs, musical instruments, and flying machines. The Face to Face exhibit allows kids to experience what it is like to be discriminated against, teaching them tolerance and compassion. In Waterways, kids put on raincoats and play with water. Toddlers can explore an indoor nature trail or visit the PlayMaze, featuring a working bakery, service station, and construction site. Artabounds, a fully equipped art studio, is available for sculpting, painting, or making ceramics. Other exhibits include the City Hospital, On Camera, Grandparents, and the acclaimed Garbage exhibit, where children learn just how much the average family disposes of and where it goes. There is also a room filled with nothing but Lego building blocks and a Baby Pit for the infant set, filled with soft toys. The museum hosts special programs for kids during the summer months. Past programs have included Kids Create, where 2- to 5-year-olds can participate in art projects, and Bubble Thursdays, where kids enjoy all kinds of bubble fun.

Every Thursday night from 5 P.M. to 8 P.M. is "Free Family Night." In the summer, the museum is open 10 A.M. to 5 P.M., Tuesday through Sunday. During the rest of the year, the museum is also open on Monday 10 A.M. to 5 P.M. Admission is $5. Infants under one are admitted free.

For information: Call the Chicago Children's Museum at (312) 527-1000. The museum is located on Navy Pier at 700 E. Grand Ave.

Chicago Tribune's Freedom Center

Take your family on a tour of the production center of the award-winning *Chicago Tribune* newspaper. The tour offers a bird's-eye view of all that goes into the printing, bundling, and delivery of a major newspaper. Before the tour, guests watch a short video reviewing the history of the *Tribune*; then they can walk through the five-story production plant, observe the 10 printing presses in action, and view the packaging area where the newspapers are assembled.

Four guided tours are offered every Tuesday through Friday between 9:30 A.M. and 1:30 P.M. A maximum of 50 people are allowed on each tour, with one chaperone required for every 15 children. Children under 10 years of age are not permitted on the tour owing to safety regulations. Reservations are necessary. The facility is disabled-accessible.

For information: Call (312) 222-2116. The Tribune Freedom Center is located at 777 W. Chicago Ave.

Kohl Children's Museum

Located just north of the Loop in suburban Wilmette, the Kohl Children's Museum is a delightful, hands-on learning place for children. Kids will enjoy Bubble Science, Food Fun, Pulley Play, Dig into the Past, Kitchen Chemistry, and the Mini Supermarket. They can ride a Chicago Transit Authority train, shop at a grocery store, and sail a Phoenician sailing ship. For toddlers, there is a Duplo building-block room and water play area. The art and technology center and Orbit the Robot are also very popular. The museum hosts many special events throughout the year, as well as daily songs, stories, and crafts.

Admission is $4 for adults and children and $3 for seniors. Infants 1 year and under are admitted free. Hours are Tuesday through Saturday 9 A.M. to 5 P.M. and Sunday noon to 5 P.M. The museum is closed on Monday during the winter.

For information: Call the Kohl Children's Museum at (847) 251-6950. The museum is located at 165 Green Bay Rd. in Wilmette.

Kraft Kids Concerts at Ravinia

Every summer Kraft General Foods sponsors a series of family-oriented concerts at the Ravinia Festival in Highland Park, Illinois. These concerts feature some of the best children's entertainers, including singers, musicians, dance companies, and comedians, in an open-air 3,300-seat pavilion. The concerts are usually held at 11 A.M. on Saturdays. Clowns entertain throughout the grounds before and after the shows. Tickets are priced at $5 for the pavilion and $3 for the lawn. Refreshments are available for sale in the park. Parents are welcome to take along a picnic lunch to enjoy on the lawn. The Ravinia Festival box office usually opens in late May.

For information: Call (773) RAVINIA (728-4642); fax (708) 266-0641; E-mail RavFest@aol.com; or write to Ravinia Festival Box Office, PO 896, Highland Park, IL 60035.

Lambs Farm

Lambs Farm is a nonprofit vocational training center that employs men and women with mental disabilities. The farm hosts all kinds of special events and has lots of activities to keep kids busy and happy: miniature golf, arts and crafts shows, pony rides, train rides, and fire truck rides. There are also a farmyard and nursery, an ice-cream parlor, shops, and a restaurant.

Admission is $1.50 per person per activity. Miniature golf is $2.50 per person. The facility is open all year 9 A.M. to 6 P.M. The shops are closed on major holidays.

For information: Call Lambs Farm at (847) 362-4636 for general information, or (847) 362-6774 for special events. The Farm is located at Rockland Rd. and I-94 in Libertyville.

Lincoln Park Zoo

Lincoln Park Zoo is a wonderful rarity—a free zoo. Located in the heart of Lincoln Park, the zoo features the largest group of great apes in captivity. A working farm is also located within the grounds, giving children an idea of life on a farm, including chores. In the animal nursery, kids can pet baby animals. Children also enjoy the feedings of the elephants, sea lions, apes, and lions. Check the information areas for feeding times. Paddleboats can be rented on the Lincoln Park Lagoon.

Admission is free. Parking is $6. The zoo is open daily 9 A.M. to 5 P.M.

For information: Call (312) 742-2000.

McDonald's Museum

We all know that McDonald's is the eating establishment of choice for most kids; so take them to the McDonald's Museum and show them how it all began. The McDonald's Museum is a re-creation of the first McDonald's restaurant, which opened in Des Plaines, Illinois, in 1955. The red-and-white-tiled restaurant even displays the original "Speedee" road sign. The counter and kitchen contain the original equipment from the days when the burgers were grilled and fresh potatoes were used. Mannequins are dressed in the 1955 uniforms complete with paper hats. In the basement, visitors can view historical photos, memos, advertisements, and a short video presentation. Four 1955 cars are parked in the lot.

The museum is open from April 15 through October 16. Hours are 10 A.M. to 4 P.M. Wednesday through Saturday and 1 P.M. to 4 P.M. on Sunday in the summer. Spring and fall hours vary, so call ahead. Admission is free.

For information: Call (847) 297-5022. The museum is located at 400 N. Lee St. in Des Plaines.

Museum of Science and Industry

The Museum of Science and Industry is one of the world's premier science museums and has thousands of hands-on interactive science exhibits for children of all ages. Visitors can catch a glimpse of the future in the "Virtual Reality" lab in the award-winning "Imaging: The Tools of Science" exhibit, climb aboard a real Boeing 727 airplane cantilevered from the museum's balcony in the "Take a Flight" exhibit, experience full-motion action in a realistic F-14 Tomcat flight simulator in the 10,000-square-foot "Navy: Technology at Sea" exhibit, and see live television programs from around the globe in "The World, Live!" theater in the "Communications" exhibit. A fanciful new children's exhibit, "The Idea Factory," is an 8,000-square-foot learning space designed to captivate toddlers through 10-year-olds with hundreds of colorful contraptions. Kids love the German U-505 submarine, the dollhouse, the circus exhibit, and the working coal mine.

General admission for the museum is $6 for adults and $2.50 for children ages 6 to 12. Children 5 and under are free. Admission is free on Thursday. The museum is open 9:30 A.M. to 4 P.M. Monday through Friday and 9:30 A.M. to 5:30 P.M. Saturday, Sunday, and most holidays.

For information: Call (800) GO TO MSI (468-6674), or (773) 684-1414 inside the Chicago area. The museum is located at 57th St. and Lake Shore Dr.

Navy Pier

Navy Pier, recently renovated and reopened, offers spectacular views of the Chicago skyline and Lake Michigan. Families enjoy a festival atmosphere complete with vendor carts and street performers in the summer. Kids will love splashing in the "magic water" fountain in front of the pier. The Family Pavilion holds the Chicago Children's Museum, a large-screen theater, shops, and restaurants. The Crystal Gardens is a glassed-in paradise filled with palm trees, exotic plants, and fountains. A reflecting pool converts to a skating rink in the winter. The Skyline Stage hosts a variety of music, dance, theater, and films throughout the year. Best of all are the carousel ($1 per ride) and the 150-foot-tall Ferris wheel ($2 per ride).

Navy Pier is open daily, free of admission charges.

For information: Call (312) 595-7437. Navy Pier is located at 600 E. Grand Ave.

Shedd Aquarium

The John G. Shedd Aquarium is the largest aquarium in the world, with more than 200 tanks and 7,000 specimens. Two of the favorite exhibits are the coral reef, where divers feed the fish several times a day, and the Oceanarium, a re-creation of a Pacific Northwest coastline with whales, dolphins, and otters. The aquarium also hosts a "Shedd's Family Overnight" program in which families can spend the night in the aquarium and be treated to a behind-the-scenes tour.

Admission is $10 for adults and $8 for kids ages 3 to 11 and seniors. Children under the age of 3 are admitted free. Thursday is free for everyone. The aquarium is open 9 A.M. to 5 P.M. Monday through Friday and 9 A.M. to 6 P.M. on weekends. It is closed Christmas and New Year's Day.

For information: Call (312) 939-2426. The aquarium is located at 1200 S. Lake Shore Dr.

Wacky Pirate Cruise

The Wacky Pirate Cruise, offered by Mercury Cruiseline, tours the city by boat along the Chicago River and Lake Michigan. Kids wear paper hats bearing skulls and crossbones. Buccaneer Bob hosts the tour, distributing kazoos to the kids and encouraging lots of fun.

The tour is $8 for passengers 12 and older and $5 for children 11 and younger. The cruises start at 10 A.M. and run throughout the day, Thursday through Sunday, from mid-April until mid-October. Call for cruise times.

For information: Call Mercury Cruiseline at (312) 332-1353.

Dallas, Texas

Dallas Museum of Natural History

The Dallas Museum of Natural History, located in Fair Park, is a wonderful place to take kids to learn about dinosaurs and such. Also in Fair Park, you'll find a collection of museums housed in art moderne buildings on 277 acres. There is something for everyone in the family here. The museums are the Hall of State, the African-American Museum, the Age of Steam Railroad Museum, the Dallas Aquarium, the Dallas Civic Garden Center, and the Science Place, which is described in detail in this section. Children love the trains, fish, and dinosaurs. The Dallas Museum of Natural History showcases Texas wildlife dioramas, an interactive urban "safari," a live insect zoo, a miniature paleo dig, and, of course, dinosaurs. The museum also offers children's after-school workshops and sleepovers.

The Dallas Museum of Natural History is open 10 A.M. to 5 P.M. daily. Admission is $4 for adults and $2.50 for children ages 3 to 18 and seniors. Children 2 and under are admitted free. Admission is free Monday from 10 A.M. until noon.

For information: Call (212) 421-3466. The museum is located at 3535 Grand Ave. in Fair Park.

Dallas World Aquarium

The Dallas World Aquarium is famous for its triangular-shaped tunnel tank. Visitors walk through the tunnel while sharks, ribbon eels, giant clams, and sea horses swim around them. The coral reef and terrarium with black-foot penguins are also fun for the small set.

Admission is $5 for adults and $3 for children ages 3 to 11. The aquarium is open 10 A.M. to 5 P.M. daily.

For information: Call (214) 720-1801. The aquarium is located at 1801 N. Griffin St.

Dallas Zoo

The Dallas Zoo displays more than 1,500 mammals, reptiles, and birds. The Wilds of Africa, a 25-acre simulated natural environment, is a fantastic exhibit, and parents will have to drag younger children away from the prairie dog village. Another favorite of youngsters is the huge flamingo exhibit. A monorail tours the zoo for those with tired feet.

Admission is $5 for visitors 12 and up, $4 for seniors, and $2.50 for kids ages 3 to 11. Children under the age of 3 are admitted free. Parking is $3. The zoo is open daily 9 A.M. to 5 P.M., except Christmas.

For information: Call (214) 670-5656. The zoo is located in Marsalis Park, at 621 E. Clarendon Dr.

Fort Worth Zoo

The Fort Worth Zoo displays more than 850 species. For kids who love snakes, alligators, and lizards, the herpetarium is one of the largest reptile exhibits in the world. The African Diorama and the James R. Record Aquarium are also great for children. The zoo's Education Complex offers multimedia programs at 1 P.M. and 3 P.M. on weekends for those who want to learn more about animals and their habitats.

Admission is $5.50 for adults, $3 for children ages 3 to 12, and $2.50 for seniors. Children under the age of 3 are admitted free. Wednesday is half-price-admission day. The zoo is open daily 10 A.M. to 5 P.M. During the summer, the zoo is open 10 A.M. to 5 P.M. Monday through Friday and 10 A.M. to 6 P.M. on weekends and holidays.

For information: Call (817) 871-7050. The zoo is located at 1989 Colonial Pkwy. in Fort Worth.

The Science Place

The Science Place is an interactive museum that kids will enjoy. The Body Tech exhibit is a big hit with its hands-on displays about human life and health. Kids can interact with robotic dinosaurs, ride in the Gyro Chair, lift 1,000-pound weights, walk into a giant cell, build a house, and watch lightning bolts shoot across the room. Children also love the bee exhibit, observing live bees at work, and the electricity demonstration. An on-site planetarium offers sky shows and the TI Founders IMAX Theater offers a 79-foot dome screen.

Admission is $6 for adults and $3 for children and seniors. The museum is open 9 A.M. to 5:30 P.M. Monday through Friday and 9:30 A.M. to 10 P.M. on weekends.

For information: Call (214) 428-5555. The museum is located at 1318 Second Ave. in Fair Park.

Denver, Colorado

The Bookies

The Bookies is a one-of-a-kind bookstore brimming with personality and bowls of pretzels for little browsers. There are toys to play with and baskets of puppets and stuffed animals to keep children entertained while their parents are combing the shelves. With more than 40,000 titles to choose from, not to mention puzzles, games, and crafts, this is no easy task. All merchandise is 10 to 15 percent off suggested retail prices.

The Bookies is open 10 A.M. to 6 P.M. Monday through Saturday and noon to 5 P.M. on Sunday.

For information: Call (303) 759-1117. The store is located at 4315 E. Mississippi Ave.

Children's Museum

The Children's Museum is a powerhouse of hands-on fun and learning for kids 12 and under. Children can try out the kid-size basketball court, shop in the miniature grocery store, visit a real television studio, and ski down a miniature mountain (see the listing for KidSlope in this section). Toddlers will enjoy Goldilocks's house, and preschoolers can dive into a sea of plastic balls. Older kids can play computer games and make wooden toys. Also featured are a science lab, theater performances, and an outdoor playground.

Admission is $5 for visitors ages 3 to 59, $3 for seniors, and $2 for children ages 1 to 2. Friday evenings are free for everyone. The museum is open 10 A.M. to 5 P.M. Tuesday through Sunday. Toddler hour is 9 A.M. to 10 A.M. Tuesday and Thursday, allowing younger kids to enjoy the museum before the bigger kids arrive.

For information: Call (303) 433-7444. The museum is located at 2121 Children's Museum Dr.

Colorado State History Museum

The Colorado State History Museum is a popular attraction for youngsters. Kids love the period costumes from the frontier days, the Indian relics, and the life-size dioramas which demonstrate how gold-miners, pioneers, and Mesa Verde cliff dwellers used to live.

Admission is $3 for adults, $2.50 for students and seniors, and $1.50 for children. The museum is open 10 A.M. to 4:30 P.M. Monday through Saturday and noon to 4:30 P.M. Sunday.

For information: Call (303) 866-3682. The museum is located at 1300 Broadway.

Denver Art Museum

The Denver Art Museum houses top collections of pre-Columbian, Spanish Colonial, and Asian art. There are also modern, contemporary, African, and Oceanic galleries. The museum is particularly known for its American Indian collection, where display halls completely re-create another time and place.

The museum is very family-friendly. Kids can pick up "Eye Spy" games on each floor of the building; the games list items for them to look for as they tour the galleries. There is also a Kids Corner where children can participate in unsupervised art projects; a new project is available each month.

On Saturdays admission to the museum is free, and events are geared toward children and families. On the first Saturday of each month, kids ages 5 to 9 can attend workshops designed especially for them. On the remaining Saturdays of each month, "Family Backpacks" can be checked out. The backpacks are filled with games and activities for use as families walk through the galleries. The activities help children (and their parents) learn how to appreciate art. The museum has also recently established programs for 3- to 5-year-olds, 6- to 12-year-olds, and 8- to 12-year-olds, including arts and crafts, gallery games, and sleepovers.

The museum is free for everyone on Saturdays. On other days admission is $3 for adults, $1.50 for kids ages 6 to 18 and seniors, and free for children under the age of 6. The museum is open 10 A.M. to 5 P.M. Tuesday through Saturday and noon to 5 P.M. on Sunday.

For information: Call (303) 640-4433. For information about family and kid programs, call (303) 640-KIDS. The museum is located at 100 W. 14th Avenue Pkwy.

Denver Firefighters Museum

What child would pass up the opportunity to climb up and ring the bell on a shiny fire truck? The museum, housed in Old Fire

House No. 1, which was built in 1909, displays authentic fire-fighting equipment from the nineteenth and twentieth centuries. Kids will love trying on boots, coats, and hats; listening to stories of historic fires and rescues; and watching a fire-safety video featuring Donald Duck and Jiminy Cricket.

Admission is $2 for those 12 and older and $1 for those 11 and under. The museum is open 10 A.M. to 2 P.M. Monday through Friday year-round and on Saturday during the summer months.

For information: Call (303) 892-1436. The museum is located at 1326 Tremont Pl. next to the Denver Mint.

Denver Public Library's Children's Library and Story Pavilion

When the Denver Public Library realized that more than one million children's books were checked out by residents each year, they decided that children needed a special place. The newly renovated 12,500-square-foot Children's Library and Story Pavilion demonstrates Denver's emphasis on the importance of reading for children. The library is filled with cozy reading spaces, "fantasy walls," and a computerized Kid's Catalog that uses pictures to help kids find the books they want. The library also sponsors story times, author visits, and special events throughout the year.

There is no admission charge. The library is open 10 A.M. to 9 P.M. Monday through Wednesday, 10 A.M. to 5:30 P.M. Thursday through Saturday, and 1 P.M. to 5 P.M. on Sunday. Every Saturday and Sunday at 2 P.M. a children's program is presented at the Story Pavilion; the program varies each week. Story time is every Wednesday at 10 A.M., 10:30 A.M., and 1:30 P.M. and Saturday at 11 A.M.

For information: Call (303) 640-6200. The library is located at 10 W. 14th Ave.

KidSlope at the Children's Museum

This very popular artificial kid-size ski slope is a great place for youngsters to learn to ski and snowboard. Ski instructors give 2-hour group lessons that teach kids the basics of skiing and get them ready for the real slopes. The classes teach the same basics that beginner classes teach at the resorts for a fraction of the cost. The slope is open year-round. Because the classes are popular, be sure to book in advance. Registration is required.

Ski lessons are $8 for kids 4 and up, with equipment included. Snowboard lessons are $10. Classes are 10 A.M., 12:30 P.M., and 3 P.M. Tuesday through Sunday.

For information: Call (303) 433-7444. The KidSlope is located next to the Children's Museum at 2121 Children's Museum Dr.

United States Mint

The United States Mint in Denver, one of the four U.S. Mints, produces pennies, nickels, dimes, quarters, half-dollars, and specialty coins. In operation since 1863, the mint stamps coins from enormous prefabricated rolls of metal. Visitors can watch metal coils weighing close to 10,000 pounds being pressed into "blanks," discs ready to be stamped with the coin design, and then stamped. Kids love the shaker, where coins that are not the proper size are weeded out. You can also stamp your own souvenir coin on the Mint Standard press purchased in 1946 for the first Franklin D. Roosevelt dimes. The display of gold bullion is mind-numbing, as is the room full of money waiting to be counted.

Admission to the mint is free. Because of the popularity of the tour, tickets are distributed first come, first served beginning at 8 A.M. Guided tours are every 10 to 15 minutes from 8 A.M. to 2:45 P.M. in the summer. From mid-September to mid-May, tours leave every 15 to 20 minutes from 8:30 A.M. to 3 P.M. The mint is closed for inventory usually during the last week in June and the first week in July. Call the mint for exact dates if you are planning a visit at that time.

For information: Call (303) 844-3331 or write to United States Mint, Tour Information, 320 W. Colfax Ave., Denver, CO 80204-2693.

Indianapolis, Indiana

Children's Museum

The Children's Museum is a magical place for children. For kids who prefer hands-on fun, the museum boasts a simulated limestone cave for spelunking, a turn-of-the-century carousel, a furnished Hoosier log cabin, a real mummy, antique fire engines, and the largest collection of toy trains on public display. Kids can dig for dinosaurs, listen to African-American stories, climb a rock wall, and ride a turn-of-the-century carousel. Also offered are interactive displays exploring natural and physical sciences and a host of special programs held throughout the year.

Admission is $6 for adults, $5 for seniors, and $3 for kids 18 and under. From March to Labor Day, the museum is open daily 10 A.M. to 5 P.M. From September through February, the museum is closed on Mondays, Thanksgiving, and Christmas. On the first Thursday of each month, the museum is open 10 A.M. to 8 P.M. Strollers may be rented.

For information: Call (317) 924-5431. For recorded information call (800) 208-KIDS or (317) 924-KIDS. The museum is located at 30th and Meridian Streets.

Conner Prairie

Conner Prairie is a 25-building, living-history settlement that captures and displays the spirit of life in 1836. It is a wonderful place where children can learn what life was like in the 1830s. Kids can watch a doctor, a potter, a blacksmith, and an innkeeper performing their duties as they would have at that time. A restaurant serving nineteenth-century, country-style dinners caps off the authentic experience.

Admission is $9 for adults, $8.50 for seniors, and $6.50 for children ages 6 to 12. Children under the age of 6 are admitted free. The settlement is open 9:30 A.M. to 4:30 P.M. Tuesday through Friday, 9:30 A.M. to 5 P.M. Saturday, and 11:30 A.M. to 5 P.M. Sunday.

For information: Call (800) 966-1836 or (317) 776-6000. Conner Prairie is located at 13400 N. Allisonville Rd. in Fishers.

Hook's American Drug Store Museum

To experience an authentic antique soda fountain, take the kids to Hook's, located at the Indiana State Fairgrounds. The museum is a monument to a unique part of America's past—the corner drugstore. The store is furnished in ash and walnut cabinetry dating back to 1849. Kids will enjoy the old-fashioned eyeglasses, toiletries, mortars and pestles, and candies.

Admission is free. Friday through Sunday, parking is $2 at the Fairgrounds, but tickets will be validated. The museum is open 11 A.M. to 4 P.M. Tuesday through Sunday and is closed on holidays.

For information: Call (317) 924-1503. Hook's is located at 1180 E. 38th St. in the Indiana State Fairgrounds.

Indianapolis Motor Speedway Hall of Fame Museum

No trip to Indianapolis would be complete without a visit to the Speedway Museum. All kids enjoy seeing the 30 Indianapolis 500–winning cars on display. For history buffs, a number of classic and antique cars are the draw.

Admission is $2 for adults. Kids 16 and under are admitted free. The track tour is an additional $2. The museum is open 9 A.M. to 5 P.M. daily.

For information: Call (317) 484-6747. The museum is located at 4790 W. 16th St.

Indianapolis Zoo

The Indianapolis Zoo is a world-class zoo, with more than 3,000 animals on display at its 64-acre downtown site. The animals reside in spacious "biomes," collections of simulated natural habitats, including waters, deserts, forests, and plains. Famous for its exhibit of free-roaming lizards and birds, the zoo also offers a carousel and bumper boats; rides on ponies, camels, and elephants; and the Encounters Exploration Center where kids can play hands-on games and interact with live animals. Kids flock to the Coca-Cola Dolphin Show and the Fun Factory.

Admission is $9 for adults, $6.50 for seniors, and $5.50 for children ages 3 to 12. Children 2 and under are admitted free. Parking is $3. The zoo is open 9 A.M. to 4 P.M. Monday through Friday and 9 A.M. to 5 P.M. weekends and holidays. Summer hours may be longer, so call ahead. Admission and parking are free the first Tuesday of each month 9 A.M. to noon.

For information: Call (317) 630-2001. The zoo is located at 1200 W. Washington St.

Kids Ink Children's Bookstore

Kids Ink is a full-service bookstore that, in addition to carrying a vast selection of titles, offers lots of free, innovative activities for kids. The store hosts story hours for toddlers and preschoolers on Tuesday and Friday mornings. Parents can call the store to register their children and check on dates and times. Kids Ink also features "Terrific Tuesdays," where kids can participate in special activities, from 2 P.M. to 7 P.M. Past events have included marbling paper, puppet shows, making musical instruments, designing bird houses, and redecorating the Kids Ink bathroom. All activities are free.

Kids Ink is open 10 A.M. to 8 P.M. Monday through Thursday, 10 A.M. to 6 P.M. Friday and Saturday, and 1 P.M. to 5 P.M. Sunday.

For information: Call Kids Ink at (317) 255-2598. The store is located at 5619 N. Illinois St.

Los Angeles, California

California Museum of Science and Industry

The California Museum of Science and Industry is the second-largest science museum in the United States. Lots of interactive exhibits encourage children to play and learn. Kids can generate their own electricity; play with bubbles and spirals; learn about saving and investing money; and test their own pulse, flexibility, and blood pressure. In the Aerospace Hall, children can even fly a jet fighter.

Admission to the museum is free. IMAX tickets are $6.25 for adults, $4.75 for students with ID, and $3.75 for children ages 4 to 12 and seniors. The museum is open daily 10 A.M. to 5 P.M., except Thanksgiving, Christmas, and New Year's Day.

For information: Call (213) 744-7400. The museum is located at 700 State Dr. in Exposition Park.

Griffith Park

With more than 4,000 acres, Griffith Park is the largest municipal park in the country. The facilities include three golf courses, tennis courts, a wilderness area and bird sanctuary, a carousel, pony rides, and picnic areas. There is lots of room for kids to run around. The park also is home to the Los Angeles Zoo (described later in this section); Travel Town, an unusual outdoor museum displaying old railroad engines, cars, and fire trucks; Griffith Observatory, a 500-seat planetarium and twin-refracting telescope; and the Hall of Science.

For information: Call (213) 665-5188.

Kidspace

Kidspace is a children's museum with hands-on activities and interactive exhibits. Children can play disc jockey, visit Eco-Beach complete with wave machine, operate a camera in a TV studio, watch entertaining performances, and participate in workshops and special events. For your little ones, Toddler Territory gives tots their own space. Critter Caverns let kids ages 5 and older explore animal habitats. Parents will find an Information Station at each exhibit that offers suggestions for hands-on interaction with the exhibit, related activities families can do at home, and books for those who want to learn more.

Admission is $5 for visitors ages 3 to 64, $3.50 for seniors, and $2.50 for 1- to 2-year-olds. During the school year, the museum is open 1 P.M. to 5 P.M. on Wednesday, 10 A.M. to 5 P.M.

Saturday, and 1 P.M. to 5 P.M. Sunday. During summer vacation and school vacations, the museum is open 1 P.M. to 5 P.M. Sunday through Thursday and 10 A.M. to 5 P.M. on Friday and Saturday.

For information: Call (818) 449-9143. The museum is located at 390 S. El Molino Ave. in Pasadena.

Los Angeles Children's Museum

The Los Angeles Children's Museum offers kids workshops and performances, as well as hands-on, interactive exhibits. In City Streets with working traffic lights, kids can ride fire trucks and buses. In Sticky City, small children can build towers with foam and Velcro. Kids enjoy recording music in the sound studio, shadow boxing, exploring the Cave of the Dinosaurs, and creating their own animated crayon cartoons. Kids can learn valuable lessons about recycling at Club Eco.

Admission is $5 per person. Children under the age of 2 are admitted free. The museum is open Saturday and Sunday year-round 10 A.M. to 5 P.M. During summer vacation, the museum is also open 11:30 A.M. to 5 P.M. Tuesday through Friday. The museum is closed July 4th and Labor Day.

For information: Call (213) 687-8800. The museum is located at 310 N. Main St.

Los Angeles Zoo

The Los Angeles Zoo is home to 1,500 animals, birds, and reptiles. Tiger Fall, an 18-foot waterfall, adds to the enchanting atmosphere of this zoo. At the base of Tiger Fall, seals frolic playfully. There are fantastic mountain habitats and a cave with bats and barn owls. Kids can enjoy animal shows at the Zoorific Theater and meet animals of the Southwest at Adventure Island.

Admission is $8 for adults, $5 for seniors, and $3 for kids ages 2 to 12. Children under the age of 2 are admitted free. The zoo is open daily 10 A.M. to 5 P.M., except on Christmas.

For information: Call (213) 666-4650. The zoo is located at 5333 Zoo Dr. in Griffith Park.

Museum of Flying

The Museum of Flying is a great place for kids, filled with interactive exhibits on aircraft design, maintenance, and aviation history. The museum is home to the World Cruiser *New Orleans,* the first plane to fly around the world, and more than 40 other aircraft. A runway viewing area allows visitors to watch WWII and other planes take off and land. In the Children's Interactive area, children can climb into cockpits, build model airplanes, and listen on headphones to actual communications from a real airport's control tower.

Admission is $7 for adults, $5 for seniors and students, and $3 for children 3 to 17 years of age. Children under 3 are admitted free. The museum is open 10 A.M. to 5 P.M. Wednesday through Sunday.

For information: Call (310) 392-8822. The museum is located at 2772 Donald Douglas Loop North in Santa Monica.

Natural History Museum of Los Angeles County

The Natural History Museum houses exhibits highlighting the cultural and technological changes of the twentieth century, including a great American history wing. Kids get a kick out of the skull of a *Tyrannosaurus rex,* a 14½-foot megamouth shark, the hall of gems and minerals, the hall of birds, and the taxidermy collection. The Ralph M. Parsons Discovery Center has entertaining and educational hands-on exhibits for kids, including polar bear teeth and x-rays of a snake. Kids can make crayon rubbings of fossils and dig for dinosaur bones. The Insect Zoo, with live tarantulas and scorpions, is a big hit with the small set, too.

Admission is $6 for adults, $3.50 for students 13 to 18 and seniors, and $2 for kids ages 5 to 12. Kids under the age of 5 are free. There is no admission fee the first Tuesday of each month. The museum is open 10 A.M. to 5 P.M. Tuesday through Sunday and on Monday holidays.

For information: Call (213) 744-DINO. The museum is located at 900 Exposition Blvd.

Miami, Florida

A. D. Barnes Park

A. D. Barnes Park is a 62-acre park with lots of special features, including a tot lot play area, jogging and bicycle paths, a wheelchair-accessible tree house, and a solar-heated swimming pool that is also accessible by wheelchair. The Sense of Wonder Nature Center and Trail is available to families on Saturday mornings. Families can take nature walks, participate in hands-on activities, and view animal exhibits.

The park is open daily 7 A.M. to 7 P.M. (with later hours in the summer) and is free to everyone.

For information: Call (305) 665-1626. The park is located at 3701 SW 72nd Ave.

Fairchild Tropical Garden

The Fairchild Tropical Garden is 83 acres of tropical and subtropical plants and trees, with the largest collection of palms in the United States. The garden features 11 lakes, a rain forest, a rare-plant house, and a one-acre plot left in its natural condition after Hurricane Andrew hit so that scientists can study the patterns of regrowth. Tram rides and walking tours are available.

Admission is $8 for adults. Children under the age of 13 are admitted free. The garden is open 9:30 A.M. to 4:30 P.M. daily, except Christmas.

For information: Call (305) 667-1651. The garden is located at 10901 Old Cutler Rd.

Metrozoo

The Metrozoo is a cageless zoo covering 290 acres and is home to 250 species of rare and exotic animals. The animals reside in re-creations of the habitats of Asia, Eurasian steppes, European forests, and African jungles and plains. The Wings of Asia exhibit features a free-flight aviary with more than 300 birds. Visitors can walk through a rain forest with a lookout tower, a swing bridge, and waterfalls. There are daily shows and feedings along with PAWS, a petting zoo where children can ride elephants, pet animals, and watch amphitheater shows. Koalas and rare white Bengal tigers keep the kids captivated. An air-conditioned, complimentary monorail runs through the zoo every 45 minutes. There is also a large playground with kiddie rides and paddleboats for those who are tired of watching the animals have all the fun.

Admission is $8 for adults and $4 for children 3 to 12. Children under 3 are admitted free. The zoo is open daily 9:30 A.M. to 5:30 P.M.

For information: Call (305) 251-0400. The zoo is located at 12400 SW 152nd St.

Miami Seaquarium

The Miami Seaquarium is home to 10,000 specimens of fish, reptiles, and sea mammals. Tide pools, jungle islands, and a huge reef tank under a geodesic dome make this aquarium special. Kids love the sea lion and dolphin shows and the "halfway house" for injured manatees. The real stars of the aquarium are Lolita (the 10,000-pound killer whale), Flipper, and Salty the Sea Lion.

Admission is $18.95 for adults and $13.95 for kids ages 4 to 12. Children under 4 are admitted free. The aquarium is open daily 9:30 A.M. to 6:30 P.M.

For information: Call (305) 361-5705. The aquarium is located at 4400 Rickenbacker Causeway.

Miami Youth Museum

The Miami Youth Museum features rotating and permanent interactive exhibits that enchant and educate. Most of the exhibits are geared to preschoolers and older children. Kids can visit a mini-neighborhood complete with a dentist's office, a fire station, and a grocery store. The "Hot Off the Press" newspaper exhibit is popular with kids, and the "Metro-Dade Safe Neighborhood" is a big hit with parents.

Admission is $4 for everyone. The museum is open 10 A.M. to 5 P.M. Monday through Friday and 11 A.M. to 6 P.M. on weekends.

For information: Call (305) 446-4386. The museum is located at 3301 Coralway.

Monkey Jungle

Kids will love watching monkeys roam freely in the Monkey Jungle, a 20-acre reserve inhabited by 500 primates. They can tour through habitats that re-create the conditions in Asian, South American, and African jungles by way of enclosed walkways that run through the park. The monkeys are free; the visitors are caged. Kids are allowed to feed some of the monkeys, which is always exciting for them. The park also offers very entertaining shows with chimps, including a monkey swimming-pool show.

Admission is $11.50 for adults and $6 for kids ages 4 to 12. Children under the age of 4 are admitted free. The park is open daily 9:30 A.M. to 5 P.M.

For information: Call (305) 235-1611. The park is located at 14805 SW 216th St.

Museum of Science and Space Transit Planetarium

How can parents pass up 150 interactive exhibits designed to introduce children to the wonders of science? The Museum of Science allows kids to view a killer whale skull; fly with the help of antigravity mirrors; and visit a wildlife center full of turtles, snakes, and birds. The observatory is open on weekend evenings free of charge, and the planetarium holds fantastic multimedia sky and laser shows, including one designed especially for preschoolers.

Admission is $6 for visitors ages 13 to 61 and $4 for children 3 to 12 and seniors. Children under 3 are admitted free. The museum is open daily 10 A.M. to 6 P.M.

For information: Call (305) 854-4247. The museum is located at 3280 S. Miami Ave.

Parrot Jungle and Gardens

At the Parrot Jungle and Gardens, children can observe parrots, peacocks, flamingos, cockatoos, and macaws in an authentic subtropical setting. They can also watch trained bird shows and visit the wildlife exhibits featuring alligators, turtles, and iguanas. The alligator pool, parrot island, cactus garden, and Flamingo Lake are favorites with the youngsters. A children's petting zoo and playground round out the program.

Admission is $11.95 for adults, $10.95 for seniors, and $7.95 for kids ages 3 to 12. Children under the age of 3 are admitted free. The park is open daily 9:30 A.M. to 6 P.M. The Parrot Cafe opens at 8 A.M. for breakfast.

For information: Call (305) 666-7834. The park is located at 11000 SW 57th Ave.

Minneapolis–St. Paul, Minnesota

Children's Theatre Company

The Children's Theatre Company, the largest theater for children in the United States, presents a season of adventurous plays each year. The 746-seat theater is the setting for 350 performances of children's classics and contemporary literature annually. Past performances have included *Little Women, Cinderella, The Hobbit, Don Quixote,* and *The Reluctant Dragon.*

Hours and admission vary from production to production, so call for schedules. On average, ticket prices range from $10 to $28 per show. Lap passes for children 3 and under are $6 each.

For information: Call (612) 874-0400. The theater is located at 3rd and 24th Streets in Minneapolis.

Como Park

With more than 300 acres, Como Park is the largest park in St. Paul, with a 70-acre lake, a small zoo, a golf course, a Japanese garden, and children's rides. The conservatory is open year-round, and a lakeside pavilion provides the setting for summer concerts.

The zoo is the perfect size for little ones who may be overwhelmed by larger zoos. Favorites with the small set include Seal Island and the children's zoo. There are even indoor viewing areas for cold weather.

Admission to the zoo is free for everyone. From October through March, the zoo is open 10 A.M. to 4 P.M., and April through September, the zoo stays open until 6 P.M.

For information: Call (612) 487-8200. Como Park is located at Lexington Ave. at Midway Pkwy.

Minnesota Children's Museum

The Minnesota Children's Museum is a world of wonder. Kids will love the electromagnetic crane and the TV studio, the cloud display, and the Water Works water wheel. Preschoolers favor the ant hill in the Earth World exhibit, as only preschoolers can. The museum hosts a variety of workshops for kids and families, including Fishing Lures, Mother's and Father's Day weekends, English Tea, Sock Puppets, and Run for the Raindrops. Parents can call the museum for schedules of upcoming events.

Admission is $5.95 for visitors ages 3 to 60 and $3.95 for children 1 to 3 and seniors. Infants are admitted free. From Memorial Day to Labor Day, the museum is open 9 A.M. to 5 P.M. daily, with longer hours on Thursdays. During the rest of the year, the museum is closed on Mondays and on Easter, Thanksgiving, and Christmas.

For information: Call (612) 225-6000. The museum is located at 10 W. Seventh St. in St. Paul.

Minnesota Zoo

The 500-acre Minnesota Zoo, set in the hills of Apple Valley, is one of the nation's best. Siberian tigers, musk oxen, and moose find the extreme weather here much like home. Take a stroll down the Tropics Trails and watch fish and marine animals under water, or the Ocean Trail where sea creatures and dolphins frolic. The five-story indoor jungle is a must-see, as is the Zoolab where volunteers introduce children to animals they can touch. The Discovery Trail is a children's zoo created with families in mind. The zoo hosts special programs for families, including family zoo adventures, overnights, and preschool programs.

Admission is $8 for adults, $5 for seniors, and $4 for children ages 3 to 12. Children under 3 are admitted free. From May through September, the zoo is open 9 A.M. to 4 P.M. Monday through Friday, 9 A.M. to 6 P.M. on Saturday, and 9 A.M. to 8 P.M. on Sunday. From October through April, the zoo is open daily 9 A.M. to 4 P.M.

For information: Call (612) 432-9000. The zoo is located at 1300 Zoo Blvd. in Apple Valley.

Science Museum of Minnesota

The Science Museum is a very popular attraction for kids in Minneapolis. The hands-on exhibits highlight the wonders of science, technology, and natural history. Kids go crazy over the full-size dinosaur on display. The Omnitheater boasts the largest movie projector in the world.

Admission is $5 for adults and $4 for seniors and children ages 4 to 15. Children 3 and under are admitted free. The museum is open 9:30 A.M. to 9 P.M. Tuesday through Saturday and 10 A.M. to 9 P.M. on Sunday.

For information: Call (612) 221-9444. The museum is located at Wabasha and Exchange Streets in St. Paul.

Nashville, Tennessee

Belle Meade Mansion

The Belle Meade Mansion features a guided tour especially for children, loaded with fun facts and tidbits. This nineteenth-century antebellum mansion was once in the business of breeding racehorses.

Admission is $7 for everyone. Hours are 9 A.M. to 5 P.M. Monday through Saturday and 1 P.M. to 5 P.M. Sunday, except for Thanksgiving, Christmas, and New Year's Day.

For information: Call (615) 356-0501. The mansion is located at 5025 Harding Rd.

Cumberland Museum and Science Center

The Cumberland Museum and Science Center is home to lots of hands-on exhibits, live animals, and a planetarium. The museum offers live animal shows and science demonstrations. Younger children will enjoy the Curiosity Corner, where they can hide in a fox's den or dress up in costumes from other countries. The Kinetic Center is a two-story study of motion.

Admission is $6 for adults and $4.50 for children ages 3 to 12 and seniors. Children 2 and under are admitted free. There are additional fees for planetarium shows. The museum is open 9:30 A.M. to 5 P.M. Tuesday through Saturday and 12:30 P.M. to 5:30 P.M. on Sunday. During the summer (Memorial Day to Labor Day), the museum is open 9:30 A.M. to 5 P.M. Monday through Saturday and 12:30 P.M. to 5:30 P.M. on Sunday.

For information: Call (615) 862-5160. The museum is located at 800 Fort Negley Blvd.

Nashville Toy Museum

The Nashville Toy Museum is home to toys from the past 150 years. Kids will delight in seeing toy soldiers, antique dolls, teddy bears, trains, and cars.

Admission is $3 for adults and $1.50 for children ages 6 to 12. Children 5 and under are admitted free. The museum is open daily 9 A.M. to 5 P.M.

For information: Call (615) 883-8870. The museum is located at 2613 McGavock Pike.

Nashville Zoo

The Nashville Zoo sits on 50 beautifully landscaped acres. Kids can't get enough of the African Savanna exhibit and the Reptile House. There is a petting zoo for kids and Nashville Zoo-Rassic, featuring 12 animated exhibits of dinosaurs. Watch the Tyrannosaurus bellow and Protoceratops hatch from eggs.

Admission is $5.50 for adults and $3.50 for children ages 3 to 12 and seniors. Children 2 and under are admitted free. Summer hours are 9 A.M. to 6 P.M. daily; winter hours are 10 A.M. to 5 P.M. daily.

For information: Call (615) 370-3333. The museum is located on 1710 Ridge Rd. Cir. in Joelton.

Tennessee State Museum

The museum hosts a variety of exhibits designed to portray life in Tennessee throughout history, complete with a working gristmill, a horse-drawn fire engine, mastodon bones, Daniel Boone's rifle, an Egyptian mummy, and a reconstructed log cabin. Kids love the Museum Experience Room, where they can enjoy a variety of sensory experiences that teach them about Tennessee's history. Across the street, the War Memorial Building houses the Military Museum, which contains exhibits from conflicts ranging from the Spanish-American War to World War II. Highlights for kids include a deck gun from the USS *Nashville*, General Dwight Eisenhower's jacket, and a soldier's belongings.

Admission to the museum is free for everyone. The museum is open 10 A.M. to 5 P.M. Tuesday through Saturday and 1 P.M. to 5 P.M. on Sunday. The museum is closed Mondays, New Year's Day, Easter, Thanksgiving, and Christmas.

For information: Call (615) 741-2692. The museum is located at 505 Deaderick St.

New Orleans, Louisiana

Audubon Institute (*Audubon Zoo, Aquarium of the Americas,* and *Louisiana Nature Center*)

You get three times the fun at the Audubon Institute in New Orleans. A family membership here entitles you to admission to the world-renowned Audubon Zoo, the Aquarium of the Americas, and the Louisiana Nature Center. One of the world's leading zoos, the Audubon Zoo enchants children with its rare white alligators, Louisiana Swamp Exhibit, Reptile Encounter, Butterflies in Flight, World of Primates, and Pathways to the Past (an interactive exhibit that takes kids back to the time when dinosaurs roamed the earth). The Embraceable Zoo, a petting zoo, is also a favorite of children.

After a morning at the zoo, hop on a riverboat for a cruise to the Aquarium of the Americas, which is quickly earning a reputation as one of the best aquariums in the country. Take a walk along a coral reef through an underwater tunnel; watch the sharks swim around the base of an oil rig replica; stroll through a misty tropical rain forest; and play with the penguins in the Living in Water gallery, which includes stage shows, hands-on graphics, and video presentations. There are even touch pools when looking isn't quite enough.

Finally, visit the Louisiana Nature Center and get up close and personal with nature. The center includes a planetarium and 86 acres of trails through woods and wetlands. There are hands-on exhibits along the way. On weekends, catch a laser rock show in the planetarium.

The Audubon Institute offers family programs for its members. Sail on an oyster schooner, sleep overnight in the aquarium or the zoo, enjoy a moonlight canoe trip and cookout, attend a workshop in Mother & Daughter Wilderness Skills, or go on a Twilight Trek. For children, there are classes such as Pondering Penguins, Nature Make 'n' Take Crafts, Animal Athletes, and Caring for Critters. Toddlers have their own special programs.

Family membership for all three facilities costs just over $100 per year and offers free admission to the zoo, aquarium, and nature center; access to members-only entrances; a subscription to the AIM newsletter and *Audubon Institute Quarterly* magazine; discounts for the riverboat cruise between the zoo and the aquarium, the gift shops, facility rental for private parties, tickets for fund-raisers, and education programs; and invitations to special family events. You can become a member of the facilities separately or to only two if you prefer.

For information: Call (504) 861-5105 or write to the Audubon Institute, PO Box 4327, New Orleans, LA 70178-4327.

City Park

In City Park, kids can get some exercise and spend time outdoors. The 1,500-acre park is home to beautiful live oaks, lagoons, botanical gardens, and boating, canoeing, golf, tennis, and fishing facilities. A little children's amusement park offers puppet shows, storytelling, a carousel, and pony rides. The annual events, "Ghosts in the Oaks" at Halloween and "Celebration in the Oaks" at Christmas, are big hits with children.

Hours and admission times vary, so call ahead.

For information: Call (504) 482-4888.

Jackson Square

Jackson Square is a public plaza surrounded by shops, restaurants, the Cabildo and Presbytere museums, and St. Louis Cathedral. The plaza has a festival atmosphere, with street performers, local artists showing their wares, and tap dancers. Just across Decatur Street is the Moon Walk along the Mississippi River. Jackson Square is the heart of New Orleans and a fun, inexpensive way to spend an afternoon. The plaza is bordered by Chartres, St. Ann, St. Peter, and Decatur Streets and is within walking distance of the Jax Brewery.

Le Petit Theatre du Vieux Carre

Le Petit Theatre du Vieux Carre is a children's theater in the French Quarter. Hours and admission vary with production. Tickets are usually about $14 to $18 for adults and $10 to $14 for students.

For information: Call (504) 522-2081. The theater is located at St. Peters and Chartres Streets in the French Quarter.

Louisiana Children's Museum

The Louisiana Children's Museum is an educational playground, with most of the activities designed for children 12 and under. There is lots of hands-on fun, including a coffee factory, mini-supermarket, TV studio, and hospital. Kids can steer a tugboat, bicycle ride with a skeleton, help build a Mardi Gras float, crack a safe, and see their own shadows glow. Two exceptional exhibits are Body Works, where children learn the importance of health and fitness by testing their own skills, and Challenges, where kids can experience the realities of how physically challenged people accomplish daily activities. The First Adventure Toddler Playscape keeps little ones occupied and happy with developmentally appropriate toys and activities. The Lab has 45 stations where kids can explore and experiment with the principles of physics and math. The museum also offers live demonstrations, theatrical presentations, and science workshops.

Admission is $5 for everyone over 1 year of age. Infants under the age of 1 are admitted free. The museum is open 9:30 A.M. to 5:30 P.M. Tuesday through Saturday and noon to 5:00 P.M. on Sunday. During the summer, the museum is also open on Monday 9:30 A.M. to 5:00 P.M. The museum is closed on New Year's Day, Mardi Gras, Easter, July 4th, Thanksgiving, and Christmas.

For information: Call (504) 523-1357. The museum is located at 420 Julia St.

New Orleans Streetcar

One of the best bangs for your buck in New Orleans is a streetcar ride up St. Charles Avenue. The streetcar (don't let the locals hear you call it a "trolley") goes right through the Garden District, past the beautiful, grand homes along the avenue. The streetcar passes Tulane and Loyola universities, Audubon Park, and a number of shops and eateries.

You can also ride the Riverfront streetcar, which shuttles people along the Mississippi River between Riverwalk and the French Quarter.

Fare for the streetcar is $1.25.

New York City

American Museum of Natural History

The American History Museum, the largest in the world, is not to be missed. The museum, thought by many to be the best in the United States, houses more than 30 million specimens and artifacts. The dinosaur exhibits, such as the five-story-tall *Barosaurus,* are enchanting and awe-inspiring. Kids enjoy the lifelike animal dioramas, the dinosaur "mummy," and the hall of minerals and gems. Children 5 and older will enjoy the Discovery Room, where they can explore science through hands-on activities. The museum hosts a variety of family workshops and dance, music, and storytelling programs for kids.

Admission is $8 for adults, $6 for students and seniors, and $4.50 for children ages 2 to 12. Children under 2 are admitted free. The museum is open 10 A.M. to 5:45 P.M. Sunday through Thursday and 10 A.M. to 8:45 P.M. on Friday and Saturday, except for Thanksgiving and Christmas.

For information: Call (212) 769-5000, or (212) 769-5920 for recorded information. The museum is located at Central Park West and 79th St.

Bronx Zoo Wildlife Conservation Park

The Bronx Zoo, the country's largest municipal zoo, covers 265 acres and is inhabited by more than 4,000 animals. The animals are separated from visitors by moats, not cages. Kids clamor around Jungle World and the Himalayan exhibit with pandas and snow leopards. The Bengali Express monorail through the Wild Asia exhibit is also a big attraction. In the children's zoo, kids 8 and under can pet and feed the animals, climb a rope spiderweb, try on a turtle shell, sit in a giant bird's nest, and slide down a hollow tree.

Admission is $6.75 for visitors ages 13 to 64 and $3 for children 2 to 12 and seniors. Children under 2 are admitted free. There is no admission charge on Wednesday. Parking is $6. From April through October, the zoo is open 10 A.M. to 5 P.M. Monday through Friday and 10 A.M. to 5:30 P.M. on weekends. From November through March, the zoo is open daily 10 A.M. to 4:30 P.M.

For information: Call (718) 367-1010. The zoo is located at 2300 Southern Blvd. in the Bronx.

Brooklyn Children's Museum

The best part of the Brooklyn Children's Museum is the imaginative corrugated-metal tunnel entrance with neon lighting. This hands-on educational playground is full of exciting learning opportunities with bright graphics and an invigorating atmosphere. The big favorites with kids are the waterwheel and the walking piano. In Night Journeys, kids learn about sleep, beds, and dreams and can try out a life-size re-creation of an Egyptian leather-strap bed. Children can rid themselves of bad dreams by describing the dream on paper and then shoving it into the mouth of Baku, the dream eater. The museum also hosts a daily variety of "action" workshops and programs.

The suggested donation for admission is $3. The museum is open 2 P.M. to 5 P.M. Wednesday through Friday and noon to 5 P.M. on weekends and most holidays.

For information: Call (718) 735-4400. The museum is located at 145 Brooklyn Ave. in Brooklyn.

Central Park

No visit to New York City would be complete without a ride on the antique carousel in Central Park. Choose one of 58 painted, hand-carved horses and take a twirl. Afterward, kids can sail toy boats in "the sail-boat pond," climb on the Alice in Wonderland statue, and feed the ducks. Families can also take a ride in a horse-drawn carriage for about $35 for 30 minutes.

The carousel costs $.90 per person. From May through September, it is open 10:30 A.M. to 5:30 P.M. Monday through Friday and until 6:30 P.M. on weekends. From October through April, the carousel runs daily 10:30 A.M. to 4:30 P.M., weather permitting. The park is bordered by 121st St., Fifth Ave., 59th St., and Central Park West.

Children's Museum of Manhattan

The Children's Museum of Manhattan is home to five floors of interactive exhibits geared to toddlers, preschoolers, and older children. Toddlers enjoy the sandy beach and the Family Learning Center; and preschoolers and older kids get a kick out of the Urban Tree House and the Sussman Environmental Center. Kids can climb through a 14-foot ear, compose and record their own music, and be a talk-show guest. The museum sponsors parent and child classes and special events, including Drum Circles, summer games, and Double Dutch jump-rope demonstrations. Daily events include sing-alongs, art projects, and story times.

Admission is $5 per person. Senior admission is $2.50. Children under 2 are admitted free. The museum is open 1:30 P.M. to 5:30 P.M. Monday, Wednesday, and Thursday and 10 A.M. to 5 P.M. Friday through Sunday. Summer hours extend 10 A.M. to 8 P.M. Wednesday and 10 A.M. to 5 P.M. Thursday through Monday.

For information: Call (212) 721-1234. The museum is located at 212 W. 83rd St.

Children's Museum of the Arts

The Children's Museum of the Arts helps open doors to art appreciation for children. Through hands-on, interactive exhibits with art-related themes, children can learn about art and create some of their own. Kids are encouraged to design and make collages, clay models, and paintings.

Admission is $5 on weekends and $4 Tuesday through Friday. The museum is open noon to 6 P.M. Tuesday through Friday and 11 A.M. to 5 P.M. on weekends.

For information: Call (212) 941-9198. The museum is located at 72 Spring St.

F. A. O. Schwarz

Imagine two floors of colorful oversized stuffed animals (some as big as Mom and Dad), trains, dolls, and kid-size cars, all beckoning your children to try them out. That's F. A. O. Schwarz, a toy store unlike any other toy store. It is magnificent. The best part about it is that kids can try out Legos, video games, real kid-size cars, and all kinds of toys. They will have a blast. The unfortunate part is that the merchandise is very expensive. It is only a good deal if you can get out of the store without buying anything.

F. A. O. Schwarz is open 10 A.M. to 7 P.M. Monday through Thursday, 10 A.M. to 8 P.M. Friday and Saturday, and 11 A.M. to 6 P.M. Sunday. Call the store to hear about special events.

For information: Call (212) 644-9400. The store is located at Fifth Ave. and 58th St.

Hayden Planetarium

The Hayden Planetarium, located at the American Museum of Natural History, offers two special sky shows just for kids on weekends. In addition to the shows, children will enjoy the spectacular collection of astronomical displays on meteorites, comets, and space vehicles.

Tickets are $5 for adults and $2.50 for children ages 2 to 12. Reservations are required. From October through June, the planetarium is open 12:30 P.M. to 4:45 P.M. Monday through Friday, 10 A.M. to 5:45 P.M. on Saturday, and noon to 5:45 P.M. on Sunday. From July through September, the planetarium is open 12:30 P.M. to 4:45 P.M. Monday through Friday and noon to 4:45 P.M. on Saturday and Sunday.

For information: Call (212) 769-5920. The planetarium is located at Central Park West and 79th St.

Metropolitan Museum of Art

The Metropolitan Museum of Art has a variety of programs for families, including a kids' newsletter that comes out three times a year and is filled with games, information about current exhibits, and schedules of programs at the Met. There are lecture series for families, Saturday family films, and classes for children including junior high and high school students. Art Hunt brochures take kids through the museum by asking questions that lead them to different works of art. You can also request gallery guides for families chock-full of activities about specific exhibits at the museum. For example, in the Musical Instruments guide, children are asked to design their own lute, locate specific instruments in the exhibit, and make up their own song. At-home activities and reading lists are also included in the guides. Ask about these materials and other activities for families at the information desks.

For information: Call (212) 650-2888 or write to Metropolitan Museum of Art, 1000 Fifth Ave., New York, NY 10028-0198.

Museum of Modern Art

The Museum of Modern Art offers a host of programs for families on Saturday mornings throughout the year at a very low cost. You can take guided tours designed especially to introduce children to art, play gallery games to help learn the art of looking at art, hunt for animals and hidden images on an Arty Safari, send 4-year-olds on Tours for Tots, or watch family films.

Admission to these programs is $5 for the whole family and is limited to children ages 5 to 10 (except for the Tours for Tots for 4-year-olds). MoMA also hosts family festivals and other events throughout the year.

For information: Write to Family Programs, Museum of Modern Art, 11 W. 53rd St., New York, NY 10019.

New York Hall of Science

The New York Hall of Science is the only hands-on science and technology museum for children in New York City. Children can explore the world of color, light, and perception in Seeing the Light, discover the magic of Feedback through self-sensing machines, see the world's first three-dimensional dynamic model of a hydrogen atom, and burn energy at the Structures playground and construction zone. The museum hosts the Discover Activities Related to Science program, which includes several workshops for families on weekends.

Admission is $4.50 for adults and $3 for children ages 3 to 15 and seniors. The museum is open 10 A.M. to 5 P.M. Wednesday through Sunday. Admission is free 2 P.M. to 5 P.M. on Wednesday and Thursday.

For information: Call (718) 699-0005. The museum is located at 111th St. and 48th Ave. in Flushing Meadows Corona Park.

Staten Island Children's Museum

The Staten Island Children's Museum is part of the Snug Harbor Cultural Center, which sits on 80 acres overlooking New York Harbor. The museum has several hands-on exhibits, including Building Buildings, where kids can play in a construction site. Portia's Playhouse is a children's theater full of costumes, props, and theater equipment. The museum also hosts Walk-In! workshops where children can create and experiment with arts and crafts. Kids can also learn the magic behind magic tricks, explore a pirate ship, crawl through an ant farm, and create mazes.

Admission is $4 per person. Children under the age of 2 are admitted free. The museum is open noon to 5 P.M. Tuesday through Sunday, with extended hours in the summer.

For information: Call (718) 273-2060. The museum is located at 1000 Richmond Ter. at the Snug Harbor Cultural Center on Staten Island.

Philadelphia, Pennsylvania

Franklin Institute Science Museum

This huge, hands-on science complex opens up worlds of wonder for creative minds and busy hands. The institute is made up of the Science Center, the Mandell Center, and the Pendleman Omniverse Theater and Planetarium. In the Science Center, kids can walk through a heart 15,000 times its actual size, watch light bend, board a T-33 Jet Trainer, and ride the 350-ton Baldwin locomotive. There are daily demonstrations on how lightning works and what energy is. The planetarium offers shows on black holes, satellite technology, and constellations, as well as laser light shows. Kids will also enjoy the Omniverse Theater and the Mandell Center.

The institute advises calling directly for hours and admission fees, as they differ for each facility.

For information: Call (215) 448-1200. The institute is located at 20th and Ben Franklin Pkwy.

Philadelphia Zoo

The Philadelphia Zoo, established in 1859, is the oldest zoo in the United States. The zoo consists of 42 acres of mammals, reptiles, and birds residing in natural-habitat displays. The zoo is home to America's first white lions, Jezebel and Vinkel. The zoo's most popular exhibits include the Carnivore Kingdom, the Rare Animal House, and Bear Country. Kids use special "elephant" keys to activate the Talking Storybooks, pet and feed barnyard animals in the Children's Zoo, and climb inside a four-story tropical tree in the Treehouse. An elevated monorail is available for tired feet. There are also camel, elephant, and pony rides.

Admission is $8.50 for adults and $6 for children 2 to 11 and seniors. Admission to the Treehouse is an additional $1. The zoo is open 9:30 A.M. to 4:45 P.M. Monday through Friday and 9:30 A.M. to 5:45 P.M. on weekends and holidays. From December to February, the zoo is open 10 A.M. to 4 P.M. daily.

For information: Call (215) 243-1100. The zoo is located at 3400 W. Girard Ave.

Please Touch Museum

The Please Touch Museum is a hands-on museum designed for children 7 years of age and younger. The museum ensures that all the activities are educational, fun, and safe. Kids can visit a Russian kindergarten, listen to lullabies from around the world, drive a bus, operate a cargo crane, sail a boat, dig for potatoes, create sound effects, or read the evening news on camera. There is a garden spot for children 2 and under. Be sure to visit the Tortoise Lounge, the Pegafoamasaurus, and Baby's World. The museum also offers workshops and activities for children, including entertaining performances and plays.

Admission is $6.95 per person. Children under the age of 1 are admitted free. Regular hours are 9 A.M. to 4:30 P.M. daily. Between July 1 and Labor Day, the museum stays open until 6 P.M. On Sunday mornings between 9 A.M. and 10 A.M. you may "Pay What You Wish," making a voluntary donation instead of paying an admission fee. Strollers are not permitted in the gallery, but there is a place to park them while you are inside.

For information: Call (215) 963-0667. The museum is located at 210 N. 21st St.

Thomas H. Kean New Jersey State Aquarium at Camden

While not technically in Philadelphia, the Thomas H. Kean New Jersey State Aquarium is just across the river. The aquarium features an amazing 760,000-gallon ocean tank, a trout stream, and a petting tank full of skates, rays, starfish, and small sharks. The Conservation Puppet Theater stages shows that teach children the importance of protecting coral reefs.

Admission is $10.95 for adults, $9.45 for seniors and students, and $7.95 for children ages 3 to 11. Children under 3 are admitted free. The aquarium is open daily 10 A.M. to 5 P.M.

For information: Call (800) 616-JAWS (616-5297). The aquarium is located at 1 Riverside Dr. in Camden, New Jersey.

Phoenix, Arizona

Heard Museum

The Heard Museum was founded in the late 1920s and focuses on native cultures of the southwestern United States. The award-winning Native Peoples of the Southwest exhibit traces the history of the region from 15,000 B.C. to the present. The Old Ways, New Ways exhibit is a hands-on way for children to learn about the cultures of the Southwest Zuni, Northwest Coast Tsimshiam, and the Great Plains Kiowa peoples. Another favorite of kids is the gallery of Hopi kachina dolls.

Admission is $5 for adults, $4 for seniors and students, $3 for children ages 13 to 18, and $2 for children ages 4 to 12. Children under 4 are admitted free. Admission is free Wednesdays 5 P.M. to 8 P.M. The museum is open 9:30 A.M. to 5 P.M. Monday through Saturday, staying open until 8 P.M. on Wednesday, and noon to 5 P.M. Sunday.

For information: Call (602) 252-8840. The museum is located at 22 E. Monte Vista Rd.

Phoenix Zoo

The Phoenix Zoo rests on 125 acres with more than 1,200 animals living in its naturalistic habitats. The zoo is known for its oryx herd and its dedication to endangered species. The displays of Arizona's natural habitats are inspiring, from deserts to 10,000-foot peaks. The new Forest of Uco exhibit features spectacled bears and howler monkeys. The zoo is organized into 5 trails: the Tropics Trail, Africa Trail, Arizona Trail, Desert Trail, and Children's Trail (which winds through kid-size exhibits and ends up at the playground).

Admission is $8.50 for adults ages 13 to 59, $7.50 for seniors, and $4.25 for children 3 to 12. Children 2 and under are admitted free. The zoo is open daily 9 A.M. to 5 P.M. Summer hours are 7 A.M. to 4 P.M., May 1 through Labor Day.

For information: Call (520) 273-7771. The zoo is located at 455 N. Galvin Pkwy.

Rawhide's 1880s Western Town

Rawhide's 1880s Western Town is a replica of an entire Old West town on 160 acres of natural desert. There are 20 shops and galleries, a shooting gallery, and an authentic blacksmith shop and general store. Kids can get arrested by a U.S. marshal, ride a stagecoach, pet a sheep, pan for gold, and ride a burro. The Rawhide Museum has historical items on display, including Geronimo's moccasins. A petting ranch, Kid's Territory, lets kids get into the action. The town also hosts sunset hay wagon rides, desert cookouts, Native American dancers, and the Rawhide Rough Riders Western Show.

Admission is free for everyone. Individual attractions range from $.50 to $3. From October to May, the town is open 5 P.M. to 10 P.M. Monday through Thursday and 11 A.M. to 10 P.M. Friday through Sunday. From June to September, the town is open 5 P.M. to 10 P.M. daily.

For information: Call (602) 502-1880. The town is located at 23023 N. Scottsdale Rd. in Scottsdale.

Portland, Oregon

Children's Museum

The Children's Museum in Portland has lots of fun "please touch" exhibits for children from infants to age 10. Kids can experiment with pumps, drawbridges, and a bubble wall; shop for, sort, and ring up groceries; make clay creations to take home; learn how people in other cultures live; and play in the playground at Lair Hill Park. There is even a Baby Room where infants can discover new textures and adventures. Other exhibits include the Kid City Medical Center, fire engines, a railroad, and The How, Why, and Wow of Motion. The museum also sponsors activities for kids all week long.

Admission is $3.50 per person. Children under the age of 1 are admitted free. The museum is open 9 A.M. to 5 P.M. daily. Mondays and Thursdays are family days at the museum; no groups are allowed on those days so that there is more room for families to play and learn together.

For information: Call (503) 823-2227. The museum is located at 3037 SW Second Ave.

Metro Washington Park Zoo

The zoo is located in Washington Park, one of Portland's oldest parks, with wonderful views of both the city and mountains. In the park you'll also find the International Rose Test Gardens (free, and open daily from dawn to dusk), the authentic Japanese Gardens, the World Forestry Center, the Vietnam War Memorial, and the Hoyt Arboretum.

The Washington Park Zoo is known for the 26 Asian elephants born there, the most successful breeding herd anywhere in the world. Kids love the polar bear and penguin exhibits, which can be viewed from both above and below the surface of the water. The Alaskan tundra exhibit, featuring grizzly bears, wolves, and musk oxen, is also a favorite of the small set.

Admission is $5.50 for adults, $4 for seniors, and $3.50 for kids 3 to 11. There is no charge for children under the age of 2. Admission is free on the second Tuesday of each month 3 P.M. to closing. The zoo is open daily 9:30 A.M. to 4 P.M. in the winter, 9:30 A.M. to 5 P.M. in the fall and spring, and 9:30 A.M. to 6 P.M. in the summer.

For information: Call (503) 226-1561. The zoo is located at 4001 SW Canyon Rd.

Oregon Museum of Science and Industry (OMSI)

The Oregon Museum of Science and Industry covers 2½ city blocks with its six large halls, Omnimax theater, planetarium, and the USS *Blueback* submarine. Exciting exhibits teach children about fascinating scientific phenomena. Kids can view the Transparent Woman, a see-through model whose organs light up; experience a simulated earthquake; trace the growth of a human fetus; and, for older children, ponder ethical issues concerning organ transplants and life-support systems. The Discovery Space is a place where children 7 and under can explore air, sand, and water.

For information: Call (503) 797-4000. The museum is located at 1945 SE Water Ave.

Weather Machine

The Weather Machine is a whimsical mechanical sculpture that predicts the next day's weather. Every day at noon, trumpets blare, water sprays, and one of three symbols appears to depict the next day's weather. A gold sun heralds fair skies; a blue heron means clouds and drizzle; and a copper dragon warns of stormy weather.

The fountain is located at Pioneer Courthouse Square.

San Antonio, Texas

Hertzberg Circus Museum

You can't go wrong taking your children to the Hertzberg Circus Museum. Kids love all the circus memorabilia, including posters, photos, and costumes. Favorite exhibits include a miniature circus and Tom Thumb's miniature coach. The museum boasts over 20,000 pieces of circus history as well as a hands-on exhibit and special children's programs.

Admission is $2.50 for adults, $2 for seniors, and $1 for children 3 to 12. The collection is open 10 A.M. to 5 P.M. Monday through Saturday and 1 P.M. to 5 P.M. on Sundays and holidays from May to October.

For information: Call (210) 207-7810. The museum is located at 210 Market St.

La Villita

La Villita is a picturesque little Spanish town of charming cobblestone lanes nestled in the center of San Antonio. The town is more than 250 years old and is the original civilian settlement of San Antonio. Kids can watch the arts of glassblowing, weaving, doll making, and pottery here. There is no admission fee. The shops are open daily 10 A.M. to 6 P.M.

For information: Call (210) 224-INFO (224-4636) or (210) 207-8610. La Villita is located off Nueva, between Alamo and S. Presa Streets.

San Antonio Zoo

The San Antonio Zoo is located in beautiful Brackenridge Park, where dramatic cliffs provide a spectacular backdrop for animals living and playing in natural surroundings. The zoo boasts one of the largest animal collections in the United States, with more than 3,000 specimens including koalas, African antelope, exotic birds, and endangered whooping cranes. Kids enjoy Monkey Island, the outdoor hippo pool, the open bear pits, and the

$3 million children's zoo, featuring a Tropical Tour boat ride. Elephant and camel rides are available for children. You can take a tour on the Brackenridge Eagle mini-railway or the Skyride cable cars for a panoramic view of the city.

Admission is $6 for adults and $4 for children ages 3 to 11 and seniors. Children under the age of 3 are admitted free. The zoo is open daily 9:30 A.M. to 5 P.M., with longer hours in the summer.

For information: Call (210) 734-7183. The zoo is located at 3903 N. Saint Mary's St. in Brackenridge Park.

San Francisco, California

Bay Area Discovery Museum

The Bay Area Discovery Museum has a host of interactive exhibits aimed at children 1 to 10 years of age. The newest exhibit at the museum, Powerhouse, lets kids learn the dynamics of waterpower by using machines to pump water into a reservoir. The museum's strong point is its programs for kids. The variety of activities includes the annual Soapbox Derby complete with Soapbox Car Construction Clinics. There are also museum sleepovers for families, workshops for toddlers and preschoolers, Friday-night performances by storytellers and entertainers, arts and crafts activities, and many other inventive diversions.

Admission is $7 for adults and $6 for children. Infants under the age of 1 are admitted free. Summer hours (from June 15 to September 15) are 10 A.M. to 5 P.M., Tuesday through Sunday. School-year hours are 9 A.M. to 4 P.M. on Tuesday and Thursday and 10 A.M. to 5 P.M. on Friday, Saturday, and Sunday. Holiday hours are 10 A.M. to 5 P.M. The museum is closed Thanksgiving, Christmas, New Year's Day, Easter, and July 4th.

For information: Call (415) 487-4398. The museum is located at 557 McReynolds Rd. in Sausalito.

California Academy of Sciences

The California Academy of Sciences is a complex of three museums located in Golden Gate Park: the Natural History Museum, the Morrison Planetarium, and the Steinhart Aquarium. (Also in the park, you'll find a vintage carousel and playground.) Upon arrival, kids receive a map of the "Hidden World of the California Academy of Sciences" designed to make the museums more fun and interesting for them. In the Hands-On Science exhibit, kids play interactive science and nature games. Other big hits are Foucault's Pendulum and Safe Quake, a simulation of a huge earthquake. The planetarium offers special family shows (call 415-750-7141 for schedules).

Admission is $7 for adults, $4 for kids 12 to 17 and seniors, and $1.50 for kids 6 to 11. Children under the age of 6 are admitted free. Admission is free for everyone the first Wednesday of each month. From Labor Day to July 3, the academy is open daily 10 A.M. to 5 P.M. and from July 4th to Labor Day daily 10 A.M. to 7 P.M.

For information: Call (415) 750-7145. The museum is located in Golden Gate Park.

Exploratorium

The Exploratorium at the Palace of Fine Arts in San Francisco is the ultimate adventure in sensory experience. Dr. Frank Oppenheimer founded the museum in 1969 as a museum of "science, art, and human perception" to encourage learning through direct personal experience. With more than 650 exhibits, the museum allows kids to touch, smell, manipulate, and experience science in a memorable way that makes learning fun and exciting. The subject areas covered are light, color, sound, music, motion, animal behavior, electricity, heat and temperature, language, patterns, hearing, touch, vision, waves and resonance, and weather.

One of the highlights of the Exploratorium is the Tactile Dome, a 13-room, pitch-black environment that visitors must feel their way through. To help visitors along, each room is a different texture. Other features of the museum include creating vortexes in tubes of water, generating one's own electricity, freezing water in a vacuum, bending light, spinning in the momentum machine, and exploring chaotic motion. For parents of toddlers, there is an interactive environment designed for young children.

Admission to the museum is $9 for adults, $7 for students, $5 for kids ages 6 to 17, and $2.50 for children ages 3 to 5. Children under the age of 3 are free. A visit to the Tactile Dome costs $12 and includes museum admission. The museum is open daily 10 A.M. to 5 P.M. in the summer and is closed on Mondays from Labor Day to Memorial Day. On Wednesday, it's open until 9:30 P.M. On the weekends, films (free to museum visitors) are shown in the 175-seat McBean Theater.

For information: Call (415) 563-7337. For recorded information, call (415) 561-0360. The museum is located at 3601 Lyon St.

Lombard Street

Every child visiting San Francisco needs to take a trip down Lombard Street, otherwise known as "the crookedest street in the world." The 1000 block of Lombard Street is located between Hyde and Leavenworth Streets, winding down from Russian Hill. Kids will love a drive or a walk down the zigzagging, steep street that they've seen in numerous movies and TV shows. There is usually a line of cars waiting to drive down the street, so a walk might be the answer. Keep in mind that the walk down is steep and going back up can be strenuous.

Museum of Children's Art

At the Museum of Children's Art, kids can view works created by other children from all over the world. Lots of art supplies are on hand so that children can create their own masterpieces.

Admission is free for everyone. The museum is open 10 A.M. to 5 P.M. Monday through Friday, 11 A.M. to 5 P.M. on Saturday, and noon to 5 P.M. on Sunday.

For information: Call (510) 465-8770. The museum is located at 560 Second St. in Oakland.

Oakland Zoo

The Oakland Zoo offers 50 exhibits on 100 acres. The Flamingo Plaza and African Veldt are not to be missed. In the children's zoo, kids can pet and feed domestic animals and watch alligators. There are also a railroad ($.75 per person) and small carnival rides for children 3 and up.

Admission to the zoo is $5 for adults and $3 for children ages 2 to 14 and seniors. Children under the age of 2 are admitted free. Parking is $3. The zoo is open (weather permitting) 10 A.M. to 5 P.M. daily during the summer and 10 A.M. to 4 P.M. daily during the fall and winter. In the spring, the zoo is open 10 A.M. to 4 P.M. Monday through Friday and 10 A.M. to 5 P.M. on weekends. The zoo is closed on Thanksgiving and Christmas.

For information: Call (510) 632-9525. The zoo is located at 9777 Golf Links Rd. in Knowland Park in Oakland.

Pier 39

Pier 39 is a reconstructed pier turned into a popular entertainment complex filled with shops, restaurants, a double-decker Venetian carousel, and Underwater World—a 50,000-square-foot aquarium featuring California Marine Life. The best part of the pier is what happens on the docks below it. Hundreds of lazy sea lions loll in the sun on the docks, occasionally having territorial disputes or diving into the water for a swim. Kids and parents alike will be unable to take their eyes off these engaging animals.

For information: Pier 39 is located on Fisherman's Wharf.

San Francisco Zoo

The San Francisco Zoo is famous for its Gorilla World, Penguin Island, Koala Crossing, and Primate Discovery Center, where kids can participate in fun computer/slide programs and hands-on experiments. The Doelger Primate Discovery Center displays 15 species of rare and endangered monkeys and includes more than 20 interactive learning exhibits. Visit with creatures of the night in the Kresge Nocturnal Gallery. Kids can pet barnyard animals and watch baby lions being bottle-fed at the 7-acre Children's Zoo and can come face-to-face with creepy crawlers at the Insect Zoo. There are also a deer park, nature trail, chick hatchery, nature theater, railroad, carousel, and playground.

Admission is $7 for adults ages 16 to 65, $3.50 for kids 12 to 15 and seniors, and $1 for children 3 to 11. Children under 3 are admitted free. Admission is free for everyone the first Wednesday of each month. The zoo is open daily 10 A.M. to 5 P.M.; the children's zoo is open daily 11 A.M. to 4 P.M.

For information: Call (415) 753-7080. The zoo is located at 45th and Sloat Blvd.

Seattle, Washington

Children's Museum

The Children's Museum, located in the Seattle Center, lets kids play and learn their way through cultural exhibits, time zones, and mountain wilderness areas. There is an infant-toddler area with a giant soft ferryboat for climbing. The museum hosts several intergenerational programs and workshops. The museum's newest exhibit, MindScape, is a "weblike high-tech studio environment." Kids between 8 and 14 use high-tech equipment to play interactive problem-solving games, superimpose themselves onto a surfboard, and compose their own music.

Admission to the museum is $4.50. Hours are 10 A.M. to 6 P.M. Tuesday through Sunday, except for New Year's Day, Thanksgiving, and Christmas. On Saturday the museum is open until 7 P.M.

For information: Call (206) 441-1768. The museum is located in Center House at 305 Harrison St.

Pacific Science Center

The Pacific Science Center is a popular hands-on science museum for children. The museum offers astro-space displays, an operating oceanographic model of Puget Sound, a laserium, and a Northwest Indian longhouse. Kids can freeze their own shadows, study the Doppler radar in the Weather Center, play Virtual Hoops, explore the Science Playground, and blast off in Starship PSC. The museum also offers planetarium, laser, and IMAX shows.

Admission is $7.50 for adults, $5.50 for kids ages 6 to 13 and seniors, and $3.50 for kids ages 2 to 5. Children under 2 are admitted free. Tickets to the IMAX theater cost an additional $2. From June through September, the museum is open daily 10 A.M. to 6 P.M. From October through May, the museum is open 10 A.M. to 5 P.M. Monday through Friday and 10 A.M. to 6 P.M. on weekends. The museum is closed Thanksgiving and Christmas.

For information: Call (206) 443-2001. The museum is located at 200 Second Ave. North.

Seattle Aquarium

The Seattle Aquarium offers a wonderful look into the marine life of Puget Sound. The domed viewing room allows visitors to be surrounded by giant octopus, starfish, dogfish sharks, rock cod, red snapper, scallops, shrimp, and anemones. The aquarium is known for its Salmon Ladder. Try to stop by in the fall when the salmon return to spawn. Kids love the Coconut Crab exhibit, the family of sea otters, and the tropical fish. There are also an exhibit on pollution in Puget Sound, an interactive tide pool, and a discovery lab.

Admission is $7.15 for adults ages 19 to 64, $5.70 for seniors, $4.70 for kids 6 to 18, and $2.45 for children 3 to 5. Children under 3 are admitted free. From Labor Day to Memorial Day, the aquarium is open daily 10 A.M. to 5 P.M. From Memorial Day to Labor Day, the aquarium is open daily 10 A.M. to 7 P.M.

For information: Call (206) 386-4320. Hearing-impaired people can call the TDD/TTY line, (206) 386-4322. The aquarium is located at Pier 59 in Waterfront Park.

Seattle Children's Theatre

The Seattle Children's Theatre is committed to providing families with safe, fun, enriching entertainment. Families can share the excitement of live performances and follow up with animated discussions and related activities, such as reading the story the play was based on or acting out the play at home. Live theater unleashes young imaginations and introduces young minds to literature and history.

Most of the theater's plays are geared to children ages 8 and up; however, the theater offers a Doorway to Theatre series for younger children featuring plays created for the 4-and-up set. Past performances have included *Romeo and Juliet, The Odyssey, Pinocchio,* and *The Secret of Skullbone Island* (a Hardy Boys adventure).

Ticket prices are $17.50 for adults and $11.50 for children, students, and seniors. Tickets can be purchased for 3-, 4-, 5-, or 6-play series as well.

For information: Call (206) 441-3322 or write to Seattle Children's Theatre, P.O. Box 9640, Seattle, WA 98109-0640.

Woodland Park Zoo

The Woodland Park Zoo is home to more than 300 species of animals that reside in a series of bioclimatic exhibit zones. Visitors can stroll through the Tropical Rain Forest, Tropical Asia, African Savanna, Temperate Forest, or the Northern Trail. Children will delight in the ocelots, poisonous dart frogs, hippos, bald eagles, elephants, orangutans, brown bears, and otters. Kids will also enjoy a romp with barnyard animals at the Pacific Northwest Family Farm or a crawl through kid-size animal homes at the Habitat Discovery Loop.

Admission to the zoo is $8 for adults, $7.25 for seniors and students, $5.50 for kids ages 6 to 16, and $3.25 for children 3 to 5; children 2 and under are admitted free. Parking is $3.50. The zoo opens at 9:30 A.M. every day of the year. From October 31 to March 14, the zoo closes at 4 P.M.; from March 15 to October 30 the zoo closes at 6 P.M.

For information: Call (206) 684-4800. Hearing-impaired people can call the TDD line, (206) 684-4026. The zoo is located at N. 55th St. and Phinney Ave. N.

Washington, D.C.

Bureau of Engraving and Printing

The tour of the Bureau of Engraving and Printing is very popular with youngsters. The presses here print all the U.S. currency and stamps. Grade-schoolers and teens get the most from the tour.

Admission is free. The bureau is open 9 A.M. to 2 P.M. Monday through Friday and is closed on federal holidays. From June through August, evening hours from 4 P.M. to 7 P.M. are offered.

For information: Call (202) 874-3109, or (202) 874-3188 for recorded information. The bureau is located at 14th and C Streets.

Capital Children's Museum

The Capital Children's Museum has hundreds of hands-on exhibits combining arts, science, humanities, technology, and fun. Children can drive a bus, create yarn art, take charge of the city room, dance in a Mexican Plaza, dress up in period costumes, navigate a maze, get lost in a bubble, and feed animals.

Admission is $6. Children 2 and under are admitted free. The museum is open 7 days a week 10 A.M. to 5 P.M. except from Labor Day to Easter, when the museum is closed on nonholiday Mondays.

For information: Call (202) 543-8600. The museum is located at 800 Third St. NE.

Federal Bureau of Investigation

Young crime fighters will get a kick out of a visit to the FBI. The tour includes the history of the FBI, crime labs, a firearms demonstration, a collection of confiscated valuables, and a question-and-answer session with a special agent.

Admission is free. The bureau is open 8:45 A.M. to 4:15 P.M. Monday through Friday.

For information: Call (202) 324-3447. The FBI is located between 9th and 10th on E St. NW.

Geographica: The World at Your Fingertips

Geographica is an interactive exhibit located in Explorers Hall on the first floor of the National Geographic Society's headquarters. The museum of geography and exploration uses high-tech communication tools to stimulate the imagination. Kids can touch a tornado, play the continent game, explore the solar system, monitor the weather in Kenya, or travel through time to the early history of life on our planet. The centerpiece of the exhibit is Earth Station One, a 72-seat amphitheater facing an 11-foot-diameter globe. During a simulated orbital spaceflight 23,000 miles above the earth, visitors view our planet's geography from space and answer questions from a "pilot" narrator by pushing buttons at their seats. All the responses are tallied and displayed on video screens alongside the globe.

Admission is free. Explorers Hall is open 9 A.M. to 5 P.M. Monday through Saturday and holidays and 10 A.M. to 5 P.M. on Sunday. It is closed on Christmas. The facilities are handicapped-accessible.

For information: Call (202) 857-7588. The museum is located at 1145 17th St. NW.

Smithsonian Institution

You could spend a month at the Smithsonian Institution and never run out of things to see and learn. The Smithsonian consists of 14 museums and the National Zoo in Washington, D.C.

(There are also two museums in New York City.) The Smithsonian Information Center should be your first stop. The information center will get you going with a 20-minute video presentation, interactive touch-screen programs in six languages, electronic wall maps, scrolling screens featuring daily events, free guides in seven languages, and volunteer information specialists to answer questions and help plan your visit.

The museums that make up the Smithsonian Institution are the Smithsonian Institution Building, otherwise known as "The Castle"; the Anacostia Museum, featuring African-American history and culture; the Arthur M. Sackler Gallery, featuring changing exhibitions of Asian art; the Arts and Industries Building, featuring the materials acquired from the 1876 Centennial Exposition in Philadelphia; the Freer Gallery of Art, featuring Asian art and nineteenth- and twentieth-century American artists including James McNeill Whistler; the Hirshhorn Museum and Sculpture Garden, featuring modern art and contemporary visual expression; the National Air and Space Museum, featuring airplanes, spacecraft, missiles, rockets, and other flight-related technology; the National Museum of African Art, featuring an extensive collection of African art; the National Museum of American Art, featuring 37,500 paintings, sculptures, graphics, pieces of folk art, and photographs by American artists; the National Museum of American History, featuring objects that embody the nation's scientific, technological, and cultural heritage; the National Museum of Natural History, featuring more than 120 million objects, including the Hope diamond, dinosaurs, Native American artifacts, and a replica of an African bush elephant; the National Portrait Gallery, featuring portraits of the men and women significant to American history; the National Postal Museum, featuring the nation's postal history; and the Renwick Gallery, featuring twentieth-century crafts. You'll also enjoy the National Zoological Park, featuring approximately 5,000 animals of 500 different species, and the Smithsonian Gardens.

There are special attractions for children throughout the Smithsonian. Families will want to visit the carousel; the Discovery Theater; the Discovery Room and Insect Zoo in the Natural History Museum; the Hands On History Room, the Hands On Science Center, and the Demonstration Centers in the American History Museum; the IMAX films in the Air and Space Museum; the Discovery Center at the Postal Museum; and the Zoolab, the Bird Resource Center, and the Reptile Discovery Center at the National Zoo. Strollers are permitted in all museums and the zoo.

Admission to the Smithsonian museums and to the National Zoo is free. There are also free tours and free activities throughout the year. Most of the museums are open 10 A.M. to 5:30 P.M. daily, with extended hours in the spring and summer. The zoo is open 8 A.M. to 6 P.M. daily, with longer hours in the summer. The Smithsonian's Information Center is open 9 A.M. to 5:30 P.M. daily. All museums are closed on Christmas.

For information: Call (202) 357-2700, or Dial-A-Museum at (202) 357-2020 for recorded information. Hearing-impaired people can call the TTY line at (202) 357-1729. Or write to Smithsonian Information, Smithsonian Institution, MRC 010, Washington, DC 20560.

Chapter Six

Fifteen Other Attractions Kids Shouldn't Miss

Boeing Tour Center, Everett, Washington

Families with older children will enjoy the tour at the Boeing airplane plant in Everett, Washington. For safety reasons, children must be 50 inches or taller to accompany the tour. The factory resides in the largest manufacturing building in the world: 10½ Kingdomes would fit inside. The factory doors alone are about the size of a football field. On the tour, visitors can watch actual airplanes being made, including wing assembly, engine installations, and final assembly. The factory produces wide-body, twin-aisle airplanes: 747s, 767s, and 777s. Kids will especially enjoy the airplane painting hangars, which are humidity and climate controlled. The airplanes are painted by hand using an electrostatic process.

The 90-minute tour is free of charge. Tickets are available first come, first served. Tours are scheduled Monday through Friday at 8 A.M., 9 A.M., 10 A.M., 1 P.M., and 2 P.M. from June through September. From October through May, there isn't an 8 A.M. tour. Tour space is limited, so, arrive early.

For information: Call the Boeing Tour Center at (206) 544-1264 or, if calling from Washington, Oregon, Idaho, or British Columbia, at (800) 464-1476.

Cane Island Flower Farm, Beaufort, South Carolina

The Cane Island Flower Farm is a magical place. Picture your-self standing in a field of yellow daffodils as far as the eye can see. You can pick as many as you like for just 10 cents a stem. Every year my mother picks bushels of daffodils here and overnights them to all her friends and relatives who live up north, where it is still the dead of winter. The daffodils bloom from about Valentine's Day to the Ides of March; prospective vis-itors should call the farm for more accurate harvest dates. Toward the end of daffodil season, Cane Island Flower Farm hosts a Daffodil Festival with live music, refreshments, and lots for kids to do, including arts and crafts, storytelling, treasure hunts, a petting zoo, and a visit from Flora the Elephant. Fam-ily ticket rates are available, and all the proceeds benefit local charities.

For information: Call the Cane Island Flower Farm at (803) 524-4120.

Cape Cod Potato Chips, Hyannis, Massachusetts

In 1980, Cape Cod Potato Chips began in a little shop making 200 bags of chips a day. Today, the company makes 150,000 bags of chips a day using the same kettle-cooked process and high standards of quality. Each potato delivery truck is sampled and tested before it is accepted. Potatoes are then peeled and individually inspected. The potatoes are washed and sliced and then put directly into a kettle fryer. When the chips are done, the excess oil is spun off in a centrifuge. Then they are seasoned and packaged.

The factory tour covers all the chip-making steps. Guests will also see popcorn made and packaged at a rate of 17 bags a minute. The free, self-guided tour ends with a free bag of chips and a visit to the retail store. The factory is open to the public 10 A.M. to 4 P.M. Monday through Friday.

For information: Call Cape Cod Potato Chips at (508) 775-3206. The museum is located at 100 Breeds Hill Rd.

Carnegie Museums, Science Center, and Library, Pittsburgh, Pennsylvania

The Carnegie Museums, Science Center, and Library offer four museums in one place and something for everyone in the family. The Carnegie Museum of Natural History showcases the *Tyrannosaurus rex,* treasures from an Egyptian tomb, the sarcophagus known as "Chantress of Amun," and the Hall of African Wildlife. Kids will love the Discovery Room where they are invited to touch everything. The Carnegie Museum of Art exhibits impressionist and postimpressionist paintings, decorative arts, sculpture, film, and architecture. The Andy Warhol Museum will captivate even the most sullen teenager. More than 3,000 works of art from Warhol's Factory are displayed here. The Carnegie Science Center is a hands-on, interactive museum with exhibits to capture the imagination of all kids, from toddlers to teenagers. There are more than 250 exhibits on such subjects as curveballs, cryogenics, WWII submarines, and miniature railroads. You can also visit the Carnegie Library of Pittsburgh and the Carnegie Music Hall and Performing Arts.

The Carnegie Science Center hosts family overnighters periodically throughout the summer. Overnighters enjoy an Omnimax film, a late-night laser show, unique demonstrations, a planetarium show, 250 hands-on exhibits, themed activities, family workshops, a snack, breakfast, free parking, and a souvenir. The cost is approximately $60 for a family of four.

Admission to the Carnegie Museum of Art and the Carnegie Museum of Natural History is $5 for adults and $3 for students and children ages 3 through 18. The museums are open 10 A.M. to 5 P.M. Tuesday through Saturday and 1 P.M. to 5 P.M. on Sunday. Call for information on summer and holiday hours. The Carnegie Science Center is open 10 A.M. to 5 P.M. Monday through Thursday and 10 A.M. to 6 P.M. Friday through Sunday. Admission is $5.75 for adults and $4.25 for children ages 3 through 18. The Andy Warhol Museum is open 11 A.M. to 6 P.M. on Wednesday and Sunday and 11 A.M. to 8 P.M. on Thursday, Friday, and Saturday. Carnegie has a special Explorer Pass, which offers admission to all four museums for one low price: $14 for adults and $8 for children ages 3 to 18.

For information: For information about the Carnegie Museum of Art and the Carnegie Museum of Natural History, call (412) 622-3131. For information on the Carnegie Science Center, call (412) 237-3400. For information on the Andy Warhol Museum, call (412) 237-8300.

Christa McAuliffe Planetarium, Concord, New Hampshire

The Christa McAuliffe Planetarium is a 92-seat theater where even the littlest scientist can explore space in an exciting and inspiring one-hour show. The show takes place on a domed screen overhead, enhanced by wraparound sound, multi-image animation, and computer graphics. There are currently five shows to choose from. "Destiny or Discovery" takes you into the past to Christopher Columbus's discovery of America and into the future to experience life onboard a space habitat. In "Pathfinders," the mission is to rescue three crew members from a spaceship spinning out of control in the year 2058. "Skybound" is a more traditional planetarium show letting visitors view the current night sky. "Through the Eyes of Hubble" lets you see footage from NASA's Hubble Space Telescope. A special show for preschoolers complete with singing Sesame Street characters, "Wonderful Sky" lets children delight in the wonders of the sky, rainbows, stars, and sunsets.

The planetarium also hosts several activities just for kids, where they can make model rockets, attend workshops for young astronomers, and participate in Astronomy Days for the whole family.

Admission is $6 for adults and $3 for students and children ages 3 to 17. On Fridays, there are three matinees, with admission $3 for everyone. Reservations are recommended.

For information: For show schedules and reservations, call (603) 271-STAR (271-7827) or write to Christa McAuliffe Planetarium, 3 Institute Dr., Concord, NH 03301.

Crayola Factory at Two Rivers Landing, Easton, Pennsylvania

The Crayola Factory at Two Rivers Landing is a new facility with more than a dozen interactive exhibits that encourage creativity. Kids can watch Crayola crayons and markers being made. They can also color on the walls of a giant glass tunnel; climb the media maze, triggering lighting and audio surprises along the way; add their artistic touch to an ever-changing three-dimensional sculpture; and create posters, name tags, and greeting cards on computers.

Admission to the Crayola Factory is $6 for adults and children. Children under 2 are admitted free. The factory is open 9:30 A.M. to 5 P.M. Tuesday through Saturday and noon to 5 P.M. on Sunday. The factory is open on Monday on the following holidays: Martin Luther King Jr. Day, Presidents' Day, Memorial Day, Labor Day, and Columbus Day. The factory is closed on New Year's Day, Easter, Thanksgiving, and Christmas. There is a McDonald's restaurant on-site and a Crayola Store. Children should wear appropriate clothing (they might get colored on).

For information: Call (610) 515-8000 or write to Crayola Factory, 30 Centre Sq., Easton, PA 18042-7744.

Hallmark Visitors Center, Kansas City, Missouri

The Hallmark Visitors Center presents guests with 14 exhibits. Enter a room filled with giant pencils, paints, and brushes and watch a film about how the artists at Hallmark create designs. Watch artists create the "dies" used in die cutting or embossing. Learn how cards are made and watch a press operator demonstrate the processes used in manufacturing cards. Press a button and watch a bow machine create a bow.

Admission is free. The Hallmark Visitors Center is open 9 A.M. to 5 P.M. Monday through Friday and 9:30 A.M. to 4:30 P.M. on Saturday. Call the center for special holiday hours.

For information: Call (816) 274-5672, or for reservations, call (816) 274-3613. The visitors center is located in Hallmark Square, at 2450 Grand Ave.

Jelly Belly Candy Trail at the Herman Goelitz Candy Co., Fairfield, California

The whole family will enjoy a trip to the Herman Goelitz Candy Co., where 40 million Jelly Belly beans are produced each day, along with 100 other confections. "Trail Guides" will lead guests along an elevated walkway above the factory floor and distribute samples during each of the three stages of production, all the while explaining why each Jelly Belly takes 7 to 10 minutes to create. The tour ends in the factory store, where you can buy bags of Belly Flops, candies that don't meet the standards for size and color.

The Jelly Belly Candy Trail is a quarter-mile long and takes about 30 minutes to walk through. The free tours are given on a first-come, first-served basis Monday through Friday 9 A.M. to 2 P.M. The factory is closed holidays, April 1, and the last week of June through the first week of July.

For information: Call (707) 428-2838 for tour information or write to the Jelly Belly Candy Trail, 2400 N. Watney Way, Fairfield, CA 94533. For a free Jelly Belly Menu, call (800) JB-BEANS (522-3267).

Magic House, St. Louis Children's Museum, St. Louis, Missouri

The Magic House is one of the most popular children's museums in the United States, with more than 300,000 visitors a year. Situated in a three-story Victorian house, the museum hosts more than 70 hands-on exhibits designed to refine gross motor skills, enhance a child's self-concept, and build self-esteem.

This museum has an exhibit for everyone, even the youngest visitors. "A Little Bit of Magic" is designed for 1- to 7-year-olds, with ball pits, doorbells to ring, and a miniature mouse house. In other exhibits, kids can manipulate magnets, slide down a three-story slide, send secret messages to friends, puzzle over optical illusions, and visit the "Touch Tunnel."

Admission is $3.50 for adults and children and $2.50 for seniors. Children under 2 are admitted free. During the school

Libraries

Local libraries are an indefatigable source of fun for kids. Kids enjoy the whole experience of going to the library, selecting their own books, and checking them out, just as you did when you were a kid. But today's libraries offer kids a whole lot more than they used to. Go to your library and visit the children's section. You're liable to encounter puppet shows, magicians, and crafts projects going on. Many libraries offer a variety of programs and services that are either free or inexpensive. Story times, children's play areas, workshops, after-school programs, and family activities are found at many libraries around the country.

"Catch 'Em in the Cradle" is a new program that is catching on around the country. In this program, library information kits containing information on stimulating language development through games, songs, and other activities are distributed to new parents through hospitals, adoption centers, and prenatal classes. Older kids can surf the Internet at most libraries, call homework hot lines, and attend term-paper clinics. Parents can often find parenting workshops and support groups.

year, the museum is open 1 P.M. to 5:30 P.M. Tuesday through Thursday, 1 P.M. to 9 P.M. Friday, 9:30 A.M. to 5:30 P.M. Saturday, and 11:30 A.M. to 5:30 P.M. Sunday. During the summer, the museum is open 9:30 A.M. to 5:30 P.M. Tuesday through Thursday, 9:30 A.M. to 9 P.M. Friday, 9:30 A.M. to 5:30 P.M. Saturday, and 11:30 A.M. to 5:30 P.M. Sunday. Parking is free. On the third Friday of each month, the museum hosts Free Family Night; parents and up to four of their own children are admitted free 5:30 P.M. to 9 P.M.

For information: Call (314) 822-8900 or write to the Magic House, 516 S. Kirkwood Rd., St. Louis, MO 63122.

Monterey Bay Aquarium, Monterey, California

The Monterey Bay Aquarium is an innovative facility dedicated to preserving the abundance of life in the oceans of the world. The centerpiece is the Outer Bay, a million-gallon indoor ocean that is home to some animals that have rarely been exhibited in an aquarium before: blue and soupfin sharks, ocean sunfish, green sea turtles, barracuda, pelagic stingrays, and tuna are displayed. Never before has ocean life been presented on such a grand scale.

Home of the tallest aquarium exhibit in the world, the aquarium transports you to the dramatic Kelp Forest: three stories of swaying kelp fronds and all the life they sustain. The Octopus and Kin exhibit delves into the relationships between octopuses, chambered nautiluses, and other sea life. The always delightful sea otters can be seen from above and below in their new two-story exhibit.

Children will enjoy the feeding shows and the touch pools, where they can feel bat rays, decorator crabs, and sea stars. There is also an exhibit just for them: "Flippers, Flukes & Fun" is filled with hands-on displays that show children how sea mammals such as whales and dolphins adapt to life in the ocean. Kids can don flippers to see how fish swim, wrap themselves in simulated "blubber," and squeak with dolphins.

The aquarium is open 10 A.M. to 6 P.M. daily, except during summer and holidays when it opens at 9:30 A.M. Admission is $13.75 for adults, $11.75 for kids ages 13 to 17 and full-time students, and $6 for children ages 3 to 12. Children under the age of 3 are admitted free. Family memberships are available for $75 per year. Benefits include free admission for two adults and children between the ages of 3 and 21, express entry through the members' entrance, monthly members' nights, previews of special exhibitions, a subscription to *Shorelines*, and discounts at the gift store and bookstore. Families enjoy special programs such as behind-the-scenes tours, art workshops, Supper in the Sea, Otter Adventures, Sea Life Book-Making, and Sea Babies.

The aquarium is ideally located on historic Cannery Row, made famous in John Steinbeck's book. After visiting the aquarium, you can spend time scuba diving, kayaking, in-line skating, bicycling, or exploring the rich tide pools. There are more than a hundred shops and several restaurants in the area.

For information: Call (408) 648-4888 or write to Monterey Bay Aquarium, 886 Cannery Row, Monterey, CA 93940-1085.

MOSI, Tampa, Florida

Science has never been more fun than at the MOSI in Tampa. This state-of-the-art 47-acre facility is home to the only IMAX DOME theater in Florida and Tampa's only planetarium. The Saunders Planetarium offers special family shows throughout the week, covering such topics as a preview of that night's skies, constellation identification, and the latest issues in astronomy. The most exciting visit in the museum is the GTE Challenger Learning Center, dedicated to the memory of the *Challenger* crew. The exhibit features a mission control simulator and a spacecraft simulator; visitors can experience the challenges of space travel from both sides of the atmosphere. Back on earth, shrink down to the size of a bug and tour the Garden Shed, making your exit through a crack in the planks. Crawl through a gopher tortoise habitat, explore anatomy Inside the Human Machine, navigate the wheelchair course to understand the challenges of disabled people, anchor the news at the WFLA Newschannel 8 News Desk, and ride out a simulated Florida thunderstorm. Toddlers can blow off steam in the Kids-In-Charge space.

Family memberships are available for $50 per year for five family members; additional family members are $5 each. Benefits for family memberships are unlimited free admission; five MOSIMAX theater tickets (additional tickets given for each additional family membership bought); discounts for special programs, Science Stores, restaurants, birthday parties, and additional MOSIMAX tickets; special members' parking area and entrance; and free or discounted admission to 150 other Association of Science and Technology Centers (ASTC) member museums and science centers around the world. Families can participate in camp-ins, Funshops, Great Escapes, summer science camps, lectures, and seasonal activities.

Admission to the museum is $8 for adults 19 and over; $7 for students ages 13 to 18, college students with a valid ID, and seniors; and $5 for kids ages 2 through 12. Children under 2 are admitted free. MOSIMAX-only and combination tickets for the museum and MOSIMAX theater are also available. Operating hours are seasonal. Call for details.

For information: Call the MOSI reservation line at (800) 995-MOSI (995-6674) or the recorded information line at (813) 987-6100, or write to MOSI, 4801 E. Fowler Ave., Tampa, FL 33617-2099.

Orlando Science Center

The Orlando Science Center is an innovative children's museum with lots to offer. Kids can take a peek in The Gater Hole, create a tornado, "see" what sound looks like, build dams and canals, and touch live animals. Kids can also trade objects of nature with the museum by bringing in one of their own. The more they know about their item, the more trading points they earn. The museum also offers "Science-sational" demonstrations, planetarium sky shows, overnight camp-ins, and laser shows.

Admission to the museum is $6.50 for adults and $5.50 for children. The museum is open 9 A.M. to 5 P.M. Monday through Thursday and Saturday, 9 A.M. to 9 P.M. on Friday and noon to 5 P.M. on Sunday. The museum is closed on Thanksgiving and Christmas.

For information: Call (407) 896-7151. The museum is located at 810 E. Rollins St.

Purina Farms, Gray Summit, Missouri

Located near St. Louis, Purina Farms is a wonderful place to spend some time with our four-legged friends. Children can cuddle puppies and dogs, take part in an audience-participation dog show, visit the 28-foot Victorian cat house, cheer dogs through an obstacle course, milk a cow, and play in a hayloft. A hands-on exhibit demonstrates how Ralston makes pet foods. Visitors can also enjoy wagon rides; a children's play area and maze; interactive exhibits that teach children about animals; a barn full of horses, cows, sheep, pigs, and chickens; a gift shop; and a snack bar.

Admission and parking are free, but reservations are required. From Memorial Day through Labor Day, the facilities are open 9:30 A.M. to 3 P.M. Tuesday through Sunday. In spring and fall, the facilities are open 9:30 A.M. to 1 P.M. Wednesday through Friday and 9:30 A.M. to 3 P.M. on weekends.

For information: Call (314) 982-3232 or write to Purina Farms, 200 Checkerboard Dr., Gray Summit, MO 63039.

Space Center Houston

Space Center Houston brings to life the incredible story of NASA's manned-spaceflight program. The exhibits highlight the past, present, and future of the space program. Find out what's happening this very minute at NASA at the Mission Status Center, repair a satellite on the MMU trainer, try on a real space helmet, or land the space shuttle on a simulator. Kids and parents alike will be awestruck by the *Apollo 17* command module and the *Saturn V* rocket. There is also a five-story movie screen which allows visitors to experience space through the eyes of an astronaut. The museum also hosts a variety of educational and day camp programs for kids.

Admission is $11.95 for adults and $8.50 for children. From Memorial Day to Labor Day, the museum is open 9 A.M. to 7 P.M. daily. From Labor Day to Memorial Day, the museum is open 10 A.M. to 5 P.M. Monday through Friday and 10 A.M. to 7 P.M. on weekends.

For information: Call (800) 972-0369 or (713) 244-2100 or write to Space Center Houston, 1601 NASA Rd. 1, Houston, TX 77058.

Vermont Teddy Bear Company, Shelburne, Vermont

Delight your children by taking them on a tour of the whimsical home of the "Great American Teddy Bear." Kids can watch these lovable teddy bears brought to life by true teddy bear craftspeople. The lively tours last about a half hour. Families can walk right into the factory and see how the bears are handcrafted. The tour ends at the Bear Shop, filled with hundreds of adorable bears. Visitors receive a souvenir "button bear."

The tours are $1 for adults. Children ages 17 and under are free. The factory is open 9 A.M. to 6 P.M. Monday through Saturday and 10 A.M. to 5 P.M. on Sunday.

For information: Call (802) 985-3001 or write to Vermont Teddy Bear, 2236 Shelburne Rd., Shelburne, VT 05482.

PART THREE

Traveling Family Style

Chapter Seven

Family-Friendly Resorts

Resort vacations are a good way to solve the family vacation dilemma. By catering to the needs of both parents and children, resorts give families the opportunity to spend time together as well as allow for parents and children to have time on their own. Most family-oriented resorts offer day camps and evening programs for kids. Parents who want to play a round of golf, have a romantic dinner, or just spend the day lounging around the pool can. Kids enjoy the activities that are tailored to their ages and interests. Plus, there are lots of opportunities for the whole family to spend time together. Resorts are popular destinations for families.

Resort vacations can be economical, as well. Some resorts offer packages that include all activities and meals. These vacations are great for parents who don't want to think about the mounting costs of jet ski rentals, arts and crafts classes, and tennis lessons.

The prices listed in this section are based on 1996 rates. In an effort to offer as many specifics as possible, I have included current programs and amenities; these may change slightly over the course of time, but the details will give parents a better idea of exactly what each resort offers.

Arrowwood—A Radisson Resort, Alexandria, Minnesota

With views of lovely Lake Darling, guest rooms at Arrowwood are refreshing retreats from the pressures of everyday life. One-, two-, and three-bedroom suites, decorated in charming country decor, are available with such amenities as fireplaces, lofts, kitchens, and whirlpool spas. Arrowwood is a year-round resort with activities for every season, including golf, tennis, swimming, sailing, skiing, skating, sledding, biking, boating, and horseback riding. Guests will enjoy the full-service marina with fishing boats, waterskiing, sailboats, paddleboats, jet skis, canoes, and Windsurfers. Other recreational facilities and activities include an 18-hole golf course, a 30-horse stable, indoor and outdoor pools, indoor tennis, beach volleyball, a playground, groomed cross-country trails, snowmobiles, sledding hills, ice-skating, and horse-drawn sleigh rides.

For children ages 4 to 12, Camp Arrowwood offers adult-supervised activities. The kids' days are filled with swimming, fishing, arts and crafts, and nature walks. The camp runs 7 days a week 9 A.M. to 2 P.M.

Upon arrival, families will receive a brochure listing all the "Family Fun" activities available. There are pizza and T-shirt–painting parties, family beach cookouts, family scavenger hunts, kids' night out, beach bonfires, sunset cruises, water games, and a rodeo.

For information: Call Radisson Reservations Worldwide at (800) 333-3333 or contact your travel agent.

Crowne Plaza Resort, Hilton Head Island, South Carolina

The Crowne Plaza Resort at Hilton Head is a four-diamond luxury resort, located on 12 miles of white, sandy beaches.

Camp Castaway is a fully supervised, structured program for children 3 to 12 years of age. The camp is open 8:30 A.M. to 5 P.M., with full-day and half-day sessions, all summer and some Saturdays in the spring and fall. The counselors are CPR certified and first-aid trained. Children ages 3 to 5 are admitted to the morning program, where they can finger paint, build sand castles, hunt for shells, and feed turtles. Kids from 6 to 8 may fish in the lagoon, play games on the beach and in the pool, and make crafts. Older kids, from 9 to 12, participate in team-building and cooperation activities, such as tennis, golf, bike tours, and scavenger hunts. Camp Castaway also sponsors children's evening programs. The evening programs follow special themes around which all the activities and games are centered. The evening programs run from 6:30 P.M. to 10 P.M. Wednesday through Saturday in the summer and on Friday and Saturday from September through May.

The Crowne Plaza Resort offers special Family Funspree packages that include Carolina Buffet Breakfasts for two each morning, one complimentary in-room movie, 1-day bicycle rental for up to four people, and two free pizzas delivered to your room. Children 12 and under eat free from the kid's menu when accompanied by a dining adult. Rates for these packages start at $119.50 per night.

For information: Call the Crowne Plaza Resort at Hilton Head Island at (800) 334-1881.

French Lick Springs Resort, French Lick, Indiana

In response to nineteenth-century America's growing appetite for mineral waters and natural beauty, Dr. William Bowles built the French Lick Springs hotel in 1834 in the midst of three bubbling mineral springs. The hotel burned down in 1897 and was rebuilt in the early 1900s and became the unofficial summer retreat of the Democratic party in the 1930s. Graced with a beautiful setting, a grand building, and lots of recreational amenities, the French Lick Springs Resort has become a favorite of families. Patrons can take advantage of two 18-hole golf courses, a driving range, 18 tennis courts, two swimming pools, six bowling lanes, a game room, a health spa, 30 miles of horseback riding trails, chuck wagon rides, and several restaurants (including an ice-cream parlor). Kids ages 5 to 12 can join the

Pluto Club during spring break and the summer season. (Supervised kids' activities are also available Saturdays and holidays throughout the rest of the year.) Children participate in such activities as monster bubbles, balloon volleyball, beanbag olympics, parachute games, storytelling, silly science projects, picnics, water games, sand sculptures, and flashlight shows. For teens, the resort hosts teen events including horseback riding, bowling tournaments, and miniature golf.

Special holiday packages are available for Mother's Day, Memorial Day, July 4th, Labor Day, Thanksgiving, Christmas, New Year's Eve, Valentine's Day, and Easter, with rooms starting at $89 per night. Double-occupancy rooms with meals included are available for $149 per night.

For information: Call the French Lick Springs Resort at (800) 457-4042 or (812) 936-9300.

Holiday Inn SunSpree Resort
Lake Buena Vista, Florida

The Holiday Inn SunSpree Resort Lake Buena Vista was built for families. Each room features a video player, electronic door lock and safe, microwave, refrigerator, coffeemaker, and free daily coffee packet. To keep the refrigerator stocked, pop down to Pinky's mini-market for provisions. A childproofing kit is available free upon request. Beepers can also be rented for quick communication between parents and children. Complimentary cribs, high chairs, sleeping bags, and board games are also available. Free shuttles run daily to the Magic Kingdom Park, the Epcot Center, and the Disney-MGM Studios Theme Park. Hotel guests can work out at the fitness center for free. Other amenities include golf, tennis, jet skiing, parasailing, bass fishing, and hot-air balloon rides.

The hotel also features Kidsuites. Each suite includes a mini-kitchenette with microwave, mini-refrigerator, and coffeemaker and an adult room with a TV, a video player, a clock radio, an electronic safe, and a telephone. The highlight of these suites is the kids' room, brightly decorated around a fun theme, such as Noah's Ark, Max the Raccoon's Family Treehouse, a clown's tent, a western frontier jailhouse, a polar bear igloo, Little Caesar's

Playland, and a lunar space capsule. The rooms also include a color TV, video player, Super Nintendo, single bed and two bunk beds, clock, radio/tape players, and a fun phone.

At Max's Fun Time Parlor, families can gather every night to participate in bingo, karaoke, and other fun events. Families can engage in a number of activities: swimming, billiards, water basketball, and Ping-Pong. Parents who want to enjoy a quiet meal alone can send their kids to their very own restaurant, where they can watch cartoons, eat their favorite foods, and make their own ice-cream sundaes under the supervision of the hotel staff.

Camp Holiday is a year-round child-care program in which kids can spend their days creating artistic masterpieces, playing games, and having fun under the watchful eyes of the state-licensed staff. The camp is open 8 A.M. to midnight for children ages 2 through 12. There are nightly variety shows, puppet shows, and kids' karaoke.

When dining at the resort's restaurants, kids under the age of 12 eat breakfast, lunch, and dinner free from the Special Kid's Menu when accompanied by a dining adult. Kids have their own check-in desk where they receive a free fun bag full of goodies, including two game-room tokens. At night, Max the Raccoon, the hotel mascot, will tuck the kids into bed, if requested.

For information: Call (800) FON MAXX (366-6299) for reservations or contact your travel agent.

La Mansión del Rio, San Antonio, Texas

From humble beginnings as a two-story school built in 1852, La Mansión del Rio was once home to St. Mary's University and the San Antonio Law School. The building was lovingly renovated into its current status as a beautiful hotel in 1966, keeping as close to the original plan as possible. Located on San Antonio's famous River Walk, the hotel combines historic charm with the bustle of a busy city. Amenities include a courtyard swimming pool, garden courtyards, and 24-hour room service.

There are a wide range of seasonal activities for kids at the hotel and lots of attractions for kids in San Antonio, including the Alamo, River Walk, the San Antonio Zoo, the Fiesta Texas theme park, the Hertzberg Circus Collection, La Villita, and Sea

World. From Memorial Day to Labor Day, the hotel offers a number of field trips for children to local attractions.

Special packages, including transportation and tickets to Sea World or Fiesta Texas, are available.

For information: Call (800) 292-7300 or (210) 225-2581 or contact your travel agent.

Marriott's Marco Island Resort and Golf Club, Florida

The Marco Island Resort has everything families look for in a world-class resort: an 18-hole golf course designed by Joe Lee, three swimming pools, 16 tennis courts, a health club, sailing, windsurfing, waterskiing, parasailing, beach volleyball, and a wide, sandy beach known for its amazing array of seashells. The Beach Bandits program for kids ages 5 to 13 operates 7 days a week and keeps kids busy with activities such as arts and crafts, sandcastle building, swimming, and movies. Lunch and an afternoon ice-cream break are provided. Special programs, such as Saturday-night pizza parties, are offered all year long. Kids can also take advantage of the wading pools, playgrounds, and miniature golf course. Five restaurants serve everything from family fare to theme buffets to fine Italian cuisine. Baby-sitting is available.

If inclement weather is detected on the horizon, the resort quickly trots out its rainy-day program: family scavenger hunts, supervised children's games, bingo, crafts, and an ice-cream social. Board games and playing cards are available at the concierge desk for families who want a little quiet time together.

The Marriott's Marco Island offers 3-, 5-, and 7-night family packages, starting at $690. The packages for up to five family members include a pool- or ocean-view room, family breakfast each morning, an evening pizza dinner, a picnic lunch, a round of miniature golf, a complimentary children's program for one day, a movie, cribs and roll-aways, a sailboat ride, a bike tour or tennis clinic, and a souvenir gift. The family package is not available in late December.

For information: Call the Marriott's Marco Island Resort and Golf Club at (800) 438-4373, (800) 228-9290, or (941) 394-2511 or contact your travel agent.

Norfolk Waterside Marriott, Virginia

Nestled in the heart of revitalized downtown Norfolk, the Norfolk Waterside Marriott offers a variety of attractions for the whole family to enjoy. The hotel looks out over the Virginia Waterfront and provides easy access to Virginia Beach, the historic Williamsburg/Jamestown areas, Newport News, Portsmouth, and Hampton. Surrounded by beaches and Colonial history, the first-class accommodations and special programs for kids make the Norfolk Waterside Marriott a bonanza of a family vacation. The 404-room hotel boasts an atrium-enclosed rooftop pool, three whirlpools, a sauna, and a health club.

Upon check-in, children will receive a "Mission: Vacation!" package, including milk caps from local attractions, a full-color souvenir map of the Virginia Waterfront, a coloring book and crayons, and a Mission Log. Kids can win prizes by using the Mission Log to record answers to questions about area attractions. Also included in the package are special offers from places such as Busch Gardens/Water Country USA, the Children's Museum of Virginia, NAUTICUS, the National Maritime Center, the Virginia Air and Space Museum, the Virginia Living Museum, Spirit of Norfolk, the American Rover, and the Virginia Zoo.

For information: Call (800) 228-9290 or (804) 627-4200 or write to Norfolk Waterside Marriott, 235 E. Main St., Norfolk, VA 23510.

The Pointe Hilton at Squaw Peak, Phoenix, Arizona

The southwestern flavor of The Pointe Hilton at Squaw Peak, set in the middle of the Sonoran Desert, is difficult to resist. When selecting accommodations, you can choose from a two-room suite or a one- or two-bedroom casita, which is a two-level villa. Activities include golf, tennis, desert jeep tours, and hot-air ballooning. Kids will have a ball at the Hole-in-the-Wall River

Sealed with a Kiss Travel Kits

To help ease the challenge of traveling with children, take along a SWAK package, a gift box filled with 10 to 20 games, toys, puzzles, and crafts to keep kids occupied along the way. Each box is custom-designed for the specific sex, age, and interests of your child and how you're traveling—by air, car, or boat. The travel packs come in sturdy drawstring plastic bags and are filled with items specially chosen to provide entertainment without taking up much space to carry or play. The kits, for children ages 3 and up, contain many items that are hard to find, would cost more if purchased individually, and are not disposable. The toys and games can be used again and again.

Many SWAK customers are repeat customers. One reason is that Sealed with a Kiss keeps careful records of its packages, and a child never receives the same item twice. The travel kits cost $30. Sealed with a Kiss also makes kits for campers. Camp care packages cost $25. Both travel and camper kits can be custom made to fit the special needs of disabled children.

For information: Call Sealed with a Kiss at (800) 888-7925.

Ranch, a 9-acre water park with a 130-foot water slide, waterfalls, a sports pool, and a lazy river for floating. On rainy days, kids can also check out books and games at the lending library. Coyote Camp, for children ages 4 to 12, features a wide variety of activities, including everything from crafts to scavenger hunts to desert explorations. The resort's amenities include seven swimming pools, a health club and spa, three restaurants, a shopping boutique, a game room, and an 18-hole putting course.

Room rates run from $149 to $399 per night. Prices include a full breakfast, access to the Hole-in-the-Wall River Ranch, a daily pass to the Fitness Centre, and a USA *Today* newspaper Monday through Friday. You can also take advantage of the Hilton Family Plan: no charge for children, regardless of age, when they stay in their parents' room.

For information: Call (800) 934-1000.

Rocking Horse Ranch, Highland, New York

The Rocking Horse Ranch provides a more casual atmosphere for families who want an active vacation. The resort is located on 500 acres in the Shawangunk Mountains. A lovely lake, apple orchards, and the largest stable of saddle horses in the East make for an inviting getaway vacation. The all-inclusive price lets parents relax without worrying about mounting activity bills and includes expert instruction, most of the equipment, and the all-you-can-eat choice menu meals. The friendly staff is happy to help, and the resort offers several services to make your stay as pleasant as possible, including a 24-hour coffeepot, nightly entertainment, all-day instruction, a giant fireplace and conversation pit, a 24-hour desk, kids' night patrol, and a nursery.

Kids can burn energy in the Western Town Playground, get creative in the arts and crafts programs, and splash in the kids-only pool, all under the supervision of an experienced staff. Families can find lots to do together, too, including horseback riding, waterskiing, fishing, tennis, volleyball, basketball, archery, paddleboating, nature walks, classes, and scheduled activities. Guests who are still looking for something to do can choose from horse-drawn hayrides, handball, softball, shuffleboard, horseshoes, bocci, croquet, miniature golf, cocktail parties, guitar sing-alongs, the Round-Up Room Nightclub, dancing, skiing, tobogganing, tubing, ice-skating, sleigh rides, a fitness gym, a video arcade, theme parties, contests, scavenger hunts, bingo, talent shows, a petting zoo, pizza parties, ice-cream sundae parties, and marshmallow roasts.

The all-inclusive rates range from $120 to $160 per adult per night and $60 per child (ages 4 and over) per night. Children under the age of 4 stay free of charge. The resort also offers specials and packages throughout the year.

For information: Call (800) 647-2624 or (914) 691-2927 for information and reservations.

Smugglers' Notch, Vermont

Smugglers' Notch is a resort dedicated to the family. Skiing is combined with children's programs, child care, ski schools, a heated pool, ice-skating, snowshoeing, and family entertainment such as karaoke, bonfires with hot cocoa, and family game nights. Newborns and infants can spend the day at Alice's Wonderland Child Enrichment Center; children ages 3 to 6 can try Discovery Ski Camp, a full-day program with lunch; kids ages 7 to 12 can participate in either Adventure Ski or Snowboard Camp; and teenagers can check out Mountain Explorers and Outer Limits, a place for teens to dance and mingle.

Vacation packages include slopeside lodging, lift tickets, group lessons, and free family activities. Supersaver and No-Frills packages are available. Children 6 and under stay free when room occupancy rates are met.

Smugglers' Notch also offers summer fun for the whole family. Families can enjoy self-guided nature trails, llama treks, water-sliding, family game nights, canoeing, fishing, shuffleboard, horseshoes, bonfires, volleyball, and the Vermont Country Fair. Alice's Wonderland is a full-certified enrichment center for newborns and toddlers, with giant fish tanks, sand and water tables, a Pirate Ship Playground, a petting zoo, a sandbox, water play, and a supervised crib room. There are also programs for older kids: Little Rascals for children ages 2½ to 3 featuring mini-hikes, singing, and imaginative play; Discovery Dynamos for 3- to 5-year-olds featuring nature treasure hunts, arts and crafts, and water play; Adventure Rangers for kids 6 to 12 featuring all-day adventures, team sports, and Giant Rapid River Rides; and Mountain Explorers for 13- to 17-year-olds featuring obstacle courses, dance parties, and Lagoon Lunacy. The World of Water is made up of two full-sized pools, three water slides, two toddlers' pools, and Little Smugglers' Lagoon. June is Special Value Month with free child care for kids ages 6 weeks to 2 years.

Summer packages include lodging, FamilyFest full-day programs for kids, unlimited Giant Rapid River Rides, unlimited water-sliding, pools, hot tubs, and evening entertainment. Other activities included with packages are sock hops, bonfires, sing-alongs, miniature golf, daily hiking trips, and walking tours. Summer packages for families for seven days/seven nights start at $1,089 for a studio that sleeps four and go to $2,285 for a five-bedroom condominium that sleeps ten. Several other packages are available.

For information: Call your travel agent or call Smugglers' Notch at (800) 451-8752, fax (802) 644-1230; the E-mail address is smuggs@together.net.

Sonesta Beach Resort, Key Biscayne, Florida

If your family is looking forward to a tropical vacation with all the trappings, the Sonesta Beach Resort at Key Biscayne is the place for you. The hotel is located on a secluded tropical island surrounded by soft, sandy beaches and crystal-clear water. When you are ready for a little more company, Miami is only minutes away. There is a lot to do at the resort: swim in the Olympic-size swimming pool, relax in the whirlpool, dance the night away at Desires Lounge, work out at the health club, enjoy a massage at the spa, play tennis, or golf at the renowned Key Biscayne Golf Course.

Kids will scamper off to the pool, playground, and game room. All the restaurants and room service offer children's menus. Baby-sitting is available. The Sonesta Sandbox, for children ages 3 and 4, has sessions from 9 A.M. to noon and 1 P.M. to 4 P.M. For older kids (ages 5 to 13), Just Us Kids runs from 10 A.M. to 10 P.M. Biking, water sports, tennis, volleyball, and basketball are available on-site. In Miami, Monkey Jungle, Parrot Jungle, the Miami Seaquarium, and the Metrozoo are only a few of the many attractions available.

Family packages include breakfast, free ice cream, and supervised children's programs. Cribs are free, and roll-aways cost $35 per night. Children under the age of 12 stay free when sharing a room with parents.

For information: Call Sonesta reservations at (800) SONESTA (766-3782) or the hotel directly at (305) 361-2021 or contact your travel agent.

Sundial Beach Resort, Sanibel Island, Florida

Located on beautiful Sanibel Island in the Gulf of Mexico, Sundial Beach Resort has all the makings of a fabulous family vacation: white, sandy beaches, dolphins diving in the surf, perfect shelling conditions, and every activity under the sun. Choose between one- and two-bedroom condominium suites with kitchens that can be stocked with food before you even arrive. Recreational activities include swimming, tennis, golf, a game room, a fitness room, and the Environmental Coastal Observatory with a 450-gallon touch tank. Guests can also take a short cruise to one of several nearby islands, join a water-sports party, try backwater fishing, enjoy a hands-on sea-life encounter accompanied by a marine biologist, or rent a bicycle, kayak, water float, Sunfish, Hobie Cat, or just an umbrella to place over your complimentary lounge chair.

Kids can call the Sundial-a-story telephone line to hear bedtime stories or check out toys, games, VCRs, and tapes from the library. Children ages 3 to 12 can join the Children's Club, which operates 9:30 A.M. to 3 P.M. daily. There is a Kids Night Out on weekends and some weekdays for evening diversions. Families can participate in daily activities, including aqua-size, sand sculptures, Kitchen Kids, poolside chair massages, hermit crab races, and educational Discovery Programs at the Environmental Coastal Observatory.

Room rates start at $176 per night. Children ages 12 and under stay free in their parents' room. Full-size cribs, play yards, roll-away beds, strollers, and high chairs can be rented. You can also request bed rails and baby gates. Several packages are available, including the Shell Pail Vacation: 8 days/7 nights in a condominium suite with kitchen, a welcome tropical cocktail, one hour of tennis court time per day, daily housekeeping, dinner at Windows on the Water, and a shell pail and shovel for each child, starting at about $1,100.

For information: Call the Sundial Beach Resort at (800) 237-4184.

Tribesman Resort, Branson, Missouri

The Tribesman is a family favorite for summer vacations. The resort is located in the Ozarks, on Table Rock Lake in a quiet wooded glen. Families can choose from a variety of lodging options, including one- to four-bedroom kitchenettes, Dutch houses, Swiss houses, and a reunion complex. There is a lot to enjoy here: swimming, fishing, boating, pontoon boats, canoeing, paddle boats, hydro bikes, a game room, a play area, and shuffleboard. During the summer, families can participate in a number of scheduled weekly events, such as an ice-cream social, a kids' fishing tournament, a hot dog picnic, a scavenger hunt, and water games.

The Tribesman offers many programs and amenities each summer just for kids, including a find-Geronimo contest, a catch–Old Charlie contest, a fishing hole just for kids, a metal-detector treasure hunt, the Buttermilk stagecoach, fishing lessons, an indoor toddler playroom, and storytellers. The resort also offers kids' night out for children ages 5 to 11.

The rates for rooms during the summer season start at $58 for one-bedroom apartments and go to $156 for a two-story cottage. Children ages 4 and younger can stay free of charge.

For information: Call the Tribesman at (417) 338-2616.

The Tyler Place on Lake Champlain, Highgate Springs, Vermont

The Tyler Place is one of the few resorts that welcomes newborns, infants, and toddlers with open arms; it's a place where the wishes and needs of families come first. This family-owned resort's philosophy is that families on vacation should have time to spend together, time to pursue individual interests, and time for parents to be a couple. Their carefully planned children's programs and attention to detail make this philosophy a reality. The staff has been known to rent a local movie theater during a rainy week and to send a counselor to entertain a sick child in his or her room.

The resort is set on 165 acres of meadows, lawns, and woodland on beautiful Lake Champlain. Guests can choose from 27 fireplace cottages and 23 suites in the modern country inn or the Victorian guest houses with separate rooms for children and oversize beds for parents. Meals, lodging, sports, activities, entertainment, and programs for children are included in the rate. Guests can enjoy swimming, tennis, windsurfing, fishing, Sunfish sailing, kayaking, canoeing, rowboating, biking, and aerobics. Breakfast, lunch, and dinner offerings include healthy choices and foods that kids love. Younger children eat in their own nearby dining room, and teens eat before adults. For families who want to share meals, a family breakfast room and picnic baskets are provided.

The children's programs are the highlight of The Tyler Place. There are several options for infants and toddler care. Parents can hire a parents' helper to provide individual care for children. This is a very flexible program: you can hire a helper for a couple of hours a day or have one stay with you for your entire visit. You can also bring your own nanny from home. The only charge for bringing a nanny is a $3-per-day fee to cover the linens, and you must provide for the children's and nanny's meals (several options help make this situation hassle free). You can also enroll your children in one of the daily supervised programs.

The infant program (newborn to 18 months) features one-on-one parents' helper care, developmental toys, musical games, sand and water play, wading pools, Bye Bye Buggy rides, and an activity center with cribs, high chairs, jumpers, and changing and nap areas. The Toddler program (18 months to 2½ years) features a morning program, arts and crafts, a petting zoo, story times, water toys, a playground, theme parties, the red wagon fleet, a secret garden, and an activity center with cribs, high chairs, jumpers, and changing and nap areas. Junior Midgets (2½ to 3 years) features a child/counselor ratio of 3 or 4 to 1, hayrides, pontoon boat rides, nature walks, storytelling, singing and musical games, cooking projects, lawn games, quiet time, and movie night. Senior Midgets (4 to 5 years) features rowboat rides, parachute games, soccer, kickball, swimming, a reading loft, and a midget playground. Juniors (6 to 7 years) features kayaking, arts and crafts, picnics, ice-cream parties, softball, capture the flag, and scavenger hunts. Preteens (8 to 10 years) features windsurfing, bumper rides, canoeing, lacrosse, basketball, cookouts and campfires, and an indoor pool party with a DJ. Junior Teens (11 to 13 years) features waterskiing, windsurfing, kayaking, bike and canoe trips, tennis tournaments, broomball, team sports, a rec room, and a pizza party. Senior Teens (14 to 16 years) features waterskiing, windsurfing, a pontoon boat party, canoe and bike trips, team sports, tie-dye projects, movies, a rec room, bonfires, Pictionary, and an indoor pool party with a DJ. The programs operate in the mornings and evenings, leaving the afternoons for family time.

All-inclusive rates cover lodging, all meals, sports and recreational facilities, informal evening entertainment, children's programs, and infant and toddler care. Prices range from $81 to $174 per night for the first two persons. Fees for additional adults and children range from $45 to $98 per night. Rates are lower in May, June, and September. A 10 percent service charge is added to your bill to eliminate the need for tipping.

For information: Call The Tyler Place at (802) 868-4000 or (802) 868-3301.

Chapter Eight

Family Vacations

 More and more families today are taking active, adventurous vacations. Parents are looking for programs that are fun, educational, and different from the traditional two-weeks-at-the-beach vacation. In an effort to give families what they want, vacation packagers are creating special family programs that answer both parents' and children's needs. Families can join archaeological digs, go whitewater rafting, learn about environmental issues, explore historic landmarks, or sing and dance to traditional American music. New family adventures are springing up every day.

Canyonlands Field Institute Family Camps, Moab, Utah

The Canyonlands Field Institute (CFI) hosts two family camps each year in a spectacular setting. These camps are an adventurous and educational way for families to share an exciting summer vacation together. The Horsethief and Ruby Canyon Camp is perfect for families with younger children. The minimum age is six. Enjoy a relaxing, calm float down the scenic Colorado River. Instructors teach families about river-running and low-impact camping techniques. Stop along the way to explore side canyons and learn about the natural and cultural history of the area.

The Westwater Canyon Camp is for the more adventurous families with kids ages 12 and up. This is a thrilling white-water rafting trip (Class I, II, and III) through breathtaking wilderness. During breaks from the excitement on the water, your guide will lead you through Indian ruins and ancient Indian rock art and teach you about the natural and cultural history of the Canyonlands. Your family will enjoy camping out and using low-impact camping techniques.

Both camps, running from 3 to 4 days, allow a maximum of 25 campers and are led by River Guides and Trip Leaders certified in Emergency Response and CPR. Prices range from $265 to $350 for children and $330 to $440 for adults, with $15 discounts for CFI members.

For information: Call the Canyonlands Field Institute at (800) 860-5262.

Conservation Summits

Conservation Summits are weeklong adventures that allow families to experience a beautiful outdoor setting while learning about nature, wildlife, and environmental issues. The Summits are sponsored by the National Wildlife Federation, and prices are competitive with other family vacations. In 1996, the program fees were $325 per adult, $275 per teen, and $250 per child. Lodging and meal prices ranged from $350 to $800 for adults and $108 to $400 for children for the entire week. There are two annual Summits in two different locations. The venues change each year. Previous locations include Kenai Fjords National Park in Alaska and Rocky Mountain National Park in Colorado. The programs offer a unique mix of outdoor adventures, hands-on learning, and practical take-home skills specially designed for preschoolers, youths, teens, and adults. Events include outdoor classes, field trips, hikes, square dancing, and sing-alongs. In addition to general activities for entire families, the Summits provide special programs for kids in four different age groups. The Teen Adventure (ages 13 to 17) combines outdoor adventure, field studies, and group interaction that challenge both physical and mental abilities. Junior Naturalist (ages 5 to 8) and Naturalist Explorer (ages 9 to 12) fill each day with educational activities, including stream studies, wildlife investigations, bird walks, and outdoor games. Your Big Backyard Preschool Program (ages 3 to 4) lets children learn about nature through "micro-hikes," touch-and-feel expeditions, and nature crafts. All four programs are led by experienced instructors and staff. More than 50 percent of Summit participants return from year to year, so spaces fill up quickly.

For families who want shorter trips that are closer to home, Family Wildlife Weekends are available.

For information: Call the National Wildlife Federation at (800) 245-5484.

Country Dance and Song Society Family Weeks

Spend a week with your family dancing and singing to traditional American and English music; listen to storytellers, enjoy the outdoors, swim, make crafts, and learn about nature. The Country Dance and Song Society's Family Week programs at Camp Kinder Ring in Hopewell Junction, New York, and Pinewoods Camp in Plymouth, Massachusetts, are wonderfully different ways to spend your summers. The camps are for families with children 4 and up. There are lots of activities to do together and dances every night. Children who are too tired for the after-dinner dances are led to bed by a pied piper and then checked on frequently by roving baby-sitters.

In addition to the workshops and planned activities, there is plenty of time for relaxation. All campers over the age of 5 are asked to chip in with the chores, which helps create a sense of community and encourages campers to contribute ideas and suggestions for events.

Kids are divided by age into activity groups, ensuring that everyone will be happy and interested.

At Camp Kinder Ring, families sleep together in large bunkhouses with one family assigned to one room in most cases. At Pinewoods, most children over the age of 6 share a room with a roommate in a cabin close to their parents' cabin. All meals are served in the dining hall.

The 8-day camps range in price from $33 per week for children under 2 up to $482 per week for adults. These programs fill up very quickly, so it is wise to make your reservations far in advance.

For information: Call (413) 584-9913, fax (413) 585-8728, or write to Country Dance and Song Society, 17 New South St., Northampton, MA 01060.

Crow Canyon Archaeological Center Family Week, Cortez, Colorado

Established in 1984 as a not-for-profit organization dedicated to archaeological research, Crow Canyon offers an unusual and rewarding opportunity for vacationing families.

In this unique program, your family will be able to participate in actual research, working alongside professional archaeologists. The program is limited to families with kids in the seventh grade or higher and welcomes grandparents. The aim of the program is to increase the understanding of the relationships between prehistoric and contemporary cultures and the need to preserve our cultural heritage and resources. Families will join ongoing research projects and will study and contribute to the field of archaeology.

Children of middle-school age will be grouped together and spend 2½ days in the field excavating. The rest of the week they will participate in experimental archaeological activities and lab work. High school students will stick with the adults and rotate among lab work, field work, and experimental archaeology. On one day of family week, the whole family will go on a tour of Mesa Verde that will encompass all aspects of the work that the families have been doing all week. Throughout the week, evening lectures will be offered.

Baby's Away

All parents know what it's like to travel with baby: pleading with the ticket agent to let you check 12 pieces of baby equipment onto the plane or renting a U-Haul to visit Grandma and Grandpa for the weekend. There is just so much stuff to take: diapers, bottles, bibs, blankets, towels, onesies, clothes, toys, books, car seats, portacribs, etc. And that's roughing it. What you wouldn't give for a swing to lull your little one off to sleep after a busy day sight-seeing or a jogging stroller to take your baby for a run on the beach. Now you can have those luxuries on your vacation. Baby's Away will deliver to the door of your hotel or villa cribs, strollers, swings, boxes of toys, playpens, VCRs and tapes, car seats, infant seats, baby gates, joggers, humidifiers, high chairs, booster seats, rocking chairs, and just about anything else you can think of.

Baby's Away will deliver and set up equipment at Grandma's, your hotel room, or your condominium before you even arrive. You can walk into a parent's vacation paradise—all the convenient equipment without the backache.

Baby's Away currently operates at popular vacation sites in California, Colorado, Florida, Hawaii, Idaho, South Carolina, Utah, Wyoming, and also in Canada. Rental fees range from $1 to $9 per day, $6 to $54 per week. Baby's Away will soon be offering baby-sitting services, as well.

For information: Call (800) 571-0077 to find out if there's a Baby's Away at your family's favorite vacation destination.

Families will stay in either log "hogans" or the Crow Canyon lodge. The staff makes every effort to keep families together, but every now and then they are separated into guys and gals rooms. Three meals a day are included. A complete list of suggested gear will be sent to you upon receipt of your registration form. The seven-day program costs $795 for adults and $549 for students.

For information: Call (800) 422-8975 or write to Crow Canyon Archaeological Center, 23390 County Rd. K, Cortez, CO 81321-9408.

Family Adirondack Weekend, Sagamore, Raquette Lake, New York

Spend a weekend at Sagamore, the historic rustic camp of the Vanderbilts, located in a spectacular setting in the Adirondacks. There are no telephones or TV to distract you from hiking, canoeing, swimming, bowling, and relaxing. Take a guided tour of the facility and bone up on your history; learn about the Gilded Age and the heritage of the Adirondacks.

The weekend begins with Friday dinner and ends with Sunday lunch. Cost is $560 for two adults and two children ages 6 to 14. Children 5 and under stay free. Additional children are $110.

For information: Call (315) 354-5311 or write to Sagamore, PO Box 146, Raquette Lake, NY 13436.

Family Week, Sagamore, Raquette Lake, New York

Enjoy a relaxing week without phones or TVs at historic Great Camp Sagamore, once the rustic playground of the Vanderbilts in the Adirondacks. The 27-building complex is now operated by a nonprofit group dedicated to maintaining the historical integrity of the facility and its use for educational purposes. Most of the rooms are double occupancy, with twin beds and hall bathrooms. Buffet meals are served in the dining hall overlooking beautiful Sagamore Lake.

There are two family weeks each summer. During the week you will hike up mountains, tour the Adirondack Museum in

Blue Mountain Lake, explore Sagamore's lake and trails, and enjoy a day trying out Old Forge's water slides, train rides, shopping, and antiquing. You can also participate in Outdoor Skills activities.

Sagamore is famous for its semi-outdoor bowling alley and other features, including the Wigwam, the carpenter's shop, the blacksmith's shop, the boat shed, and the meeting room, complete with a billiards table and a Ping-Pong table.

Prices for Family Weeks are approximately $20 per night per child 5 and under, $40 per night per child ages 6 to 14, and $80 per night per adult.

For information: Call (315) 354-5311 or write to Sagamore, PO Box 146, Raquette Lake, NY 13436.

High Sierra Family Vacation Camp, Los Altos, California

"The Great Family Adventure" awaits you at High Sierra Family Vacation Camp located in the Sequoia National Forest. Your whole family will enjoy a week of relaxing, uncrowded recreation. You can choose to stay in a rustic cabin or the lodge. Nutritious meals with plenty of fresh fruits and vegetables are served buffet style. There are 11 weeklong sessions (but you can stay for more than one week) each summer, as well as two mini-camps and one 8-night camp.

Each day is divided into five activity periods. You choose your activities from a list that includes waterskiing, canoeing, fishing, swimming, riflery, archery, sailing, tennis, hiking, sing-alongs, pony rides, horseback riding, volleyball, horseshoes, arts and crafts, water aerobics, mock Olympics, theme nights, and overnight outings. You can participate separately or together or just enjoy some time by yourselves. There are children's and teen programs for kids from 2 to 17 years. If all that doesn't keep you busy, each week features casino night, the Friday-night variety show, a theme night, and an artist of the week. For parents with children under 2, there is the primary yard with age-appropriate toys.

The cabins hold three to eight people and are not equipped with running water or bathrooms (bathhouses are located nearby). Prices range from $95 for infants to $595 for adults for the weeklong stay. For the lodge rooms, which can accommodate two to eight people, prices range from $95 for infants to $670 for adults for the week.

For information: Call the Montecito-Sequoia Reservation Office at (800) 227-9900 or write to Montecito-Sequoia, 1485 Redwood Dr., Los Altos, CA 94024.

Kids Ski Free/Stay Free Program, Wednesday Free Program, Red River Valley, New Mexico

The Red River Ski Area in New Mexico offers two plans for fun-filled, affordable family winter vacations. The Ski Free/Stay Free program allows kids to stay and ski free when their parents stay at one of the many participating lodges in the Red River area. For each parent who stays a minimum of 3 nights and buys at least a 3-day lift ticket, one child under the age of 12 stays free and receives a lift ticket for the same number of days.

Families with children 13 and older can participate in the Wednesday Free Program, which provides your family 4 days of skiing and lodging at a 3-day price. Families staying for at least 4 days (Monday through Thursday) receive Wednesday's lodging free. Guests who buy any Red River Ski Area package, including rental equipment, lessons, and lift tickets, will receive the fourth day of the package free.

These discounts do not apply December 15 to January 1.

For information: Call (800) 331-SNOW (331-7669) or write to Ski Free/Stay Free, PO Box 900, Red River, NM 87558.

Minor Trips: A Traveler's Guide to Minor League Baseball

Minor Trips is a guide to all the minor league baseball teams in the United States and Canada. This handy little guide provides baseball fans with home schedules, phone numbers, ticket prices, and directions to the stadiums, as well as bits of trivia and other attractions located near the ballparks. When you order the $5 guide, you also receive a copy of the Minor Trips annual newsletter filled with travel tips, news from around the minor league, and changes in teams and ballparks.

For information: Write to Minor Trips, PO Box 360105, Strongville, OH 44136.

Ski NH Family Pass, New Hampshire

Variety and flexibility are the keys to the success of the Ski NH Family Pass. With this interchangeable ticket, your family has access to 14 of New Hampshire's finest ski areas. An adult can ski or snowboard for five consecutive midweek days, and a child age 12 years or younger can ski or snowboard free. The pass is easy to use and offers a flexible start date. For example, if you buy the ticket on a Thursday, you can ski Thursday, Friday, and the following Monday, Tuesday, and Wednesday. The pass can save families more than $130 and can be purchased at the following areas: Loon Mountain, Waterville Valley, Gunstock, Attitash Bear Peak Cranmore, Bretton Woods, Cannon, Mt. Sunapee, King Pine, Ragged Mountain, Pats Peak, Temple Mountain, Dartmouth Skyway, Whaleback, and The Balsams Wilderness. (Waterville Valley is highlighted on the next page.)

The adult pass cost $169 for the 1996 ski season, and for each adult pass purchased, one child receives a complimentary pass. Passes for additional children were $80 each.

For information: Call (800) 887-5464.

Squaw Valley USA

Squaw Valley USA, a ski area covering six separate peaks in the Sierras near Lake Tahoe, offers a wide variety of activities to please each member of the family. The ski area has grand hotels, cozy lodges, plenty of restaurants and shopping, and even a few nightspots for Mom and Dad. With more than 4,000 acres of ski slopes and 31 ski lifts, every member of the family will find just the right challenge to suit his or her skills. For those interested in things other than skiing, the High Camp Bath & Tennis Club offers mountain top ice skating, a heated outdoor swimming pool, bungee jumping, sundecks, and night skiing.

For the kids, Children's World is a supervised ski playground for youngsters ages 2 through 12. Along with pony tows and a kid-size ski hill, children can enjoy full- or half-day programs packed with fun activities and surprises.

A call to Squaw Valley Central Reservation allows you to book the whole package with one phone call, including lodging at one of more than 40 hotels, condominiums, and bed and breakfasts; lift tickets; ski lessons; child care; rental cars; and air-line reservations. Nightly room rates range from $22 at a hostel to $350 for a rental house.

The best part of the deal is that kids ages 12 and under and seniors can ski for $5 a day.

For information: Call Squaw Valley Central Reservations at (800) 545-4350.

Waterville Valley $39 Room and Never Bored Package, New Hampshire

Waterville Valley offers families a complete adventure vacation. Families lodge at one of the valley's eight inns, lodges, or con-dominiums, nestled below the 4,000-foot peaks of the White Mountains in New Hampshire. Although the facilities are open all year long, summer is the perfect opportunity for families to enjoy a vacation that includes activities everyone can enjoy: mountain biking, hiking, in-line skating, canoeing, paddleboat-ing, swimming, golf, tennis, trout fishing, shopping, and dining. There are more than 60 miles of clearly marked hiking trails for every level of exercise. Guests can choose tough terrain for seri-ous hiking or relaxed nature walks for families with smaller chil-dren. Another option is taking the chairlift up to the top of Snow Mountain to enjoy the view, hike, or mountain bike.

Visitors can also take advantage of the White Mountain Ath-letic Club and the Waterville Valley Summer Recreation Camp. The camp is open to 4- to 12-year-olds during the summer, with full-day and half-day options. Kids can swim, hike, listen to storytellers, play soccer and tennis, and make arts and crafts. Each week at camp is a theme week with an environmental influence on the week's activities. The Waterville Valley Recreation Department hosts activities and programs that visitors are welcome to attend, including field games, family "rec" nights, open gym, sports, and kids' night out. Several of these evening activities are supervised, so that parents wanting a quiet dinner in town are accommodated. A newly installed skateboard and in-line skate park is a favorite among kids.

Rates are $39 per person per night; however, kids can stay free in their parents' room. The package includes a variety of free activities, including a free day for the kids at the summer camp. Waterville Valley is also considering a similar winter package.

For information: Call Waterville Valley at (800) GO VALLEY (468-2553).

Chapter Nine

Establishments for Families on the Go

 Several hotels and restaurants have created family programs to encourage patronage. Traditional business hotels have started offering special services and amenities to families to fill their rooms on weekends. These hotels also recognize that more parents are taking children with them on business trips and that these children need baby-sitters, childproofed rooms, cribs, kids' menus, and activities to keep them busy. By responding to these needs, hotels are becoming more family-friendly and more accommodating, especially to the needs of smaller children.

Best Western Hotels

The Best Western Family Plan is available at most Best Western hotels in the United States. Family plan rates offer deals on up to four family members in one room and sometimes a deal on a second room. Each night of the stay at the Best Western, kids receive a new toy. Upon checking in, families receive a packet of coupons, including discounts for at least two local activities and national coupons for such companies as Thrifty Car Rental, United Artists Theaters, Koosh Toys, Six Flags Theme Parks, and American West Vacations. Families can also enter contests to win theme-park vacations and other prizes. These offers vary from hotel to hotel, so be sure to call your specific destination in advance.

For information: Call Best Western at (800) 528-1234.

Choice Hotels International

When visiting one of the more than 3,500 Choice hotels around the world, any child age 18 and under stays free. The kids must stay in the same room as their parents. Choice hotels are more recognizable under their brand names: Sleep, Comfort, Quality, Clarion, Friendship, Econo Lodge, and Rodeway. Kids can stay free with grandparents as well.

AAA members can receive a 10 percent discount at Sleep, Comfort, Quality, Rodeway, Econo Lodge, and Friendship Inns; a 20 percent discount applies to stays at Clarion Hotels and Clarion Carriage House Inns.

For information: Call (800) 4-CHOICE (424-6423) for more information on the Kids Stay Free program. For AAA discount rates, call (800) 228-1AAA (228-1222).

Club Med

Club Meds are all-inclusive resorts where families can experience a warm feeling of community, a room with a private bath, three meals a day with wine and beer at lunch and dinner, a variety of sports and organized activities, live entertainment nightly, dancing, and children's programs. There is no tipping, so you can leave your wallet in your room. Some optional items that have extra charges, such as drinks at the bar, boutique purchases, special services, and certain activities, can be signed for and paid at checkout. Several Club Meds are designed especially for families and are centered around family villages.

The Club Med family vacation includes programs for children and teens, separate clubhouses, special meals for kids, an emphasis on safety with one doctor and two nurses available 24 hours a day, free use of baby monitors, baby-sitting services, and qualified, experienced supervision. The Baby Club is for children from 4 months to 23 months and is open 9 A.M. to 5 P.M.

and 7:15 P.M. to 9 P.M. Infants and toddlers are given extra-special attention, naps, and playtime. A Baby Restaurant serves specially prepared meals for tots. The Petit Club (2 to 3 years), the Mini Club (4 to 7 years), and the Kids Club (8 to 11 years) are open 9 A.M. to 9 P.M. Kids can learn circus skills, scuba diving in the pool, pony and horseback riding, go-carting, and other activities in appropriate age groups using proper kid-size equipment. The Teen Club (12 to 17 years), open 10 A.M. to 10 P.M., lets teens meet other teens and participate in sports and other activities.

Participating Club Meds also offer Single Parenthood programs, family reunions, and family mystery vacations. Children 5 and under stay free of charge at all family villages during certain weeks of the season.

For information: Call Club Med at (800) CLUB MED (258-2633).

Days Inn Family Vacation Club

The Family Vacation Club offers savings and values to families. Members receive a 10 percent discount off the standard room rate at all Days Inn hotels nationwide and another discount at participating restaurants and gift shops. Families can also receive discounts on car rentals, entertainment, food, cruises, and airfares. Children under 12 always stay free at Days Inn hotels when they stay in the same room as their parents. The Family Vacation Club newsletter will keep members abreast of the latest benefits and special discounts.

A one-year membership to the Family Vacation Club costs $12.

For information: To enroll, ask for an application at the front desk of any Days Inn or write Days Inn Family Vacation Club, PO Box 27048, Minneapolis, MN 55427-0048.

Holiday Inn SunSpree Resorts

Holiday Inn SunSpree Resorts offer an affordable, family-friendly resort experience. The SunSpree Resorts are full-activity hotels providing a wide range of recreational facilities, ameni-

Play and Pizza Joints

A number of establishments have cropped up in recent years—Chuck E. Cheese, Circus World, Discovery Zone—where kids can eat and play all in the same facility. These are wonderful places for kids with cabin fever. They can climb, crawl, jump, and run through tunnels, ball pits, slides, and moon walks. There are kiddy rides, pinball machines, video games, and prizes to be won. When they work up an appetite, you can order a pizza or a hot dog and feed them right then and there.

I know several parents whose play groups meet at these facilities. The parents can sit and talk while the kids play. It's a great alternative to going to the park when the weather doesn't cooperate.

ties, and services designed for families. You'll find planned daily events, fitness rooms, pools, sports, the supervised KidSpree Vacation Club program, and Marketessens (a combination market/deli). The hotels are located near beaches, lakes, mountains, ski slopes, deserts, and other major attractions.

Kids stay free in parents' rooms.

For information: Call Holiday Inn SunSpree Resorts at (800) HOLIDAY (465-4329) and ask for the Resort Desk or call your travel agent.

Holiday Inn Worldwide

Holiday Inn calls itself "The Official Hotel for Family Fun." In keeping with their title, they offer the Kids Eat Free program at more than 1,300 participating hotels during the summer months and at more than 750 hotels all year long. Children ages 12 and under can eat free in hotel restaurants when accompanied by an adult and when ordering from the kids' menu. Between Memorial Day and Labor Day, kids are given a free toy at check-in. Past toys have included Carmen Sandiego™ Activity Kits, Parker Brothers® Trivial Pursuit Packs, POG™ Wild Packs, and Olympic Izzy figurines.

For information: Call (800) HOLIDAY (465-4329).

Radisson Hotels

Radisson Hotels do their best to make things easy on families, with several programs designed with families in mind. The hotel has done extensive research to create programs that have kept families' best interests at the forefront. Participating "Family Approved" hotels and resorts offer special features and services. The program's goal is to make traveling more pleasurable for parents traveling with children. The Family Approved hotels offer a children's menu filled with kids' favorites available in at least one restaurant and through room service; child-care services on-site or a list of qualified baby-sitters available; cots, cribs, and playpens; books and games that can be checked out (a professional children's librarian from Baker & Taylor books developed a list of 40 books specifically for Radisson Hotels); swimming pools; family movies; discount coupons for local attractions; and childproofing safety kits including outlet plugs, night-light, doorknob covers, window-shade cord wind-ups, soft-spot cover, floating duckie water thermometer (with complete instructions for correct usage), and a copy of "Tips for Safety at Home and When Traveling." Hotels that want to earn Family Approved status must satisfy specific safety and family-service standards.

Radisson's Family Magic program is another way for price-conscious families to get added value from their vacation budgets. Families receive coupons at check-in for a full breakfast for up to four people. Each child 12 years and younger receives a Crayola Kids Magic Activity Kit. The kit features 18 custom-designed tricks, a giant poster, a world map, and games such as a word finder and travel trivia with stickers. Radisson hotels will confirm in advance the availability of rooms with two double beds or two queen-size beds at the time reservations are made. Families requesting a second room will be offered a 25 percent discount off the Family Magic rate.

The Radisson family programs have been praised by the Center for Injury Prevention.

For information: Call the Radisson Reservation Line at (800) 333-3333.

Ritz-Carlton Hotels and Resorts

The Ritz Kids programs at Ritz-Carlton Hotels and Resorts are perfect for the times parents want to be alone together. Kids participate in fully supervised activities while their parents are away. Each hotel is in charge of designing its own program, so be sure to contact the one at your particular destination to see what's available. Some of the activities are Shoreline Shell Safaris, Children's Dinner Theater, Junior Chef Debut, Nature and Adventure Walks, Teddy Bear Teas, "Social Savvy" Etiquette Classes, and Nutcracker Brunches. Many of the hotels offer services such as theater and zoo tickets, video and board games, day camps, and nanny services.

For information: Contact each Ritz-Carlton Hotel directly or check with your travel agent.

Swissôtel

Some Swissôtels offer Kidsôtel programs for children. At Kidsôtels, children 12 and under stay free in the parents' room, or they can stay in an adjoining room at a discounted price. There are also value-priced special menus for kids. Children receive a "Barry, the Legendary St. Bernard" Kidpack at check-in. The pack includes a plush St. Bernard, a backpack, a coloring book, and crayons. Cookies and milk are available at bedtime through room service.

For information: Call Swissôtel reservations at (800) 637-9477.

Westin Hotels

Upon checking in at most Westin Hotels, ask about the Westin Kids Club program. You will receive a package containing a registration card to be filled out by you or your child, a family information sheet, and an amenity bag especially suited for your child's age group. The amenity bag is a plastic laundry bag covered with pictures for coloring. Each bag contains a safety kit with outlet plugs, a night-light, and adhesive bandages. Children up to age 3 receive an infant kit of small bottles of lotion, baby powder, shampoo, and a child's cup. Kids 4 to 6 years of age get a cup, a coloring book and crayons, and bath toys. Kids ages 7 and up receive a sport bottle and a Westin-logo ball cap. Most hotels also have available a selection of bottle warmers, high chairs, bed rails, cribs, potty seats, and jogging strollers. Emergency diapers and wipes are available either at the front desk or in the gift shop, depending on the hotel. There will be some variation in the packages from hotel to hotel. Ask your reservation representative about what services are available at your particular destination.

For information: Call the Westin Hotel Reservation Line at (800) 228-3000.

Chapter Ten

Trips for Kids Only

Many preteens and teens like to take their own vacations during the summer and at spring break. As an alternative to traditional summer camps, many programs are available for kids looking for educational and adventure vacations with peers. These programs last anywhere from a couple of days to a couple of weeks. Kids can experience the thrills of high adventure, spend time learning about nature and the environment, and get lots of fresh air and exercise.

Explorer Camps

Kids ages 11 to 18 will hike, canoe, kayak, and white-water raft their way through summer at exciting adventure camps. With three 9-day Explorer Camps to choose from, kids can select from different levels of adventure and learn valuable recreational skills. The Canoeing and Hiking Camp takes teens (ages 14 to 18) into the spectacular canyon country in Moab, Utah. The trip starts with an exploration through Arches National Park, followed by 6 days of canoeing along the Green River through the Labyrinth Canyon. Day hikes include visits to wilderness areas, prehistoric sites, petroglyphs, and ruins of early mines. The

Kayaking and Hiking Camp is also for teens ages 14 to 18 and involves kayaking down the San Juan River through the 57-mile serpentine canyon corridor known as the Goosenecks. Participants will camp on sandy beaches along the river. The Mountain Hiking and Rafting Camp is for younger kids, ages 11 to 13. Campers will spend time exploring forests, lakes, and subalpine areas in the La Sal mountains and rafting down the Colorado River through the Ruby and Horsethief canyons.

The camps cost about $700 each and are limited to groups of 13 to 20 depending on the camp. Members of the Canyonlands Field Institute receive a small discount.

For information: Call the Canyonlands Field Institute at (800) 860-5262.

Geowhiz Day Camps

The Geowhiz 4- and 5-day programs give children ages 6 to 15 a chance to explore and investigate the natural world in an unforgettable way. For kids 6 to 11, Geowhiz Kids camp hosts half-day hikes during which children can learn games and participate in field studies. The outings, which take place over a 4-day span, are organized around a central theme and are led by Canyonlands Field Institute instructors. Geowhiz Adventure, for 12- to 15-year-olds, offers full-day outings over a 5-day period. Kids hike, canoe, and raft, and they learn basic survival skills; map and compass reading; hiking and boating skills; and outdoor science. Both programs are a great way for kids to interact with nature, learn, and gain self-confidence.

For information: Call the Canyonlands Field Institute at (800) 860-5262.

Teen Adventure

Designed for teens ages 14 to 17, Teen Adventure is a challenging 12-day back-country wilderness experience that emphasizes conservation education. Six-day spring-break trips are also available. Past locations include the Blue Ridge Mountains and the Colorado Rockies for the summer trips and canoeing the Okefenokee and cycling the C & O Canal for the spring-break

The American Camping Association Guide to Accredited Camps

With thousands of children's summer camps to choose from, finding the right camp for your kids can be a daunting task. The American Camping Association, the only organization that accredits children's summer camps, has made the task easier by publishing a yearly guide to accredited camps. The camps are indexed by state, activities offered, and special clientele served. The guide covers both day and overnight camps, trip and travel programs, special-needs programs, special-emphasis camps, and religiously affiliated camps. There are also several articles on finding a camp, packing for camp, and deciding if your child is ready for camp.

Of the 8,000 camps in the United States, only about 2,100 are accredited. Each entry includes contact names, addresses, and phone numbers; session lengths; camper ages; price ranges; special focuses; programs for campers with disabilities; and activities and programs offered. The book costs $16.95 plus shipping and handling.

For information: Call (800) 428-CAMP (428-2267).

trips. Participants are required to provide their own backpacks, sleeping bags, and hiking boots. Teens will learn outdoor living skills, hike 5 to 10 miles a day, and gain leadership skills, personal growth, and self-confidence. In 1996, program fees were $705 for the summer Teen Adventures and $475–$575 for the spring Teen Adventures. Three to four trips are scheduled each summer for each location.

For information: Call the National Wildlife Federation at (800) 245-5484.

Whitewater Academy, Moab, Utah

The Whitewater Academy summer program in the spectacular Canyonlands of Utah is designed to teach teens ages 13 to 18 the skills needed to be professional white-water guides. This hands-on course instructs kids on safety and rescue issues, paddling and rowing techniques, equipment rigging, and river and desert ecology. Participants can try out their skills on the nearby Colorado and Dolores rivers. The camp lasts for a week and provides teens with an exciting adventure and a sense of accomplishment, as well as valuable skills.

Whitewater Academy allows a maximum of 20 participants and costs $495 per teen, with a $15 discount for members of the Canyonlands Field Institute.

For information: Call the Canyonlands Field Institute at (800) 860-5262.

Wildlife Camp

Wildlife Camp focuses on fun. Kids ages 9 to 13 explore and learn about nature and wild animals. Campers set out on a supervised "Quest" each morning to explore such topics as Incredible Insects, Boulder Builders, and Creepy Crawlers; learn outdoor living skills; and participate in Hobby Swaps. Two overnight camp-outs—roasted marshmallows, campfire songs, and all—are planned for each 12-day camp session. Wildlife Camp has six summer sessions in two locations—Henderson, North Carolina, and Estes Park, Colorado. In 1996 costs were $705 per child.

Wildlife Camp also offers two affordable weekends for the entire family (about $100 per adult and $80 per youth). At Family Camp, families fish, hike, canoe, sing around a campfire, and learn about nature in this 3-day "camp-within-a-camp." On the Family Trek, participants go on a 2-day backpacking trip. Families hike, tent camp, and cook on a backpacking stove.

For information: Call the National Wildlife Federation at (800) 245-5484.

Chapter Eleven

Trips for Grandparents and Their Grandchildren

 More and more grandparents are taking vacations with their grandchildren. With many grandparents and grandchildren living in different parts of the country, these trips are a wonderful way to build relationships. In support of this trend, several travel organizations do nothing but plan trips for intergenerational travel companions. Some vacation sites also offer special grandparent/grandchildren programs. This chapter should help get you going.

Grandparents' & Grandchildren's Camp, Sagamore Lodge, Raquette Lake, New York

This program is so popular that it fills up a year in advance and has quite a waiting list, and it's worth every effort to book. A week of building memories, filled with meaningful activities both indoors and out, is all that's needed to create a lifelong bond between grandparent and grandchild.

For kids ages 5 to 12 and their grandparents, this historic Adirondack lodge, built in 1897, offers two sessions each summer. The well-planned program presents patrons with a number of activities, including canoeing, crafts, storytelling, sing-alongs, and night hikes. Grandparents are invited to attend discussion groups with Arthur and Carol Kornhaber, founders of the Foundation for Grandparenting, to talk about relevant issues. While the grown-ups are talking, children play noncompetitive games. Afterward, everyone joins together for dinner. Evenings are spent square dancing, night hiking, or singing by the campfire. Parents are not allowed—only grandparents and grandchildren.

The cost for the 6-day camp is $550 for grandparents and $335 for grandchildren.

For information: Call (315) 354-5311 or write to Sagamore, PO Box 146, Raquette Lake, NY 13436.

GRANDTRAVEL

GRANDTRAVEL is a wonderful way to give children and their grandparents an opportunity to spend time together on exciting, well-planned journeys. The program, developed by a team of teachers, psychologists, and leisure counselors, sponsors 17 trips a year to locations all over the world. The trips are designed for children ages 7 to 17 and last from 8 to 15 days. Choose from tours of Washington, D.C., the Pacific Northwest, the Southwest, Hawaii, Alaska, Ireland, Switzerland, Italy, Denmark, Kenya, Australia, and China, or take theme journeys such as The American Indian Culture in the Southwest, The Grandest Canyons (including the Grand, Glen, Bryce, and Oak Creek canyons), Western Parks, Western Space, Castles of England and Scotland, Barging on the Waterways of Holland and Belgium, and A Grand Tour of London and Paris. GRANDTRAVEL journeys focus on bringing grandparents and grandchildren together in a fun, supportive, and enriching environment. Emphasis is placed on the educational opportunities each trip presents, highlighting natural, historic, and cultural attractions.

Prior to each trip, you will receive a day-by-day itinerary, maps, brochures, age-appropriate reading lists, and a Travel Advisory with guidelines for clothing, health, safety, and tipping. Accommodations are deluxe, first-class, or best-available near attractions along the way. You will travel between destinations on air-conditioned motor coaches. Children keep them-

Travel Scrapbooks

One way to preserve the memories of a special trip with Grandma and Grandpa is to create a travel journal. You can use a store-bought scrapbook or make one by fastening together sheets of construction paper. Punch two holes in the end of each sheet of paper and string together with a piece of ribbon. You can use two pieces of cardboard for the front and back covers. Your children can decorate their scrapbooks and fill them with photographs, postcards, souvenirs, ticket stubs, and memories. They can write down funny or special events and include an itinerary of their trip. They can even make two scrapbooks—one to keep and one to give to their grandparents for a birthday or holiday gift.

selves amused with guidebooks filled with entertaining anecdotes, mini-histories, and information on the things they'll see. There is also a program of games, puzzles, and crafts to keep youngsters occupied. Peer activities (adults only and children only) are offered as well.

The fees for this high-quality program range from $2,770 to $7,615 and include transportation (excluding airfare to the home city), meals, lodging, tour escort, admission fees for all events in the itinerary, tips, and all GRANDTRAVEL extras.

For information: Call (800) 247-7651 or (301) 986-0790, or write GRANDTRAVEL, 6900 Wisconsin Avenue, Ste. 706, Chevy Chase, MD 20815, or contact your travel agent.

The Sierra Club

For hearty souls who don't mind roughing it, the Sierra Club's annual trip to California's Sierra Nevada mountains for grandparents with grandchildren ages 5 and up is filled with opportunities to share and build memories together. The six-day trip offers lots of good, clean fun fishing, hiking, horseback riding, picnicking, roasting marshmallows, and singing around the campfire. Highlights of the week include a beach picnic at Donner Lake, a leisurely stroll on the Nature Trail, a tram tour of Squaw Valley, a visit to historic downtown Truckee, and a hike on the Pacific Crest Trail.

Lodging is provided by the Clair Tappaan Lodge, a rustic, two-story building near the Donner Pass, in the Sierra Nevada. The elevation of the lodge is 7,000 feet and will take a little time to get used to. The itinerary includes time to adjust. Two-person cubicles and family-sized rooms are the norm, with two men's and two women's bathrooms. The facilities include a library, a sundeck, a dining room, a sitting room for gathering, a hot tub, a volleyball court, and a horseshoe court. Everyone is expected to pitch in and do a daily chore. The facilities are clean and serviceable but not luxurious.

Grandparents and those grandchildren 12 and older must be members of the Sierra Club to take advantage of the program. The price of the trip is $390 per adult and $260 per child. You will be expected to provide your own bedding and towels, broken-in hiking boots or high-top sneakers, and basic camping gear.

For information: Call (415) 923-5588 or write to Sierra Club Outing Department, Dept. #05618, San Francisco, CA 94139.

Warren River Expeditions, Inc., Salmon, Idaho

Twice a year, Warren River Expeditions offers grandparents and grandkids special white-water raft trips down the Main Salmon River, known as "The River of No Return." The river was first discovered by Lewis and Clark in 1805 and is the longest undammed river in the continental United States. The river flows fastest in June and is tamer in August. The river and canyon are isolated and breathtaking. If rafting isn't your only interest, you have nothing to fear. The Frank Church–River of No Return Wilderness has lots of hiking trails, abandoned gold mines, side streams, hot springs, and big, sandy beaches. You can fish, hike, swim, play horseshoes, or learn the art of Dutch Oven Cooking. The Grandparents/Grandkids trips are planned especially for intergenerational groups, including appropriate activities for the adults and kids.

The trips last 6 days and include rooms in lodges with all the comforts of home. Trips are limited to 12 guests and cost about $1,400. These trips are very popular and start to fill up by mid-March. Warren River Expeditions provides life jackets, all eating utensils, and waterproof bags. A complete personal-gear check-list will be sent to you upon receipt of your deposit and your reservation.

For information: Call (800) 765-0421 or (208) 756-6387 or write to Warren River Expeditions, Inc., PO Box 1375, Salmon, ID 83467-1375. The fax number is (208) 756-4495.

PART FOUR

Resources for Parents and Kids

Chapter Twelve

Books and Booklets

 An amazing number of organizations and businesses produce free or very inexpensive materials for parents and kids. These materials cover all kinds of topics, such as safety, baby care, child development, discipline, history, children's literature, and families with special needs. Many of the organizations listed in this chapter periodically update or change their publications depending on funding, public interest, and new research. If the particular item requested is unavailable, ask for a list of current publications.

Resources for Kids

Bicycle Safety Camp

Grade-school children will enjoy this entertaining 25-minute video that teaches children to "Ride Safe and Love It." The video depicts kids singing and having fun at bicycle safety camp while learning the importance of wearing a helmet, the rules of the road, and safety tips.

The video is $9.95 and is endorsed by the American Academy of Pediatrics.

For information: Call (800) 433-9016 or write to American Academy of Pediatrics, 141 Northwest Point Blvd., PO Box 927, Elk Grove Village, IL 60009-0927.

Growth Chart

This colorful growth chart from the American Academy of Pediatrics records the progress of your children as they reach new heights. The poster is 8½ inches by 33 inches, long enough to measure your child's growth until about age 10. Tips on immunizations, nutrition, and injury prevention and other child-related information are colorfully displayed on this poster, which is illustrated with kites, skates, blocks, and toys.

The growth chart costs $5.95 per copy.

For information: Call (800) 433-9016 or write to American Academy of Pediatrics, 141 Northwest Point Blvd., PO Box 927, Elk Grove Village, IL 60009-0927.

My Word Book

Published by Modern Learning Press, *My Word Book* is a wonderful book that beginning readers and writers can use to keep track of the new words they learn and use. For each letter of the alphabet, there are several words written in big, bold print with accompanying drawings. On the facing page, kids can write new words and draw pictures of them. This combination of words and pictures lets kids label the world around them and "own" the words they use. There are also pages for the names of friends, family members, pets, colors, shapes, and "school tools." Parents who want to supplement the workbook can purchase the companion "Help-At-Home Guide."

My Word Book costs $2.50 per copy plus shipping. The "Help-At-Home Guide" is only $.55. Modern Learning Press also publishes similar books for older kids: *Words I Use When I Write* for first- and second-graders and *More Words I Use When I Write* for third- and fourth-graders. The books are $2.75 and $2.95, respectively, plus shipping and also offer "Help-At-Home Guides," available for $.55 each.

For information: Call (800) 627-5867 or write to Modern Learning Press, PO Box 167, Dept. 363, Rosemont, NJ 08556.

"The Story of Money"

Children will enjoy reading "The Story of Money," an educational piece prepared by the U.S. Mint about the history of money, how coins are made, the United States Mint in Denver, the meaning of "*E Pluribus Unum*," the Bureau of Engraving and Printing, why paper money is green, and the mysterious numbers that appear on dollar bills. You can also request "Some Fun Facts About Money" and "Shootout at the Denver Mint." All publications are free.

For information: Write to the U.S. Mint, Exhibits & Sales Division, 320 W. Colfax Ave., Denver, CO 80204-2693.

U.S. Consumer Product Safety Commission Activity Books

The U.S. Consumer Product Safety Commission has available several booklets that teach kids important principles about safety. The booklets are free and can be ordered by sending a postcard with the title and number of the publication desired. The titles for kids are "Toy Safety Coloring Book" (#283) and "Sprocketman Comic Book" (#341).

For information: Send a postcard to Publication Request, Office of Information and Public Affairs, U.S. Consumer Product Safety Commission, Washington, DC 20207.

"Wishes and Rainbows"

"Wishes and Rainbows" is a free 20-page comic book for elementary schoolchildren that teaches the basic economics of scarce resources. The book's characters explore society's reactions to such problems and educate children on fundamental economic principles.

For information: Write to Federal Reserve Bank of New York, Federal Reserve PO Station, New York, NY 10045-0001.

Resources for Parents

"10 Ways to Help Your Children Become Better Readers"

Parents will appreciate the 10 suggestions for helping children enjoy reading in this free brochure from the Center for the Study of Reading at the University of Illinois at Urbana–Champaign.

For information: Send a self-addressed, stamped envelope to Center for the Study of Reading, University of Illinois at Urbana–Champaign, 174 Children's Research Center, 51 Gerty Dr., Champaign, IL 61820.

"100 Most Frequently Asked Questions & Answers About Your Baby"

This helpful, free booklet, sponsored by The Prudential, contains the answers to 100 questions every parent asks in those early months after bringing baby home from the hospital. Covering the gambit from breast-feeding to baby-sitting, these answers advise parents on such topics as feeding, formula, solid foods, sleep, crying, bathing, teething, developmental skills, when to call the doctor, immunizations, and safety tips.

For information: Call (800) THE-ROCK (843-7625), extension 50, for a free copy of this booklet.

American Academy of Pediatrics Brochures

The American Academy of Pediatrics offers a series of free brochures to parents on a variety of topics, including:

"Acne"
"Alcohol: Your Child and Drugs"
"Allergies in Children"
"Better Health Through Fitness"
"Child Care: What's Best for Your Family"
"Choking Prevention and First Aid"
"Deciding to Wait: Delaying Sex"

"Developmental Milestones"
"A Guide to Your Children's Dental Health"
"Healthy Start: Feeding Kids Right Isn't Always Easy"
"Immunization Protects Children"
"Parent Resource Guide"
"Playground Safety"
"Right from the Start: ABC's of Good Nutrition for
    Young Children"
"Single Parenting"
"Sleep Problems and Children"
"Sports and Your Child"
"Suicide and Adolescent Depression"
"Television and the Family"
"Temper Tantrums"
"Toilet Training"
"Toy Safety"

To request these free brochures or a complete list of available brochures, send one self-addressed, stamped envelope (business size) for each request to the American Academy of Pediatrics. Be sure to indicate which brochure you want on the outside of the self-addressed envelope.

For information: Write to American Academy of Pediatrics, Dept. C — (name of brochure), PO Box 927, Elk Grove Village, IL 60009-0927.

Asthma Pamphlets

The Asthma Information Center will be happy to forward to parents free information about asthma. The packet of information includes an asthma resource guide and a series of brochures. The resource guide lists books, newsletters, organizations, support groups, and asthma and allergy disease centers. The brochures cover topics including guidelines for living with asthma, using a metered-dose inhaler, using a peak flow meter, and the dial-a-cough wheel.

For information: Write to The Asthma Information Center, PO Box 790, Spring House, PA 19477-0790.

Baby Alive Video and Book

Produced in cooperation with the American Academy of Pediatrics, this 60-minute video and book offer crucial information about keeping children safe. Hosted by Phylicia Rashad of *The Cosby Show* with the help of several medical experts, the video presents a step-by-step guide to the prevention and treatment of life-threatening situations that children 5 and under may encounter. This video helps parents feel more confident and secure about handling emergencies as they arise.

The *Baby Alive* video costs $19.95, and the companion book is $4.95.

For information: Call (800) 433-9016 or write to American Academy of Pediatrics, 141 Northwest Point Blvd., PO Box 927, Elk Grove Village, IL 60009-0927.

"Becoming Your Child's First Teacher"

Instilling in your child a love of learning should be every parent's priority. "Becoming Your Child's First Teacher" outlines the steps to creating an environment in which learning is fun, not a chore. Full of tips and wonderful illustrations, this upbeat guide discusses the importance of play and togetherness in learning, guidelines for making learning enjoyable, and the joys of reading, writing, and arithmetic.

For information: Call (800) 654-ROCK (654-7625), extension 51, for a free copy of this booklet.

"Breastfeeding Information Guide"

This free booklet from Medela®, the makers of breast pumps and other breast-feeding supplies, presents tips and advice about breast-feeding in a straightforward manner. There are detailed discussions of the mechanics of nursing and of expressing and storing milk and solutions to common problems, such as engorgement and sore nipples. A list of products available to nursing moms is also included.

For information: Send a written request to "Breastfeeding Information Guide," Medela, Inc., PO Box 660, McHenry, IL 60051-0660.

"Child Health Guide"

The American Academy of Pediatrics offers parents a copy of their "Child Health Guide," a 40-page booklet with handy charts for tracking and recording information about your child's growth, immunizations, and illnesses.

The booklet is $2.95.

For information: Call (800) 433-9016 or write to American Academy of Pediatrics, 141 Northwest Point Blvd., PO Box 927, Elk Grove Village, IL 60009-0927.

"Children's Books of the Year"

The Child Study Children's Book Committee publishes an annual list of approximately 650 recommended books from the 4,000 books evaluated each year. Books are selected on the basis of their "emotional, intellectual, and ethical impact" on children. The lists are organized by age and interest for children ranging in age from preschoolers to 14-year-olds. Both fiction and non-fiction are evaluated. A brief description of the book accompanies each title.

"Children's Books of the Year" is $6 per copy. The Child Study Children's Book Committee also publishes "Paperback Books for Children" ($6) and "Books to Read Aloud with Children of All Ages" ($5).

For information: Call (212) 875-4540 or write to Child Study Children's Book Committee, Bank Street College, 610 W. 112th St., New York, NY 10025.

"Children's Choices"

Parents are always looking for quality books that their children will enjoy. How many times have you brought home a book you just knew your child would love, only to get a mild smile as he tosses it aside and continues making mud pies on the coffee table? To solve this problem, the Children's Book Council and the International Reading Association asked 10,000 kids what their favorite books were. They compiled all their choices into a booklet for parents. The idea was so successful that they have been doing it every year since 1975. Separated into age groups from beginning readers to middle-grade readers and older, this booklet lists bibliographic information as well as short descriptions of the books. So, the next time you head to the bookstore or library, take along a copy of "Children's Choices" to help you sift through the hundreds of books on the shelves and find the ones your kids will enjoy.

For information: Send a self-addressed, 9-inch by 12-inch envelope with $.78 postage affixed to IRA, PO Box 8139, Newark, DE 19714-8139.

Consumer Information Catalog

The Consumer Information Catalog offers parents a variety of free and low-cost federal publications. Parents can receive publications covering such topics as helping children with school and homework, feeding babies, reducing lead levels in the home, preparing family disaster kits, raising drug-free children, and encouraging reading in children. Through the catalog, parents can also request book lists, baby safety checklists, health guides, and even a Deputy Fire Marshall Kit. The catalog is free and is issued quarterly.

For information: Write to Consumer Information Catalog, Consumer Information Center, PO Box 100, Pueblo, CO 81002.

"The Family Travel Guides Catalogue"

Families who are planning vacations for the whole crew will appreciate the free catalog of family travel guides from Carousel Press. The 32-page catalog lists books on camping, hiking with children, weekend adventures, sight-seeing, skiing, ranches, and resorts. There are books on specific regions, states, and cities. Books to keep kids busy on the road are also included.

For information: For a free copy of "The Family Travel Guides Catalogue," send either $1 or a self-addressed, stamped ($.55) business-size envelope to Carousel Press, FTG Catalogue, PO Box 6061, Albany, CA 94706-0061.

First Aid Chart

Everyone in your family could use a little help remembering basic first aid in an emergency. This 11-inch by 17-inch wall chart from the American Academy of Pediatrics should be placed in an easily accessible location. The chart lists treatments for emergencies in an easy-to-read manner. One side of the chart gives instructions for handling burns, eye injuries, nosebleeds, poisonings, insect stings, head injuries, seizures, and broken bones. The other side gives the procedures for choking intervention and performing CPR for both infants and children. Every family should have this vital information handy.

The double-sided chart is $2.95 per copy.

For information: Call (800) 433-9016 or write to American Academy of Pediatrics, 141 Northwest Point Blvd., PO Box 927, Elk Grove Village, IL 60009-0927.

"A Guide to Your Child's Hearing"

This free booklet from the Better Hearing Institute helps parents to identify possible hearing problems in their children. Early hearing loss can lead to delays in the development of speech and language. Early detection can help alleviate many of the challenges a hearing-impaired child faces. This booklet describes the warning signs of hearing problems, the milestones of communication development, the different types of hearing problems, and the testing, evaluation, and treatment of hearing problems.

For information: Call (800) EARWELL (327-9355) or write to Better Hearing Institute, PO Box 1840, Washington, DC 20013.

"Guidelines to Help Protect Abused and Neglected Children"

The children's division of the American Humane Society has put together a free pamphlet to help parents and others identify possibly abused children. The guidelines list indicators of a child

who may need protection and discuss the importance of reporting suspected child abuse, the role of protective services, and
the importance of early detection.

For information: Write to Children's Division, American
Humane Association, 63 Inverness Drive E., Englewood, CO
80112-5117.

Healthtouch

Healthtouch is a database created by the American Academy of
Pediatrics and Medical Strategies, Inc., that allows parents to
receive on-screen and printed information on a variety of child-
care and health subjects. This interactive computer system is
currently installed in pharmacies and retail stores around the
country.

For information: Call (800) 433-9016 or write to American
Academy of Pediatrics, 141 Northwest Point Blvd., PO Box 927,
Elk Grove Village, IL 60009-0927.

Healthy Mothers: Babies Best Start Book

Available to residents of Georgia receiving prenatal care in the
Atlanta metropolitan area, Healthy Mothers: Babies Best Start is
a free prenatal health-education incentive program designed to
encourage pregnant women to seek early and continuous prenatal care. Eligible mothers-to-be who enroll in the program
receive a free Coupons & Health Tips book filled with $1,000
worth of coupons for gifts and services, including baby products, restaurants, clothing, and prescriptions.

At each prenatal checkup, a month's worth of coupons and
gift certificates are validated by the participant's health-care
provider. The book also includes health tips and information
about pregnancy.

For information: Call (404) 607-0MOM (607-0666).

"Home Team Learning Activities"

The American Federation of Teachers has compiled a list of fun,
learning activities for grade-school children and suggestions for
parents on creating a good home learning environment. This

brochure stresses teamwork between teachers and parents to create the best possible learning situation for children.

The brochure costs $.25.

For information: Send a request for item number 592 and a check for $.25 to "Home Team Learning Activities," American Federation of Teachers, 555 New Jersey Ave. NW, Washington, DC 20001-2079.

"Let's Talk About It" Series

Mr. Rogers has some help for parents who want to improve communication between themselves and their children. The producers of *Mister Rogers' Neighborhood* offer ten 8- to 20-page booklets that encourage communication between parents and their children and reflect Fred Rogers's reassuring, informative style. The titles in the series are

"Talking with Families About Creativity"
"When You Have a Child in Day Care"
"Talking with Young Children About Death"
"Talking with Families About Discipline"
"Talking with Families About Divorce"
"When Your Family Moves"
"Talking with Families About Pets"
"When Your Child Goes to School"
"When Your Child Goes to the Dentist"
"When Your Child Goes to the Hospital"

A single copy of a booklet is free when you send in a self-addressed, stamped business-size envelope. If you would like copies of all ten, you must include a check for $2.

For information: Send a self-addressed, stamped envelope and the title of the booklet requested to Family Communications, Inc., 4802 Fifth Ave., Pittsburgh, PA 15213.

Parent Involvement Handbook

Published by Education Today and a 1995 Ed Press Award Winner for Distinguished Achievement in Educational Publishing, the *Parent Involvement Handbook* provides parents with practical

Your obstetrician is a wonderful source of free information. Most doctors give their expectant patients pregnancy packs. These packs usually consist of books on prenatal care, special offers and coupons from formula and diaper manufacturers, and a variety of materials from the makers of prenatal vitamins, including little books on baby names, breast-feeding, baby care, and vitamins, of course. Many doctors also include pamphlets from the American College of Obstetricians and Gynecologists that pertain to your particular set of circumstances. Your doctor will also probably give you some sample vitamins. In addition to your pregnancy pack, you can usually find copies of free magazines for expectant and new parents in your doctor's office.

advice on getting involved in their children's education. The book begins with the importance of parents as first teachers in establishing a positive environment for learning. Advice on selecting schools, parents' conferences, identifying learning problems, setting priorities, enrichment programs, and teens and jobs helps parents to stay involved in their children's education all the way through to college. Each chapter ends with a list of resources.

The *Parent Involvement Handbook* costs $7.95, plus $3 for shipping and handling. With it you receive a free copy of the *Education Today* newsletter.

For information: Call (800) 927-6006, extension 127, or write to EPG, 20 Park Plaza, Ste. 1215, Boston, MA 02116.

Parents in a Pressure Cooker

Parents in a Pressure Cooker by Jane Bluestein, Ph.D., and Lynn Collins, M.A., is a book designed to help parents deal with highly stressful situations. All parents want to be good parents, but every parent's limits are tested at some point. This book gives families a way to handle potentially explosive situations and to build a home based on positive discipline, acceptance, and love. A companion workbook for parents is also available. The workbook is filled with exercises to help parents help their children to become "responsible, loving, and non-codependent individuals."

Parents in a Pressure Cooker is $12.50, plus shipping; the workbook is $6.95, plus shipping.

For information: Call (800) 627-5867 or write to Modern Learning Press, PO Box 167, Dept. 363, Rosemont, NJ 08556.

Practical Parenting Song Books

Practical Parenting has three take-along books for parents who are entertaining their kids on the go. These books are perfect in the car, on the plane, or just about anywhere. Stash one in your diaper bag for boredom emergencies. Each book costs $1.

Lullaby Songs for Babies has all your favorite lullabies from "Rock-a-bye Baby" to "Beautiful Dreamer." Choose from 22 songs for singing your little one to sleep. *Sing Along Songs for Kids* includes 37 of the most popular kids' songs. Join your children in roaring choruses of "Clementine," "If You're Happy and You Know It," "John Jacob Jingleheimer Schmidt," and "On Top of Old Smoky." *Jump-Rope Rhymes* are perfect for a little outdoor release. Hop along to "Cinderella," "Coffee and Tea," "Miss Lucy Had a Baby," and "Teddy Bear."

For information: Send a self-addressed, business-size envelope affixed with two stamps, and $1 for each order, to Practical Parenting, Dept. Good Deal (LL, SING ALONG, or JR), 18326 Minnetonka Blvd., Deephaven, MN 55391.

Please identify which book you are ordering by the following department numbers:

Lullaby Songs for Babies — Dept. Good Deal-LL
Sing Along Songs for Kids — Dept. Good Deal-SING ALONG
Jump-Rope Rhymes — Dept. Good Deal-JR

Prenatal Care Pamphlets

Good prenatal care is one of the best gifts you can give your children. The March of Dimes Birth Defects Foundation is dedicated to ensuring that expectant mothers receive the information they need to give birth to healthy babies. You can receive one free copy of any of the following pamphlets by contacting the March of Dimes:

"Alcohol and Pregnancy: Make the Right Choice"
"Be Good to Your Baby Before It Is Born"
"Dad, It's Your Baby Too"
"Eating for Two: Nutrition During Pregnancy"
"Fitness for Two"
"Give Your Baby a Healthy Start: Stop Smoking"
"How Your Baby Grows"
"Pregnancy After Age Thirty"
"Stress and Pregnancy"

For information: To request a pamphlet, call (914) 997-4750 or write to March of Dimes Birth Defects Foundation, 1275 Mamaroneck Ave., White Plains, NY 10605.

"Reading and Your Adolescent"

Many parents focus on the importance of reading when their children are in elementary school and then back off as their teenagers become busier with sports, jobs, and social activities. However, research shows that adolescents who enjoy reading reap a bundle of benefits, including better grades, bigger vocabularies, better writing skills, and an easier time unraveling complex ideas. These benefits can lead to a more successful adulthood.

To encourage parental involvement in teenagers' reading, the Center for the Study of Reading at the University of Illinois at Urbana–Champaign put together this free brochure to encourage teenagers to read. The brochure offers suggestions for parents who want to create a positive environment for reading, including a bibliography of guides to books for teenage readers.

For information: Send a self-addressed, stamped envelope to Center for the Study of Reading, University of Illinois at Urbana–Champaign, 174 Children's Research Center, 51 Gerty Dr., Champaign, IL 61820.

"Safe & Sound for Baby"

The "Safe & Sound for Baby" brochure is sponsored by the Juvenile Products Manufacturers Association and is free to consumers. The brochure is filled with important safety information about car seats, changing tables, cribs, crib toys, pacifiers, bedding, carriers, swings, strollers, high chairs, baby gates, infant seats, baby walkers, and play yards. There are also tips on household dangers, electrocution, suffocation, and strangulation. Packed with good advice about the products babies come in touch with every day, this little guide is a must for parents.

For information: Send a self-addressed, stamped business-size envelope to JPMA Public Information, 236 Rte. 38 West, Ste. 100, Moorestown, NJ 08057.

"Starting School: A Parent's Guide to the Kindergarten Year"

Written by Judy Keshner, "Starting School: A Parent's Guide to the Kindergarten Year" is the key to a successful first year of school for your child. Packed with tips and advice, this 16-page booklet begins with the months leading up to the big day and follows through to the end of the year. The booklet costs $1.95 plus shipping and can be purchased from the Modern Learning Press.

For information: Call (800) 627-5867 or write to Modern Learning Press, PO Box 167, Dept. 363, Rosemont, NJ 08556.

"Toys & Play"

The Toy Manufacturers Association of America has produced a toy safety and selection guide which is free to all consumers. The booklet discusses how essential playing is to proper development in children, how to play with your children, how toys are labeled, how to select appropriate toys, and how important it is to supervise your children. Also included are a safety checklist and a toy buying guide. The booklet is also available in Spanish.

For information: Send a postcard requesting either English or Spanish edition, along with your complete name, address, and zip code, to Toys & Play Booklet, c/o TMA, 200 Fifth Ave. #740, New York, NY 10010.

"Travel with Baby"

To receive an educational booklet on safe travel for babies, as well as any special coupons available at the time of request, send $.50 and a self-addressed, stamped envelope to Cosco, Inc.

For information: Write to Cosco Promotions Fulfillment Department, 2525 State St., Columbus, IN 47201.

U.S. Consumer Product Safety Commission Pamphlets and Booklets

The U.S. Consumer Product Safety Commission has a number of free pamphlets and booklets available to parents. The materials cover varying topics on product safety, including

"Baby Product Safety Alert" (#250)
"Baby Safety Checklist" (#206)
"Bicycle Safety" (#242)
"Bunk Beds Fact Sheet" (#071)
"For Kids Sake, Think Toy Safety" (#281)
"Home Playground Safety Tips Fact Sheet" (#323)
"Poison Lookout Checklist" (#383)
"Protect Your Child" (#241)
"Protect Your Family from Lead in Your Home" (#426)
"Tips for Your Baby's Safety—Nursery Equipment" (#200)

To order a pamphlet or booklet, send a postcard with the title and number to the U.S. Consumer Product Safety Commission.

For information: Send a postcard to Publication Request, Office of Information and Public Affairs, U.S. Consumer Product Safety Commission, Washington, DC 20207.

Resources for Families with Special Needs

Braille and Talking Books

The National Library Service of the Library of Congress (NLS) provides free library services to any child who cannot read because of limited vision, who is physically unable to hold a book or turn a page, or who has a reading disability caused by an organic dysfunction. The NLS offers braille, print/braille, cassette, and disc formats free of charge. There are hundreds of children's books to choose from, including picture books and popular fiction and nonfiction in varying levels ranging from preschool to junior high. Children's magazines and music instruction materials are also offered.

For information: Write to The National Library Service for the Blind and Physically Handicapped, Library of Congress, Washington, DC 20542.

Directory of National Information Sources on Disabilities

The *Directory of National Information Sources on Disabilities* is a valuable sourcebook for locating organizations that offer services to people with disabilities. Each entry lists the organization's name, address, phone number, and type of disability, along with a description of publications and services offered. The book costs $15 to cover the shipping and handling.

For information: Call (800) 346-2742 or (301) 588-9284 or write to National Rehabilitation Information Center, 8455 Colesville Rd., Ste. 935, Silver Spring, MD 20910-3319.

"Getting Started with Food Allergies: A Guide for Parents"

This 20-page booklet from the Food Allergy Network is loaded with basic information for parents about handling their child's food allergies. The booklet discusses management strategies, shopping advice, and cooking tips and includes 10 Pantry Partner stickers which help sitters, kids, and other family members identify safe food packages.

The Food Allergy Network also produces Personalized Emergency Care Cards that list the symptoms of anaphylaxis, your child's name, and other emergency information. The cards are laminated and fit easily into wallets, backpacks, and lunch boxes.

The "Getting Started with Food Allergies: A Guide for Parents" booklet is $4 per copy. The Personalized Emergency Care Cards are $3 each.

For information: Call the Food Allergy Network at (800) 929-4040.

"A Guide to Children's Literature and Disability"

"A Guide to Children's Literature and Disability" is a bibliography of books that are written about or include characters who have disabilities. The books are categorized into specific disabilities and are identified by age or grade level. The book list is produced by the National Information Center for Children and Youth with Disabilities, which also distributes bibliographies on the following subjects: assessing children for the presence of a disability, behavior management, and mental health/mental illness. These bibliographies give parents a place to look for information that addresses their family's special needs. The bibliographies are free.

For information: Send a written request for the title you want to National Information Center for Children and Youth with Disabilities, PO Box 1492, Washington, DC 20013-1492.

Learning Disabilities Association of America Publications

The Learning Disabilities Association of America provides access to a number of publications concerning learning disabilities. Most cost less than $15. You can select from such titles as:

"Living with a Learning Disability: A Handbook for High School and College Students"
"A Parent's Guide to Attention Deficit Disorders"

"Coping with the Hyperactive Child"
"Educational Strategies for Students with ADD"
"Eagle Eyes: A Child's Guide to Paying Attention"
"Building a Child's Self-Image: A Guide for Parents"
"Help Me to Help My Child: Sourcebook for Parents of LD Children"
"Johnny Can Read"

For information: For a complete list of publications, write to Learning Disabilities Association of America, 4156 Library Rd., Pittsburgh, PA 15234-1349.

National Braille Press's Children's Braille Book Club

For the past 10 years, the National Braille Press has offered visually impaired children a wide variety of Braille versions of popular children's books so that they too can experience the joy of reading. Although Braille books are usually significantly more expensive than regular print books, the National Braille Press sells its books for the same retail price as regular print editions.

The National Braille Press also produces books for adults, calendars, basketball schedules, magazines, recipes, computer manuals, and CD-ROM, which are sold through catalogs.

For information: Write to National Braille Press, Inc., 88 St. Stephen St., Boston, MA 02115.

NICHCY News Digests

The National Information Center for Children and Youth with Disabilities publishes a number of News Digests on specific topics that relate to children with disabilities. Parents will find these 12- to 24-page booklets helpful when searching for information on parenting children with special needs. Topics available include understanding sibling issues, respite care, education for children with disabilities, sexuality education, estate planning, readings and resources for parents, directory of organizations, and assistive technology.

For information: Send a written request for the subject of interest to National Information Center for Children and Youth with Disabilities, PO Box 1492, Washington, DC 20013-1492.

NICHCY Parent's Guides

The National Information Center for Children and Youth with Disabilities offers several guides for parents of children with disabilities. The materials are free and cover the following topics:

"Accessing Parent Groups"
"Accessing Programs for Infants, Toddlers, and Preschoolers with Disabilities"
"Accessing the ERIC Resource Collection"
"Doctors, Disabilities, and the Family"
"Planning a Move, Mapping Your Strategy"
"Special Education and Related Services: Communicating Through Letter Writing"

The guides are 12 to 20 pages long and follow a Q&A format. Most guides include lists of additional resources.

For information: Send a written request for the title you want to National Information Center for Children and Youth with Disabilities, PO Box 1492, Washington, DC 20013-1492.

"Pocket Guide to Federal Help for Individuals with Disabilities"

This free guide is helpful for both disabled parents and parents of disabled children. The "Pocket Guide to Federal Help for Individuals with Disabilities" provides a summary of the government benefits and services available to individuals with disabilities. The Clearinghouse on Disability Information of the Office of Special Education and Rehabilitative Services, which is a branch of the U.S. Department of Education, has been distributing and updating this booklet for more than 18 years. Topics covered are programs for specific disability groups, vocational rehabilitation, education, employment, financial assistance, medical assistance, civil rights, housing, tax benefits, transportation, and the Americans with Disabilities Act. Contacts and addresses are given for the various agencies and organizations included.

For information: Call (202) 205-8241 or (202) 205-8723 or write to Office of Special Education and Rehabilitative Services, U.S. Department of Education, 330 C St. SW, Room 3132, Washington, DC 20202-2524.

Preschool Learning Activities for the Visually Impaired: A Guide for Parents

The key to this book is fun: parents and preschoolers having a good time and learning in the process. The 91-page, illustrated book is packed with games and activities designed to keep the minds and bodies of visually impaired children active during these important formative years. The book costs $9.50, plus $2 for shipping, and is available through the National Association for Parents of the Visually Impaired, Inc. (NAPVI). For members of NAPVI, the book is only $8.

For information: Write to NAPVI, PO Box 317, Watertown, MA 02272-0317.

Take Charge: A Guide to Resources for Parents of the Visually Impaired

Written by Dian Nousanen and Lee Rocinson, this 94-page guide provides an extensive listing of the national resources available to parents of blind and visually impaired children. A chapter is included on helping parents locate state and local resources, as well. There is also a large bibliography of books, films, tapes, magazines, and newsletters covering a broad spectrum of topics. The book is distributed by the National Association for Parents of the Visually Impaired, Inc. (NAPVI) and costs $6.50 for members and $8 for nonmembers, plus $2 shipping.

For information: Write to NAPVI, PO Box 317, Watertown, MA 02272-0317.

Book Clubs for Kids

Books of My Very Own

Books of My Very Own is a club that selects sets of books that are age appropriate. Parents are then able to decide whether or not to keep them. Age categories include baby books (6 months to 2 years), picture books (2 to 4 years), storybooks (4 to 7 years), and books for older readers (7 to 10 years). The first introductory package consists of three books. If a member chooses to accept them, he or she pays $1.95 for each book, plus shipping and handling. A free T-shirt is also included in the introductory package. Future packages of three to four books will be shipped every 5 weeks or so. Each shipment of books costs $13.95, a savings of up to 40 percent off publishers' prices. Members keep only the packages they want and can upgrade their child's age level whenever they choose. After receiving the introductory shipment, there is no obligation to buy additional books.

For information: Write to Books of My Very Own, A Division of Book-of-the-Month Club, Inc., Camp Hill, PA 17011-9849.

Children's Book-of-the-Month Club

Children's Book-of-the-Month Club has all kids' favorite characters and authors, including Richard Scary, Sesame Street, Babar, Winnie the Pooh, Simba, Maurice Sendak, Curious George, the Magic School Bus, and Shel Silverstein. Members can choose three books for $1 as an introductory offer and will receive a gift, currently a tote bag. Over the next year, members must buy three more books. Selections are divided into age groups from newborns to 12-year-olds, so it's easy to find age-appropriate gifts. Members will receive a catalog about every 3 weeks. If you want the featured selection for your child's age group, you do nothing and it will automatically be sent to you. If you don't want the selection or want to order other books, simply complete and return the order postcard. The monthly catalog is filled with books up to 50 percent off publishers' prices. Bonus points that allow you even greater discounts are earned for each book purchased.

For information: Write to Children's Book-of-the-Month Club, A Division of Book-of-the-Month Club, Inc., Camp Hill, PA 17011-9850.

Christian Parenting Today Club

The Christian Parenting Today Club offers a wide variety of books for children that teach values and faith. Most titles are religious in nature and are geared toward children ages 1 to 12. There are also books for adults on marriage, discipline, and parenting. As an introductory offer, members receive six books for $1 each, plus postage and handling. There is no obligation to buy additional books. Members will receive a catalog about once a month. If you want the featured selection, do nothing and the selection will automatically be sent to you. If you don't want the selection or want to order other books, you complete and return the order postcard. The monthly catalog is filled with books at least 15 percent off regular retail prices. Members can also earn bonus points for each book purchased that allow even greater discounts.

For information: Write to Christian Parenting Today Club, PO Box 36710, Colorado Springs, CO 80936-9902.

Crossings for Kids

Crossings for Kids is a Christian book club full of wholesome reading choices. There is a wide variety to choose from, including Richard Scary books, nursery rhymes, Barney books, board books, bibles for children, and lots of popular titles, such as *The Little Engine That Could* and *Goodnight Moon*. Not all the books are religious in nature, but all stress family values.

When members enroll, they receive three books for $1, along with a gift (currently a backpack). Members are then obligated to buy four more books over the next 2 years, at which point membership can be canceled. The books are aimed at children from newborn to 12 years of age. Members will receive a catalog about once a month and can select any book they want. If you want the featured selection, you do nothing and it will automatically be sent. If you don't want the selection or want to order other books simply complete and return the order postcard. The monthly catalog is filled with books up to 40 percent off regular retail prices.

For information: Write to Crossings for Kids, Member Service Center, 6550 E. 30th St., PO Box 6375, Indianapolis, IN 46206-6375.

Grolier Books

Grolier Books has a variety of book clubs for children, the two most popular of which are the Disney and Dr. Seuss clubs. Catch up with all the Disney favorites: Simba, Pocahontas, Snow White, Dumbo, Winnie the Pooh, and Mickey Mouse. Or get all the classic Dr. Seuss books: *The Cat in the Hat; Green Eggs and Ham; One Fish, Two Fish, Red Fish, Blue Fish; Hop on Pop;* and *And to Think That I Saw It On Mulberry Street,* among others. When joining either club, members receive eight books and a book rack for $1.99. Then, about every month, members receive two books in the mail. Each book is $4.99 plus shipping, so the monthly total is about $12.50. Members can cancel after they purchase four shipments and can return any books they don't want. Members cannot select the books they wish to receive, though.

For information: Write to Grolier Books, PO Box 1772, Danbury, CT 06816-1772.

Chapter Thirteen

Magazines and Newsletters

 Magazines and newsletters are an inexpensive way for parents to keep up to date on the latest parenting news, books, videos, and toys. Parenting magazines are filled with creative ideas for entertaining your kids, recipes for picky eaters, fun projects and activities to do at home, and current information on safety and health. Most magazine subscriptions are less than $20 a year. I know many a parent who, on the fourth rainy day in a row in the middle of summer, has been saved by an idea from a magazine.

Children's magazines are good learning tools. Kids love getting their own mail and usually devour a magazine as soon as it hits the mailbox. Parents can use children's magazines as a way to build communication and to spend time focusing on their child's interests. Most children's magazines are educational. As they hit the teen years, though, kids tend to go for pop magazines, comic books, and fashion magazines.

Newsletters usually appeal to narrower groups, such as single parents or stay-at-home dads. They offer more support and information for their particular group of interest than one would find in general parenting magazines.

Magazines for Kids

American Girl

Published by the Pleasant Company, the folks who bring us the American Girl Dolls, *American Girl* focuses on girls ages 8 to 12. This quality magazine is full of how-tos for things to do and create, hidden fun facts, "The Giggle Gang," and stories about girls all over the world.

The magazine comes out six times a year and costs $19.95 for an annual subscription.

For information: Call (800) 234-1278.

Babybug

Babybug is a magazine designed specifically for children ages 6 months to 2 years. The magazine comes in a board-book format, perfect for little hands, with rounded corners and no staples. It's packed with all the things infants and toddlers love: lots of colorful pictures, very simple stories, and rhymes.

A one-year subscription (nine issues) costs $32.97.

For information: Call (800) 827-0227.

Crayola Kids

Crayola Kids is packed with fun things to do and make: arts, crafts, stories, and games. There are activities, contests, puzzles, and articles for kids of all ages. The lively format will appeal to kids.

A one-year subscription costs $19.97.

For information: Call (800) 846-7968.

Creative Kids

Creative Kids is written by kids for kids. The purpose of the magazine is to encourage and showcase creativity in kids ages 8 to 14. All the art, articles, stories, photographs, poetry, games, contests, and special features are produced by the kids themselves. It's a wonderful way to get kids to express themselves.

A one-year subscription (six issues) costs $19.95.

For information: Write to *Creative Kids*, PO Box 8813, Waco, TX 76714.

Cricket

Cricket magazine has all the fairy stories, folk tales, science fiction, fantasy, history, biographies, poems, science, sports, and crafts needed to keep the active minds of 9- to 14-year-olds busy and stimulated. A powerhouse of reading, *Cricket* combines learning with lots of fun.

A one-year subscription (12 issues) costs $32.97.

For information: Call (800) 827-0227.

Girls' Life

Girls' Life is a magazine just for girls, full of all the kinds of things young girls like. Departments keep girls current on the latest info about entertainment, celebrities, conservation, and products. The articles feature clothes, activities, quizzes, sports, interesting girls, money, parties, and current events. Readers will learn how to throw fabulous parties, face paint, and cook cool foods and how other girls deal with issues in their lives. Articles have appeared on handling three-way friendships, whether or not girls are getting cheated in math and science, gym phobia, the coolest girl in America, and a behind-the-scenes look at beauty pageants. Your daughters can make new friends through the magazine by writing to a pen pal.

A one-year subscription (six issues) costs $14.95.

For information: Call (800) 999-3222.

Kid City

Kid City is specially formatted for kids ages 6 to 10. Filled with stories, puzzles, word games, and articles, this magazine gets kids learning without their even knowing it. *Kid City* is published by the Children's Television Workshop, the folks who bring you *Sesame Street.*

A one-year subscription (10 issues) costs $16.97. *Kid City* is not sold on newsstands.

For information: To order a subscription, call (800) 678-0613 or, in Colorado, (303) 447-9330. To request a sample copy, send a self-addressed, stamped 9-inch by 12-inch envelope to Children's Television Workshop, Magazine Group, One Lincoln Plaza, New York, NY 10023.

Ladybug

For children ages 2 to 6, *Ladybug* magazine is a wonderful first step to reading. Each issue brings to life all the best stories, poems, songs, and games young children like. The well-crafted illustrations and quality material make this magazine a favorite with parents and children. Inside the covers you will find read-aloud stories, songs, activities, and suggestions to encourage your children to explore the world around them. A section for parents is included in each issue with articles, letters, activity suggestions, and a book list.

A one-year subscription (12 issues) costs $32.97.

For information: Call (800) 827-0227.

Ranger Rick

Ranger Rick is a magazine for kids ages 6 to 12 published by the National Wildlife Federation. The magazine contains articles and activities about wildlife, nature, and the environment.

A one-year subscription (12 issues) is $15.

For information: Call (800) 432-6564.

Sesame Street Magazine

From the Children's Television Workshop, *Sesame Street Magazine* is a fun-filled magazine for children ages 2 to 8 packed with fun ways to learn and play. Each issue is brought to you by a number and letter—just like the TV show. Lots of games, activities, and stories fill the pages of this high-quality, award-winning magazine. Kids can draw, color, connect the dots, cut out, paste, and read. The magazine emphasizes family values and education. For the youngest readers, there are special Little Bird pages. For parents, *Sesame Street Parents* is sent along with each issue and is full of tips and advice, childproof recipes, and reviews of books, games, and toys.

A one-year subscription (10 issues) costs $19.90.

For information: To order a subscription, call (800) 678-0613 or, in Colorado, (303) 447-9330. To request a sample copy, send a self-addressed, stamped 9-inch by 12-inch envelope to Children's Television Workshop, Magazine Group, One Lincoln Plaza, New York, NY 10023.

Spider

Kids ages 6 and up will enjoy this lively magazine, which inspires young minds with vividly illustrated stories, poetry, articles, and activities. This magazine is perfect for beginning readers, giving them a variety of material on which to practice their new skills.

A one-year subscription (12 issues) costs $32.97.

For information: Call (800) 827-0227.

3-2-1 Contact

The Children's Television Workshop, the creators of *Sesame Street,* publish a fun, thought-provoking magazine, *3-2-1 Contact.* Children ages 8 to 12 will be fascinated by the world of science, nature, and technology that comes alive in the pages of *3-2-1 Contact.* It's filled with fun and engaging articles, games, puzzles, and experiments.

A one-year subscription (10 issues) costs $17.97. *3-2-1 Contact* is not sold on newsstands.

For information: Call (800) 678-0613 or, in Colorado, (303) 447-9330 to order a subscription. To request a sample copy, send a self-addressed, stamped 9-inch by 12-inch envelope to Children's Television Workshop, Magazine Group, One Lincoln Plaza, New York, NY 10023.

Turtle

Turtle is a magazine for preschoolers ages 2 to 5. It's filled with illustrated stories, poems, and songs to encourage the development of reading and comprehension skills. Topics covered include nutrition, exercise, and safety, as well as a variety of other subjects all presented in simple language that preschoolers enjoy.

A one-year subscription (eight issues) is $13.95.

For information: Write to *Turtle,* PO Box 7133, Red Oak, IA 51591-0133.

Magazines for Grown-Ups

Adoptive Families

For up-to-date information on adoption-related issues, *Adoptive Families* offers valuable news, advice, and resources. Subscribers also receive membership to Adoptive Families of America, a nonprofit organization that provides support and information to families who have adopted or who are considering adoption. Sections inside each issue include reviews of hard-to-find books, toys, and videos; articles about single adoptive parents; an age-by-age guide to growing up adopted; and special features on such subjects as finding a therapist, stress and marriage, and planning your adoption trip. It is a helpful magazine, filled with good advice on the particular concerns of adoptive families.

The magazine is published bimonthly, and the subscription rate is $19.95 per year.

For information: Call (800) 372-3300.

American Baby

You can pick up a free copy of *American Baby* in most obstetricians' or pediatricians' offices. Written for expectant parents, this magazine answers many of the questions pregnant women and new parents ask. With topics ranging from morning sickness to labor and delivery to baby's first visit to the pediatrician,

American Baby sets many first-time parents' minds at ease. Each issue contains articles grouped into the following topics: fashion, baby care, health and medical, and relationships.

A one-year subscription is free to expectant parents. After the first year, a one-year subscription is $13.97.

For information: Call (303) 604-1464 or write to *American Baby*, PO Box 51194, Boulder, CO 80322-1194.

Baby on the Way

From the editors of *Baby Talk* magazine and the American College of Obstetricians and Gynecologists, *Baby on the Way* focuses on the needs and anxieties of expectant mothers in a reassuring, informative way. You'll find information on maintaining a healthy pregnancy, eating right, what you'll be feeling, how babies develop, and how to cope with labor and delivery.

For information: Pick up free copies of *Baby on the Way* at your obstetrician's office.

Biracial Child

This quarterly magazine offers support for multiracial families and advice on raising healthy, multiethnic children. Raising positive, confident children is the focus of *Biracial Child*. The magazine deals with tough issues such as racism, coping, and rejection but also recognizes that biracial families have a lot more going on than just negative issues. This magazine is a positive force for multiracial families.

Biracial Child is published four times a year, and the subscription rate is $20.

For information: Call (404) 364-9690 or write to *Biracial Child*, 2870 Peachtree Rd., Ste. 264, Atlanta, GA 30305.

Child

Child is one of the most popular magazines for parents, covering a broad spectrum of information. There are monthly sections on child development, broken down by age group and covering kids from birth to the preteen years; health; family; and living.

Topics previously covered in the magazine include "Raising a Fruit and Veggie Lover," "Discipline with a Difference," "Have Baby, Will Travel," and "Science Magic." Monthly features include a discipline workshop; reviews of books, videos, and movies; pediatric news; nutrition; child safety; activities; and recipes. When you subscribe, you receive a special four-page insert that focuses on your child's particular age group.

A one-year subscription (10 issues) costs $8.97.

For information: Call (800) 777-0222.

Christian Parenting Today

Parents looking for a more spiritual approach to raising children will enjoy *Christian Parenting Today.* Articles and columns include information on the family bible, family health, dad talk, you and your spouse, and a parent's Q & A. An age-by-age development guide covers kids in utero through the teen years. There are also a parent's exchange, a marketplace, and humorous anecdotes from readers.

A one-year subscription (six issues) costs $16.97.

For information: Call (800) 238-2221.

FamilyFun

FamilyFun is chock-full of fun activities and creative ideas for families. Packed with after-school activities, hobbies, rainy-day amusements, parties, and holiday celebrations, this magazine is a must-have for parents looking for new ways to have fun. Each issue of *FamilyFun* offers tips on entertaining places to take your kids and family-friendly vacation destinations, a monthly activity calendar, ideas for sharing time and making memories with your children, complete instructions for arts and crafts and other activities, recipes for kid-approved foods, and a section on family computing, with how-tos and buying guides.

A one-year subscription (10 issues) is $14.95.

For information: Call *FamilyFun* at (800) 289-4849.

Donating Old Magazines

If your house is like mine, magazines seem to accumulate and multiply. Before I know it, I have stacks hidden in every corner. I hate to throw them away, so I have my children help me donate them. Donating teaches kids empathy with others and the value of helping others. It doesn't matter if the gesture is large or small, it's making the gesture that counts. So we donate magazines. You can donate them to hospitals, shelters, doctors' offices, schools, arts-and-crafts teachers, hospices, fire stations, libraries—almost anywhere people will be looking for something to read. If you are going to donate magazines, call the recipient ahead of time to make sure the magazines are wanted. You don't want your gesture of goodwill to turn into a burden for someone who then has to find a way to get rid of them.

FamilyPC

For families who are wired and on-line, *FamilyPC* magazine makes sense out of the mind-numbing array of computer-related information and products available. The focus on family and household uses for computers is a much needed resource in a field dominated by business. The magazine offers reviews of hardware and software, computer projects and activities, and articles such as "The Family PC Toolbox," "100 Best Products," and "Great Summer Projects."

A one-year subscription (10 issues) costs $14.95.

For information: Call (800) 413-9749 or write to *FamilyPC*, PO Box 400454, Des Moines, IA 50340-0454.

GrandParenting and Other Great Adventures

GrandParenting and Other Great Adventures is written for devoted, spiritual grandparents. It's a magazine about spending time with your grandchildren, sharing family values, and building beautiful relationships. Each issue covers subjects that are important to grandparents and includes book reviews, grandparenting advice, and feature articles such as "12 Steps to a Better Memory," "Confessions of a Mixed-Up Grandma," "7 Ways to Help Your Single-Parent Grandkids," and "Aging Myths Exposed."

A one-year subscription (six issues) costs $15.95.

For information: Call (800) 388-5509.

Healthy Kids

For reassuring advice on matters concerning kids from birth to 10 years of age, many parents turn to *Healthy Kids*. The magazine is produced by the publishers of *American Baby* and the American Academy of Pediatrics and offers the most up-to-date information on the health of children. In each issue, parents' questions are answered by pediatricians, parents' tips submitted by readers are provided, and articles are featured concerning the latest health news.

Parents can pick up free copies of *Healthy Kids* at the pediatrician's office.

For information: Call (708) 981-7944.

Mothering

Mothering celebrates the joys of bearing and raising children. With articles addressing such topics as the art of mothering, pregnancy and birth, family living, health, a child's world, and ways of learning, *Mothering* stresses the importance of good parenting and a solid family life which considers the needs of all its members.

A one-year subscription (four issues) costs $18.95.

For information: Call (800) 984-8116.

Parenting

One of the most popular general parenting magazines available, *Parenting* is noted for its reassuring advice and tons of information on every subject important to parents, from scheduling babies to beauty tips to children in crisis. With articles such as "Mom's from Mars, Dad's . . . in Orbit" and "When the Cupboard Is Bare," and contributors such as Dr. Benjamin Spock and Hillary Rodham Clinton, *Parenting* keeps current with the most up-to-date and reliable parenting information and issues. Arlene Eisenberg and Heidi E. Murkoff, the writers of the *What to Expect* books, have a monthly "What to Expect" column.

A one-year subscription (10 issues) is $18.

For information: Call (303) 682-8878.

Parents

Parents magazine is another very popular parenting magazine. Articles are grouped into such categories as Milestones, Health & Safety, Family Life, As They Grow, Working Life, Time for You, Home Style, and Fun Time. As They Grow, the age-by-age development guide, covers stages from pregnancy to 7 to 10 years old. Issues also include special sections with several articles concerning one topic.

A one-year subscription (12 issues) costs $12.97.

For information: Call (800) 727-3682.

Parents' Choice

Parents' Choice is a nonprofit organization that helps parents sift through all the children's books, toys, videos, TV shows, computer programs, CDs, on-line services, and multimedia products to find the best, highest-quality products for their children. Through their quarterly consumer guide, Parents' Choice evaluates and reviews children's products, awarding the best with a coveted Parents' Choice Award.

A one-year subscription (four issues) costs $20.

For information: Write to Parents' Choice, Box 185, Newton, MA 02168.

Twins Magazine

Twins Magazine addresses the special needs of parents of twins, triplets, and other multiples. The magazine helps parents of twins understand the impact of being a twin; keep current on the latest trends, opinions, and research; and cope with the practical aspects of raising multiples.

For information: Call (617) 965-5913 or write to *Twins Magazine*, PO Box 12045, Overland Park, KS 66282-2045.

Working Mother

Working Mother magazine is for moms who are doing it all. Articles on coping with stress, taking time out for yourself, time management, child rearing, and nutrition, along with age-by-age guides, predominate in this supportive and informative magazine. Recipes, beauty tips, and an annual list of the 100 best companies for working mothers also are offered.

A one-year subscription (12 issues) costs $12.97.

For information: Call (800) 627-0690.

Newsletters

At-Home Dad

For the growing numbers of fathers who choose to stay at home with their children, *At-Home Dad* offers support and a way to get in touch with other stay-at-home dads. Created by Peter Baylies after he was laid off from his job as a software engineer in 1994, *At-Home Dad* started out with a subscription roster of only six. He now has more than 1,000 subscribers and a network of more than 200 dads who have created play groups in 35 states. Baylies has also teamed up with Curtis Cooper, who founded Dad-to-Dad, a national organization for *At-Home Dad* readers, with new chapters popping up all over the country.

The newsletter is published quarterly and includes features on home business and finance, KidTips, father connections, recipes, and a spotlight on a new dad each issue. Each edition features a cover story on a subject relevant to these special dads.

Previous articles have been on starting play groups, single fatherhood, getting wired, and on-line chats for fathers.

A one-year subscription (four issues) costs $12.

For information: Write to *At-Home Dad*, 61 Brightwood Ave., North Andover, MA 01845-1702.

Education Today

The *Education Today* newsletter is filled with information for parents who are interested and involved in the education of their children. Aimed at families with children from preschool through high school, the newsletter features articles on issues and trends in education, suggestions for getting your children interested in learning, and reviews of educational books, software, and games.

A one-year subscription (eight issues) costs $16.95 for the standard eight-page edition and $18.95 for the math and science edition.

For information: Call (617) 542-6500 or write to EPG, 20 Park Plaza, Ste. 1215, Boston, MA 02116.

Father Times

Father Times is the newsletter of the Fathers' Resource Center, a nonprofit family-service agency dedicated to helping fathers become better parents. The newsletter covers subjects relating to fathers as involved parents. You'll find stories on support groups, programs available, legal issues, relationships, parenting, and the importance of a father's presence in a child's life.

A one-year subscription (four issues) is $20, which also entitles you to membership in the Fathers' Resource Center.

For information: Write to Fathers' Resource Center, 430 Oak Grove St., Ste. B3, Minneapolis, MN 55403.

Full-Time Dads

Full-Time Dads addresses the issues and concerns of the growing numbers of fathers who are the primary caregivers of their children. These special dads need their own support network, and that is what *Full-Time Dads* delivers. Each issue contains regular features, including the Forum, an ongoing dialogue among readers; The Single Dad; The Lighter Side; Now You're Cooking, recipes for dads and kids to make together; Opening Up, written by family therapist Bruce Linton; Full-Time Kids, a page of books, music, activities, and projects just for kids; The Savvy Advisor, a column dealing with money matters; and reviews of books, videos, movies, and products. Articles that have been featured in the past include "Top Ten List for Full-Time Dads: How to Survive in the Trenches," "Fathers and Intimacy," "Fathers in the Classroom," and "What My Father Taught Me."

Full-Time Dads also keeps a list of resources for fathers. Dads looking for hard-to-find publications, organizations, and services can send in a specific request with a $2 fee. The staff at *Full-Time Dads* will do their best to find what you're looking for.

A one-year subscription (six issues) is $26.

For information: Write to *Full-Time Dads*, PO Box 577, Cumberland, ME 04021.

Growing Child and Growing Parent

Growing Child and *Growing Parent* are monthly companion newsletters that match the age of your child. For example, if you subscribe when your child is 18 months old, your newsletter will begin with the 19-month-old edition. The parents' newsletter matches the age of the child. The newsletters cover each age monthly from birth to 6 years.

Growing Child gives you information about how your child is developing right now: what the developmental milestones for that age are, why the child is behaving in certain ways, what kinds of activities he or she is ready for, and what activities will enhance current abilities. Month by month you can follow your child's development with current, practical advice. Past newsletters have included articles on the 5-month-old's fascination with faces, how to keep the busy hands of a 12-month-old busy safely, and childhood fears at age 2 years and 4 months.

Growing Parent complements each monthly issue by offering advice on the challenges and joys of each particular age. Parents have to take care of themselves as well, and this supplement offers reassurance and advice just for them. Each issue also comes with an activity calendar that offers fun and creative suggestions for each day of the month. Some topics that have appeared in previous newsletters are "Experience More Joy—21 Ways to Free Your Spirit," "When Bad Things Happen . . . Bounce Back!," and "Down Time: Creative Ways to Relax."

The two newsletters together cost $15 for a one-year subscription (12 double issues).

For information: Call (800) 927-7289 or write to *Growing Child,* 22 N. Second St., PO Box 620, Lafayette, IN 47902-0620.

Manic Moms

Manic Moms is a humorous newsletter written for "crazed mothers." Through stories, articles, essays, poetry, fiction, Kid Quips, book and video reviews, and new product information written by parents, this newsletter shares the laughter and fun of parenting with all its readers. The newsletters have covered such subjects as carpooling, stalking runaway hamsters, dealing with the independent child, potty training, and the trials of the househusband. Each issue also includes safety tips, favorite books, recipes, cartoons, and letters from readers.

A one-year subscription (six issues) is $12.

For information: Write to *Manic Moms,* 3748 Homestead Rd., Ravenna, OH 44266-9556.

Parent and Preschooler

Each monthly issue of this newsletter for parents and professionals addresses one topic relevant to early childhood. Past issues have covered "Words to Love By: Communicating with Preschoolers" and "Social Skills: Learning to Play Together." Each issue also features a "Preschooler in the Kitchen" activity and a list of resources. The newsletter provides practical information on each of the main topics as well as theory. *Parent and Preschooler* is also available in an English/Spanish edition.

A one-year subscription (12 issues) costs $28. With it you receive three back issues.

For information: Call (800) 726-1708.

SingleMother

SingleMother came into being as a result of Andrea Engber's flipping through a magazine in a pediatrician's office. The article she was reading advised that to relieve the stress of parenting she should get her husband to pitch in more. Right then and there, she decided to do something to offer support to all the single mothers out there who don't have someone to take over the 2 A.M. shift. Out of that desire came the National Organization of Single Mothers, Inc., a not-for-profit group whose mission is to meet the needs of single mothers with a positive, proactive approach.

SingleMother is a supportive, informative newsletter for single moms who feel overwhelmed and alone. The positive messages and upbeat format make you feel less isolated and more able to handle the particular challenges of raising a child without a partner. The newsletter is loaded with resources, advice, news, and articles on such topics as "The Five Favorable Traits of Successful Single Mothers (like you!)," "Estate Planning: Keeping Your Kid's Future on Track," "Coping with Co-Parenting," "What Kids Need Is a Pampered Mom," and "How to Handle a Custody Crisis." There are also advice columns, letters, and book reviews.

The newsletter comes out six times a year and costs $12.97 for a one-year subscription. With your newsletter you receive a welcome kit that includes a list of resources, a list of members you can contact for support, and a copy of "How to Avoid Single Mother Burnout." You can also order back issues of the newsletter for $1.95 each.

For information: Call the Infoline at (704) 888-KIDS (888-5437) or write to National Organization of Single Mothers, Inc., PO Box 68, Midland, NC 28107-0068.

Single Mothers by Choice

The newsletter of the Single Mothers by Choice organization offers support and information for women who decided to have or adopt a child knowing they would be the sole parent. The group also welcomes women who are considering this option.

The newsletter features articles on artificial insemination, adoption, raising children as a single parent, personal experiences, and new babies.

A one-year subscription (four issues) is $20. Members receive the newsletter for free. Membership costs $45 per year and entitles members to a membership directory, a resource packet, a sibling registry, a private E-mail group, and a subscription to the newsletter.

For information: Write to *Single Mothers by Choice,* PO Box 1642, Gracie Square Station, New York, NY 10028.

Welcome Home

Welcome Home is a monthly 32-page journal published by Mothers at Home to support women who choose to stay home to raise their children. Each issue includes stories about the joys and challenges of parenting, articles about family life, humorous anecdotes, poetry, and a column in which readers offer solutions to another mother's problem. The encouraging and supportive tone of this journal provides comfort to many women who feel isolated and misunderstood.

A one-year subscription (12 issues) costs $18.

For information: Call (800) 783-4MOM (783-4666).

Your Child's Wellness Newsletter

Your Child's Wellness Newsletter offers up-to-date information on health issues concerning children. The newsletter covers pediatric research, new medicines and treatments, nutrition news, immunization facts, first-aid tips, and answers to readers' questions. Recent issues have discussed such subjects as DPT vaccinations, home improvements that put lead in your water, dangerous vitamins, effective ways to deal with allergies, and safety precautions at home.

A one-year subscription (six issues) is $14.95.

For information: Call *Your Child's Wellness Newsletter* at (800) 938-1915.

Chapter Fourteen

The Internet

 The Internet is full of entertainment and information for parents and kids, if you know where to find it. Navigating the Internet can be a challenge, but with a little patience and the list of fun sites in this chapter, parents and kids can come up with a wealth of free entertainment and information.

The sites listed here are divided into activities for kids and information for parents. You'll find a variety of educational and fun sites appropriate for children. Each of the main on-line services (America On-line, Compuserve, Microsoft, and Prodigy) has its own kids' area where they can play games, enter contests, and chat with each other. The on-line services also have areas for parents.

The sites included are accessible to everyone, no matter which service is used. However, bear in mind that given the fast-paced nature of the Internet, sites change addresses and reformat constantly.

Internet Sites for Kids

Adventure Online

Adventure Online is full of educational adventures geared for children from kindergarten to 12th grade. The on-line adventures include such games as a scavenger hunt in which children use their geographical knowledge to unravel clues and win prizes, and Journey North, where kids can migrate with birds and animals, travel to the Black Sea, or kayak down the Nile.

Internet address: http://www.adventureonline.com/index.html.

The Birmingham Zoo

The Birmingham Zoo, located in Birmingham, Alabama, offers all kinds of wonderful things for children to do. They can peruse an index of zoos throughout the world, sign the guest book, take an African safari, or tour the Galapagos Islands. Kids can also search for specific animals and then learn about their habits and characteristics.

Internet address: http://www.bhm.tis.net/zoo/.

The Computer Museum Network

Kids can visit the Computer Museum and "work through" a model of a computer, learning about the aspects and components that work together to make a computer run. The site offers parents guidelines to safely surfing the Internet. Also available is information about the actual Computer Museum in Boston, including membership guidelines, hours, fees, and directions. You can even print out a coupon to use for a discount on admission.

Internet address: http://www.tcm.org.

The Field Museum

Dinosaur-loving kids will go ape over the Field Museum's on-line dinosaur exhibit. Kids can "tour" the exhibit, clicking on the dinosaurs they want to learn more about and focusing on their history and evolution. This award-winning website is loaded with pictures, facts, and animated "movies." Kids can actually watch the Moropus eat and the Triceratops run. There are also interactive games for kids to play. They can even hear a recording of mammoth bone music.

Internet address:
http://www.bvis.uic.edu/museum/Dna_To_Dinosaurs.html.

Houghton Mifflin Education Place

The Houghton Mifflin Education Place is an educational website with activities, parent and teacher guides, and information on books and software. Kids can answer grade-appropriate brain-teasers in the math center. In the reading/language arts center, children can fill in the blanks to create a wacky web tale. In the social studies center, kids can play the Geonet game, saving the earth from aliens by answering questions about geography.

Internet address: http://www.hmco.com/school.

Kid Pub

Kid Pub is dedicated to encouraging creativity in children. It offers kids a place to showcase their work and read the work of others. Kids can read poems and stories written by other children, submit their own writing, and collaborate on stories with other children in other parts of the country and the world.

Internet address: http://www.kidpub.org/kidpub/.

Kids Com

Kids Com is a "communication playground" for children ages 4 to 15. At this site, kids will find a graffiti wall where they can post one-line messages to one another. The messages are monitored and censored before posting by Kids Com staffers. Children will also enjoy the story-writing games, trivia contests, and arts and crafts sections. There are tips for the technologically challenged.

Internet address: http://spectracom.com/kidscom.

Kids Craft

Created by two Australians, the Kids Craft website offers a wide selection of age-appropriate arts and crafts for children ages 5 to 12. Kids can create dream catchers, pom-pom chicks, stained glass windows, and worry dolls. The site is updated frequently with new ideas. The instructions are easy to understand—although, some of the wording and spelling is a little confusing because it is Australian. Craft ideas that are sent in by children and interested parties from around the world are also available.

Internet address:
http://www.ozemail.com.au/~teasdale/craft.html.

KidNews

KidNews is a free writing service where any child can submit articles for publication. The website offers articles from kids all over the world on such topics as news, feature stories, profiles, sports, reviews, and creative writing. The site also includes discussion areas for both kids and adults.

Internet address:
http://www.vsa.cape.com/~powens/kidnews3.html.

Lite Board

Fans of the Litebrite games will love playing Litebrite on-line. Visit the Internet site and design your own pictures. You can also view Litebrite masterpieces submitted by other viewers.

Internet address: http://asylum.cid.com/lb/lb.html.

NASA

Kids will have a blast at the NASA site. They can explore the NASA frontier, looking into the various NASA centers and learning about missions of the past, present, and future. Kids can also learn about how space exploration has helped Mother Earth.

Internet address: http://www.nasa.gov/NASA_homepage.html.

The Noodlehead Network

The Noodlehead Network has powerful and well-done videos touching on a variety of subjects, including safety in the home, energy-saving ideas, racism, and relationships with grown-ups. The videos are produced from a kid's point of view. You can also order videos made for kids by kids and follow tips for producing your own videos with just a camcorder.

Internet address: http://www.noodlehead.com.

Puzzle Archive

Kids who love brain teasers and puzzles will enjoy the Puzzle Archive. This site contains puzzles in 18 categories, including cryptology, logic, trivia, and probability. It's a great place for great thinkers to stretch their minds.

Internet address:
http://www.nova.edu/Inter-Links/puzzles.html.

Raindrop

Raindrop was designed to help children understand life and death. On this site, children can read a story about the life and death of a raindrop.

Internet address: http://iul.com/raindrop.

Scholastic Place

Scholastic Place offers lots for kids to do. It is a learning experience that is fun for all. Children can understand and appreciate the importance of getting involved in the community through world community awareness and learning about others. They can also explore the Animorphs, the Goosebumps, Harriet the Spy, the Babysitters' Club, and the Magic School Bus.

Internet address: http://www.scholastic.com/.

On-Line Services

In addition to the multitude of websites for kids and parents on the Internet, there are several on-line services that offer special interactive sites for kids and parents: America On-Line, Compuserve, Prodigy, Wow!, and Microsoft Network. These services make navigating the Internet manageable and offer their own services, including current news, sports and weather, chat rooms, bulletin boards, special interest forums, and on-line magazines. The services charge either a monthly flat rate for unlimited use or a lower monthly charge plus a charge for each hour spent on-line. All the services provide special areas just for kids with games, contests, news, and kids-only chat groups. They also provide parental controls so that kids can't wander off into areas their parents don't find acceptable. Special forums for parents are also featured. Parents can enter a chat room with other parents and discuss the basics of potty training, the difficulties of single parenting, or coping with teenage curfews. All the services offer parents and kids a great way to find others who share the same interests and stages in life.

Theodore Tugboat On-line Activity Center

Theodore Tugboat is a popular Canadian TV character. The site contains a variety of activities for children, including a coloring book and an interactive story. Children can also sign up to receive a Theodore Tugboat postcard or reserve a T-shirt. For parents, there is an overview of stories and characters and a discussion list. From this site, you can also contact other kid-oriented sites on the Internet.

Internet address: http://www.cochran.com/tt.html.

Yahooligans

Yahooligans is a search device for children that helps them locate kid-related sites on the Internet. Kids can choose from such categories as School Bell, homework help and educational programs; Science and Oddities, space exploration and environmental issues; and Around the World, global politics and ancient history. Yahooligans makes it easier for kids to find the sites in which they are most interested.

Internet address: http://www.yahooligans.com.

The Yuckiest Site on the Internet

All kinds of yucky things are waiting to be explored in this website. In worm world, Wendell the Worm leads kids through the underworld of worms, teaching children about how worms recycle, what body parts they have, and who their relatives are. There are games, stories, and poetry all about worms, too. Rodney the Roach guides kids through the world of the cockroach. Kids find out what a day in the life of a cockroach is like and all about roaches around the globe. There are even roach quizzes and activities. If they haven't already had enough, kids can ask Betty the Bug Lady about all kinds of creepy crawlers. If it gets to be too much, there are links to other kid-related web pages that aren't quite so yucky.

Internet address: http://www.nj.com/yucky/index.html.

Internet Sites for Parents

Ask Mom

Ask Mom is a great resource for traveling families. The site provides information "for kid-friendly vacationing in America." This city-by-city guide offers information on family-friendly entertainment, recreation, restaurants, hotels, emergency medical services, and 24-hour groceries and pharmacies in 29 American cities.

Internet address: http//:www.softline.com/askmom.

Big Top Productions

Big Top Productions is a software catalog and a whole lot more. In the Parent's Corner are ideas for arts and crafts such as worry dolls and tin candles as well as recipes for Wacky Popcorn and Toad in the Hole. Resources are also available for parents concerning children and computers and other parenting issues. An interactive journal invites children to post answers to the daily question or just post a note. The site has several other similar activities, including a cartoon theater. Parents can preview software from the catalog before purchase.

Internet address: http://www.bigtop.com.

Blind Children's Center

The Blind Children's Center is a resource guide to help parents of blind and partially sighted children find a variety of programs and services that are available to them. Information and referrals are provided. The Blind Children's Center also publishes a newsletter that can be viewed on-line.

Internet address: http://www.primenet.com/bcc/.

The Children's Literature Web Guide

The Children's Literature Web Guide brings together tons of information on Internet resources concerning books for children and young adults. Parents will find full-text stories, reviews, book lists, book discussion groups, information on authors and illustrators, and other websites. It is a valuable resource for parents.

Internet address:
http://www.ucalgary.ca/~dkbrown/Index.html.

The Dragonfly Toy Company

The Dragonfly Toy Company is a catalog full of products for children with special needs. All sorts of toys and games are offered. Each item is accompanied by a description of the item, the skills stimulated by the item, and a play therapist's notes on the product and its functions.

Internet address: http://www.magic.mb.ca/~dragon.

Family Education Network

The Family Education Network offers parents tips on becoming more involved in their children's education. The site features discussions on finding good child care, controlling television usage, giving children an allowance, and paying for college. Parent-related issues are also discussed, such as how to balance home and work, how to write a résumé, and how responsible parents should be for their children's misdeeds. Detailed information is available on a variety of topics. Kids will enjoy the activity center packed with science experiments, geography quizzes, and vocabulary-building exercises. The site also offers on-line versions of *Exceptional Parent,* for parents of disabled children, and *Parents' Choice,* a consumer guide for parents.

Internet address: http://www.families.com.

Family Planet

The Family Planet offers news about issues that are important to parents, including guidelines for preventing SIDS, political issues, celebrity parents, information on product recalls, and common and everyday hazards parents may not know about. Parents can also receive advice from other parents.

Internet address: http://family.starwave.com.

The Family Web Home Page

The Family Web is mostly for expectant and new parents, offering information on pregnancy, childbirth, and baby care. Parents can read other parents' birth stories and find explanations and tips on commonly occurring symptoms during pregnancy and immediately following childbirth.

Internet address: http://www.familyweb.com.

Med Access

Med Access is a source for information on health-related issues, including environmental concerns, quizzes, surveys, and recipes. Parents can search various databases for answers to questions they may have concerning their children's health. They can find out where to write for medical records, how to contact the Physician Disciplinary Board, and how to locate health information resources.

Internet address: http://www.medaccess.com.

Our Kids

Our Kids is a resource guide and support group for parents of children with special needs, such as children with Down's syndrome, autism, and cerebral palsy. The site also offers parents and kids a list of suggested books that deal with a variety of issues, including physical disabilities, dyslexia, and special education.

Internet address: http://wonder.mit.edu/ok/.

Parent Soup

One of the most popular parent-oriented sites on the web, Parent Soup offers a cornucopia of chat topics, information, activities, and recipes for parents. There is advice for pregnant parents, a list of baby names, and tips for childproofing your home. Parents will also find information on selecting a preschool, getting children to do their homework, and cutting down on TV time. There are suggestions for books, movies, and software for families. In addition, parents can access a weekly newsletter, activities, contests, and a Parent Poll.

Internet address: http://www.parentsoup.com.

Parents Place

Parents Place is an interactive site for parents. Users can talk with other parents in chat rooms about the challenges, concerns, and joys of raising children or post messages on bulletin boards. The variety of sources available to parents on this site includes a searchable database for topics of interest to parents, the Pregnancy Reading Room, and the National Parenting Center. You can link up with the Parents Place Mall to purchase books, services, and products.

Internet address: http://www.parentsplace.com.

Psych Central

At Psych Central, parents will find information, support, and resources on issues concerning mental health. The website offers a suicide help line and a symptoms list to help parents identify troubled children. There is also a list of the best Internet sites dealing with mental health.

Internet address: http://www.coil.com/~grohol/.

Rockville Creative Learning, Inc.

Visit the Rockville Creative Learning site to shop on the Internet for educational books and kits for children. All types of creative kits to entertain and educate children are available. Kids can open a dinosaur egg and put together a model of *Tyrannosaurus rex,* grow Dilithium and other crystals on the USS *Enterprise,* or create a planetarium in their living room. Parenting guides are available on diverse subjects, including raising children with learning disabilities, helping children believe in themselves, outsmarting your toddler, and keeping your child safe. This site offers a variety of workbooks, activity kits, and books for both parents and children.

Internet address: http://www.books4kids.com.

The Tide Clothes Line

Busy parents will appreciate this site; it's all about laundry and how to do it better and faster. The Stain Detective will help you get almost any stain out of almost any fabric. There are tips, time-saving ideas, product information, and even a laundry game.

Internet address: http://www.clothesline.com.

University of Pennsylvania Cancer Center Resource

The University of Pennsylvania Cancer Center Resource offers parents a place to go for information on cancer-related issues and concerns. The information is helpful to parents who have cancer or who have children with cancer. There are sections on clinical trials, frequently asked questions (FAQs), global resources, and financial concerns.

Internet address: http://www.oncolink.upenn.edu/.

Chapter Fifteen

Support Organizations and Hot Lines for Parents

 Parents need all the help they can get, and a number of support organizations and hot lines are willing to provide it. Many families have special circumstances and children with special needs. The organizations listed in this chapter are dedicated to providing information, resources, and support from people in similar situations. Most of these organizations offer memberships, which, for a yearly fee, provide parents with a variety of services, including newsletters and updates containing the latest research in their particular field of interest. These organizations provide much needed practical and emotional support to hundreds of thousands of parents around the world and are a great source of comfort to many. Most of the hot lines listed are run by trained staff and operate either 24 hours a day or during business hours.

Support Organizations

The Asthma Information Center

The Asthma Information Center offers two kinds of help. First, parents can contact the center for a list of resources, including colleges, academies, and foundations that can provide information and the names of local asthma specialists. Second, the center offers a series of brochures filled with tips, advice, and information for asthma sufferers on such subjects as using a metered-dose inhaler, helping children manage asthma, using a peak flow meter, and persistent coughing.

For information: Write to The Asthma Information Center, PO Box 790, Spring House, PA 19477-0790.

Family/Professional Resource Center
Children's Hospital Medical Center

The Family/Professional Resource Center of Cincinnati's Children's Hospital Medical Center is a free resource to *any* parent who has need of information related to the care or parenting of a child with a chronic illness, condition, or disability. The program, established in 1991, offers parents consultation, support, and help contacting other parents of children with chronic conditions. Parents can also take advantage of the Health Reference Center's computer database of up-to-date consumer health information, a wide variety of printed information, listings of local organizations and services, and referrals from an extensive resource base. In keeping with its philosophy that parents like to talk with other parents in a time of need or crisis, the center employs parents who have children with chronic conditions as "parent listeners."

For information: Call (513) 559-7606, fax (513) 559-7173, or write to Family/Professional Resource Center, Children's Hospital Medical Center, 3333 Burnet Ave., Cincinnati, OH 45229-3039.

F.E.M.A.L.E. (Formerly Employed Mothers at the Leading Edge)

F.E.M.A.L.E. is a national nonprofit organization for women who have chosen to leave their careers to stay home and raise their children. The organization offers support to all women who are coping with this dramatic change in lifestyle. Members receive a subscription to the monthly newsletter, *F.E.M.A.L.E. Forum*, and membership in a local chapter. There are currently chapters in 30 states, providing mothers with friendship, play groups, baby-sitting co-ops, support systems, and a sense of community.

The annual membership fee for F.E.M.A.L.E. is $20.

For information: For membership information, send a self-addressed, stamped business-size envelope to F.E.M.A.L.E., PO Box 31, Elmhurst, IL 60126.

Food Allergy Network

The Food Allergy Network provides parents of children with food allergies information on managing the allergies, special alerts concerning food mislabeling, and advice on reading food labels. The organization publishes a bimonthly newsletter, *Food Allergy News,* filled with the latest findings on food allergies, advice for getting children to eat well, allergy-free recipes, answers to diet dilemmas, and consumer alerts. In addition to the newsletters, the Food Allergy Network issues special mailings to notify parents of hidden ingredients in foods or of product recalls. Recently, they sent 11 special alerts in one year. In an area in which it is vital to keep up with the latest news, the Food Allergy Network helps parents cope with the challenges of keeping their allergic children safe.

A one-year membership to the Food Allergy Network is $24 and includes six issues of *Food Allergy News* and any special allergy bulletins released. A number of other publications are also available to parents.

For information: Write to Food Allergy Network, 10400 Eaton Pl., Ste. 107, Fairfax, VA 22030-2208.

Learning Disabilities Association of America

The Learning Disabilities Association of America (LDA), which has a membership of more than 60,000 people, has a variety of services available for parents of children with attention deficit disorder, dyslexia, hyperactivity, and other learning disorders. The association advocates a comprehensive approach to correcting an individual child's problem by taking into consideration the educational, physiological, psychological, and medical needs of the child. The services offered by the LDA include information and referrals, development of school programs with school systems directly, updates on current legislation, annual conferences, and a biannual newsletter, *Newsbrief*, that covers the latest news in the field.

Membership costs $25 per year.

For information: Write to Learning Disabilities Association of America, 4156 Library Rd., Pittsburgh, PA 15234-1349.

Medela®, Inc.

Medela, Inc., makers of breast pumps and other related products, is dedicated to promoting the benefits of breast-feeding for both babies and mothers. Medela offers direct support to nursing mothers through its Breastfeeding National Network (BNN), a toll-free hot line with 24-hour information on local breast-feeding specialists (see the entry under "Hot Lines") and retail and rental stores where nursing mothers can get breast pumps and accessories.

Medela also sponsors a corporate lactation program, called Sanvita. By providing companies with a managed care program run by lactation professionals, Medela encourages mothers to continue to breast-feed their children after they return to work. The Sanvita program involves prenatal breast-feeding education, maternity leave support, equipped work-site lactation centers, and work-site support by lactation professionals. Nursing women are provided with a place to express milk, with lactation consultants on-site to offer support. The program benefits companies by reducing maternal absenteeism, insurance claim costs for infants, and severity of illnesses that do occur; it benefits mothers by reducing the risk of developing breast and ovarian cancers and osteoporosis; and it benefits infants by reducing the number and duration of respiratory illnesses and the risk of developing middle-ear infections, rotavirus gastroenteritis, and bacterial meningitis.

For information: Write to Medela, Inc., PO Box 660, McHenry, IL 60051-0660.

MOMS Club

MOMS Club is a national nonprofit support group for mothers who stay home with their children. Members are directed to one of more than 260 local chapters. If there is not a local chapter in a mother's area, MOMS Club will invite her to start one and will send all the information needed. The club emphasizes the importance of not feeling isolated by the choice to stay home with one's children. They offer a support group with daytime meetings where mothers can get together for presentations by speakers, discussions, and activities. Chapters also host park play days, outings for mothers and their kids, baby-sitting co-ops, playgrounds, arts and crafts, a monthly MOMS night out, and other activities. Each chapter is required to perform a minimum of one service project per year that benefits needy children.

Local chapter dues range from $15 to $30 per year.

For information: For an information brochure, send $2 to MOMS Club, 814 Moffatt Circle, Simi Valley, CA 93065.

Mothers at Home

Mothers at Home (MAH) is for any mom who stays home with her children and has faced the favorite cocktail-party question, "What do you do?" When she responds that she stays home with her children, the other person usually says, "Wow, it must be great not doing anything all day," or simply moves on. A nonprofit organization, Mothers at Home strives to fulfill three goals: to support the choice these mothers have made, to help mothers be excellent parents, and to correct society's misconceptions about mothering today. MAH accomplishes these goals by publishing a newsletter and books, educating the media, and influencing national legislation. MAH also practices what it preaches by offering its employees a family-friendly work environment with flexible hours and a large playroom for their children in view of meeting rooms and workrooms.

For information: Call (800) 783-4MOM (783-4666) or write to Mothers at Home, 8310A Old Courthouse Rd., Vienna, VA 22182.

Mothers of Preschoolers (MOPS)

More than 45,000 mothers of children under school age meet at nearly a thousand MOPS groups in churches around the United States and in 10 countries around the world. They gather to calm each other's frazzled nerves, find friends, discuss feelings on parenting and marriage, listen to experienced teachers discuss the spiritual and practical aspects of parenting, and complete craft projects. Children receive quality care during these meetings. MOPS also publishes a free newsletter.

For information: Call (800) 929-1287 or write to MOPS International, Inc., 1311 S. Clarkson St., Denver, CO 80210.

National Association for Gifted Children

The National Association for Gifted Children (NAGC) is dedicated to educating intellectually and creatively gifted children to their full potential. Benefits for members include a subscription to *Parenting for High Potential,* a magazine for parents of gifted children; a subscription to *Gifted Child Quarterly,* a journal providing recent research developments in gifted education; a subscription to *Communique,* a newsletter reporting on updates in federal legislation, parent and public information, and announcements about upcoming NAGC activities; and discounts on NAGC materials.

A one-year membership to NAGC costs about $60.

For information: Call (202) 785-4268 or write to National Association for Gifted Children, 1707 L St. NW, Ste. 550, Washington, DC 20036.

National Association for Parents of the Visually Impaired, Inc.

The National Association for Parents of the Visually Impaired, Inc. (NAPVI) provides parents of visually impaired children with support, information, and resources. NAPVI is dedicated to helping children reach their full potential by offering outreach programs, a network for parents, and advocacy for the educational needs and welfare of blind and visually impaired children. Members receive the *Awareness* quarterly and are able to join the network of families sharing the special challenges of raising blind and visually impaired children. Members also receive discounts on NAPVI publications.

For information: Write to National Association for Parents of the Visually Impaired, Inc., PO Box 317, Watertown, MA 02272-0317.

National Black Child Development Institute

The National Black Child Development Institute (NBCDI) is a nonprofit organization dedicated to improving the quality of life for African-American children, with special emphasis on health, education, child welfare, child care, and early childhood education. The NBCDI is working to fulfill its goal by training professionals and parents to be more effective, tutoring young African Americans, researching and providing resources to aid parents, and serving the needs of community leaders supporting local and national issues relating to African-American children.

A regular one-year membership to NBCDI costs $25. Members receive subscriptions to the *Black Child Advocate* and *Child Health Talk* newsletters and discounts on NBCDI publications and annual conference fees.

For information: Call (800) 556-2234 or (202) 387-1281 or write to National Black Child Development Institute, 1023 15th St. NW, Ste. 600, Washington, DC 20005.

National Center for Missing & Exploited Children

A series of helpful pamphlets is available from the National Center for Missing & Exploited Children. The "Just In Case . . ." series covers topics such as parental guidelines for evaluating day care, hiring baby-sitters, helping runaways, finding missing children, and identifying sexual abuse. The center also offers materials on basic child safety, including a poster for children, "My 8 Rules for Safety," that lists rules in first person so they are more meaningful to children. For example, rule number one reads, "Before I go anywhere, I always check first with my parents or the person in charge. I tell them where I am going, how I will get there, who will be going with me, and when I'll be back."

For information: Write to National Center for Missing & Exploited Children, 2101 Wilson Blvd., Ste. 550, Arlington, VA 22201-3052.

National Information Center for Children and Youth with Disabilities (NICHCY)

NICHCY is an information clearinghouse that provides free information on disabilities and disability-related issues for children and youth from birth to age 22. NICHCY provides personal responses to questions on disability concerns, including specific disabilities, family matters, legal issues, and special education. They will refer you to other organizations that can help with your particular concern: national and state disability groups, professional associations, information centers, parent groups, and advocacy groups. They will also search NICHCY's databases and libraries for information and offer technical assistance to parent and professional groups. Parents can request a variety of free publications, such as state resource sheets, fact sheets on specific disabilities, issue and briefing papers, legal information, parent guides, and bibliographies. All information and services are provided free of charge. NICHCY's publications are also available on the Internet—no waiting.

For information: Call (800) 695-0285, fax (202) 884-8441, use the Internet: nichcy@aed.org, or write to NICHCY, PO Box 1492, Washington, DC 20013-1492.

National Organization of Single Mothers, Inc.

The National Organization of Single Mothers (NOSM) stresses the importance of a positive, can-do attitude. In addition to pub-

10 Ways to Help Your Children Help Others

1. Have your children help prepare meals to donate to a shelter.
2. Take your kids to a retirement or nursing home to visit with residents.
3. Let your children pick out toys to donate to Toys for Tots.
4. Encourage your teenager to shovel a neighbor's walk or rake leaves without payment.
5. Help kids go through closets and choose clothes to donate to a charity.
6. Encourage older kids to tutor younger children at school.
7. Organize a neighborhood clean-up day on your street or in a park.
8. Donate some of your children's artwork to help brighten up a pediatric unit at your local hospital.
9. Save canned goods for a food drive.
10. Take a trip to the recycling center.

lishing a bimonthly newsletter, *Single Mother,* NOSM serves as a clearinghouse of resources and information for single moms, employers, schools, and professionals. It provides research to the media and the public, educating them on the positive aspects of single motherhood and the harm in portraying single mothers by unfair stereotypes. For mothers looking for a support group, NOSM will help you find one or help you start one. Contact sheets with lists of single mothers who are willing to offer support are also available to members.

For information: Call the Infoline at (704) 888-KIDS (888-5437) or write to National Organization of Single Mothers, Inc., PO Box 68, Midland, NC 28107-0068.

National Resource Center on Child Abuse and Neglect

The National Resource Center on Child Abuse and Neglect operates a toll-free number, (800) 227-5242, that provides parents and professionals referrals and information on child abuse and neglect, statistics, and clinical consultations. Parents can request information sheets, research reviews, directories of treatment programs, and resource packets. Operated by the American Humane Association, the Resource Center mainly serves professionals but does have information in which some parents may be interested.

For information: Call (800) 227-5242 or write to National Resource Center on Child Abuse and Neglect, 63 Inverness Dr. East, Englewood, CO 80112-5117.

The Twins Foundation

For those parents doubly blessed, the Twins Foundation offers support and information geared to the special concerns of families raising twins and other multiples. The foundation supports research on twins, maintains the National Twin Registry to aid medical and scientific research, and provides an information clearinghouse and a support network for multiples and their families. As members of the foundation, you will receive subscriptions to *The Twins Letter and Research Update* newsletters and discounts on future foundation publications, covering such topics as "Should Twins Be Separated in School?," "Vanishing Twin Syndrome," and "Twins' Life Patterns" and columns such as "Twin to Twin" and "Parents Want to Know." Membership costs $15 per twin per year.

For information: Call (401) 729-1000, fax (401) 751-4642, or write to The Twins Foundation, PO Box 6043, Providence, RI 02940-6043.

Hot Lines

Adoptive Families of America

The 24-hour hot line of Adoptive Families of America offers information and referrals to support groups in the caller's area.

For information: Call Adoptive Families of America at (800) 372-3300.

American Federation of Teachers Learning Line

When your kids are bored and looking for something to do, have them call the Learning Line, sponsored by the American Federation of Teachers. This toll-free hot line for kids between the ages of 8 and 12 offers fun and innovative educational activities. The activities and experiments help kids learn about math, science, history, geography, and other subjects. A new activity is described by recorded message each week. Be sure to have a pen and paper ready to write down details.

For information: Call the American Federation of Teachers Learning Line at (800) 242-5465.

Ask-A-Nurse Connection

By dialing the national Ask-A-Nurse Connection line, you can find an Ask-A-Nurse hot line in your area. When your doctor's office is closed and you have a question concerning your child's health, call your local Ask-A-Nurse line to be connected to a registered nurse. The nurse will answer questions relating to your child's health and refer you to a doctor listed on your insurance plan. More than 200 hospitals around the country participate in the Ask-A-Nurse program.

For information: Call (800) 535-1111.

Auto Safety Hot Line

The National Highway Traffic Safety Administration's Auto Safety Hot Line is the number to call if you have any questions concerning the safety and installation of car seats. Staffers will let you know if your car seat has been recalled and can offer suggestions for proper use and installation.

For information: Call (800) 424-9393.

Beech-Nut Nutrition Helpline

Beech-Nut staff will answer callers' questions about the feeding and nutrition of babies from 8 A.M. to 7 P.M. central standard time, Monday through Friday. You can find out where to buy their products and receive a set of introductory coupons (one time only). Beech-Nut also offers a selection of more than 40 prerecorded messages on various subjects pertaining to the feeding, nutrition, and care of babies, including breast-feeding, introducing the cup, colic, allergies, sleeping through the night, spitting up, child development, feeding solids, and prenatal and postpartum care.

For information: Call the Beech-Nut Nutrition Helpline at (800) 523-6633.

Breastfeeding National Network

Medela®, Inc., maker of breast pumps and other breast-feeding products, operates a 24-hour information line that tells callers where they can rent breast pumps in their area and how to get in touch with local lactation consultants.

For information: Call the Breastfeeding National Network at (800) TELL-YOU (835-5968).

Bright Beginnings Warmline

Call the Bright Beginnings Warmline to speak with a trained volunteer about common concerns for parents, including temper tantrums, eating habits, thumb sucking, and child development. The hot line is open 9 A.M. to 9 P.M. eastern standard time, Monday through Friday, and is sponsored by the Parental Stress Center at Magee Women's Hospital in Pittsburgh, Pennsylvania.

For information: Call the Bright Beginnings Warmline at (412) 641-4546.

Consumer Product Safety Commission's Hot Line

To check on whether or not one of your child's toys, equipment, or other baby or juvenile products has been recalled, call the Consumer Product Safety Commission's Hot Line. The hot line is automated and will request the particular product's manufacturer and model number, so be sure to have that information available before you call. You can also use the hot line to report unsafe products.

For information: Call (800) 638-2772.

Gerber Hot Lines

Gerber operates two hot lines for consumers of its products. The formula hot line is open Monday through Friday 7 A.M. to 4:30 P.M. central standard time. The staff will answer your questions about Gerber formulas and bottle-feeding your baby.

The Gerber product hot line operates 24 hours a day. The hot line offers information on the care and feeding of babies and answers questions about Gerber's other products (baby food, toys, apparel, bottles, baby accessories, etc.). They will send you information for children with special feeding needs, including milk-free and citrus-free products. Gerber will also send coupons when available and will give you location information on where to find their products in your area.

For information: The number for the Gerber formula hot line is (800) 828-9119; the number for the Gerber product hot line is (800) 4-GERBER (443-7237).

Headaches Hot Line

The National Headache Foundation sponsors a headache hot line, which operates 9 A.M. to 5 P.M. central standard time, Monday through Friday. You can call the staff to ask questions about your child's headaches. Parents can receive more detailed information by sending a self-addressed, business-size envelope with three stamps affixed, along with a description of your child's symptoms, to the National Headache Foundation.

For information: Call the National Headache Foundation's Headache Hot Line at (800) 843-2256 or write to them at 428 W. St. James Pl., Second Floor, Chicago, IL 60614.

Job Survival Hot Line

The Job Survival Hot Line is operated by Nine to Five, an advocacy organization for working women and families. The hot line is open 10 A.M. to 4 P.M. eastern standard time, Monday through Friday. The staff answers questions about maternity benefits, family leave, sexual harassment, and other work-related issues.

For information: Call the Job Survival Hot Line at (800) 522-0925.

La Leche League Hot Line

La Leche League International offers nursing mothers a direct link to support and information on breast-feeding. The toll-free line is staffed 8 A.M. to 5 P.M. (CST), Monday through Friday. Staffers will answer questions over the phone and will refer you to a La Leche League representative in your area.

For information: Call (800) LA-LECHE (525-3243).

National AIDS Hot Line

The 24-hour National AIDS Hot Line provides callers with basic information on HIV and AIDS by a staff specially trained by the Centers for Disease Control. Members of the staff are not doctors and will not give out medical advice over the phone. They offer a referral service to locate testing centers, support groups, and medical treatment facilities in your area. You can also request free brochures on various subjects pertaining to HIV and AIDS.

There is also a line for people who speak only Spanish. This line operates 7 days a week 8 A.M. to 2 A.M. eastern standard time.

For information: Call the National AIDS Hot Line at (800) 342-AIDS (342-2437) for English-speaking operators and (800) 344-7432 for Spanish-speaking operators.

National Immunization Information Hot Line

State and federal health departments have been working together to ensure that all children receive immunizations. Call the National Immunization Information Hot Line to find an immunization service in your area where your child can receive free or low-cost immunizations.

For information: Call the National Immunization Information Hot Line at (800) 232-2522.

National Multiple Sclerosis Society

On the National Multiple Sclerosis Society's 24-hour information line, callers can have their questions about MS answered and get details on local chapters.

For information: Call the National Multiple Sclerosis Society at (800) FIGHT-MS (344-4867).

Scottish Rite Children's Resource Line

The Scottish Rite Children's Resource Line has a lot to offer Atlanta-area parents (although I have called it myself on several occasions even though I live near Chicago). Parents can listen to recorded messages on common childhood illnesses and emergencies, children's health, adolescents' health, parenting, and safety. Callers can also speak to a pediatric nurse about particular concerns or get referrals to Atlanta-area doctors.

For information: Call the Scottish Rite Children's Resource Line at (404) 250-KIDS (250-5437).

TwinLine

Parents with double duty can call Twin Services, a nonprofit agency that helps parents cope with raising multiples.

For information: Call the Twin Services TwinLine at (510) 524-0863.

YMCA of the USA

Call the YMCA information line to find out about YMCAs in your area. Most YMCAs offer classes and programs for kids. Your local YMCA may offer Mom and tot classes, day camps, day care, postpartum exercise classes, arts and crafts, and a variety of other activities for children at minimal fees. Call your local YMCA for schedules and fees.

For information: Call the YMCA at (800) USA-YMCA (872-9622).

Index

A

Abused children, 179–180

Activities for children
free, 45–46
using old catalogs and, 22
ways for children to help
others, 233

Activity books, 173

A. D. Barnes Park, (Miami),
75

Adler Planetarium (Chicago),
54

Adoptive Families (magazine),
200

Adoptive Families of America
(hot line), 235

Adventure Online (website),
214

Adventure vacations,
139–149

After the Stork (catalog),
17–18

Alcoholism and drinking,
29–30

Alisa Ann Ruch Burn Foun-
dation, 28

American Academy of Pedi-
atrics, 171–172, 174–175

American Baby (magazine),
200–201

*American Camping Association
Guide to Accredited Camps*,
161

American Federation of
Teachers Learning Line
(hot line), 235

American Girl (magazine),
196

American Museum of Natural
History (New York City),
85–86

Arrowwood Resort (Alexan-
dria, Minn.), 124

Art Institute of Chicago,
54–55

Ask Mom (website), 219

Ask-A-Nurse Connection
(hot line), 235

Asthma Information Center
(support organization),
225–226

Asthma pamphlets, 175

At-Home Dad (newsletter),
206–207

Atlanta (Ga.), attractions for
children, 39–44

Audubon Institute (New Orleans), 82–83
Auto Safety Hot Line, 235–236

B
Baby Alive (video), 176
Baby Clothes Wholesale (catalog), 18
Baby foods, 4–5
Baby on the Way (magazine), 201
Baby products, top 10 under $10, 7
Baby Superstore, 11–12
Babybug (magazine), 196
Baby's Away rentals, 143
Baby-sitting training programs, 32–34
Back to Basics Toys (catalog), 18
Baltimore, Md., attractions for children, 44–47
Baltimore Zoo, 44
Barnes & Noble (bookstore), 12
Bay Area Discovery Museum (Sausalito, Calif.), 98
"Becoming Your Child's First Teacher" (booklet), 176
Beech-Nut New Parents Pack, 3–4
Beech-Nut Nutrition Helpline, 236
Belle Meade Mansion (Nashville), 80

Best Western Hotels, 151–152
Bicycle Safety Camp (video), 171–172
Big Top Productions (website), 220
Biracial Child (magazine), 201
Birmingham (Ala.) Zoo (website), 214
Birthday Express (catalog), 18
Blind Children's Center (website), 220
Bluestein, Jane, 182–183
Boeing Tour Center (Everett, Wash.), 109
Book clubs, children, 192–194
The Bookies (bookstore, Denver), 64–65
Books, for special-needs children, 187
Books of My Very Own (book club), 192
Boston, Mass., attractions for children, 48–54
Boston by Little Feet tour, 48
Boston Children's Theatre, 48
Boston Common (park), 48–49
Boston Public Garden, 48–49
Boston Public Library, 49
Braille books, 187, 189
"Breastfeeding Information Guide" (booklet), 176
Breastfeeding National Network, 236

Bright Beginnings Warmline,
236–237
Bronx Zoo, 86
Brookfield (Ill.), Zoo, 55–56
Brooklyn Children's Museum,
87
Bucklebear Club, 27–28
Bureau of Engraving and
Printing (Washington,
D.C.), 105
Burn kits, 28

C
California Academy of Sci-
ences (San Francisco), 99
California Museum of Sci-
ence and Industry (Los
Angeles), 71–72
Cane Island Flower Farm
(Beaufort, S.C.), 110
Canyonlands Field Institute
(CFI), 160
Canyonlands Field Institute
(CFI) Family Camps
(Moab, Utah), 139–140
Cape Cod Potato Chips
(Hyannis, Mass.), 110
Capital Children's Museum
(Washington, D.C.), 105
Carnation Special Delivery
Club, 4
Carnegie Museums, Science
Center, and Library (Pitts-
burgh, Pa.), 111–112
"Catch 'Em in the Cradle"
library program, 115

Center for Injury Prevention,
27–28
Center for Puppetry Arts
(Atlanta), 39–40
Central Park (New York
City), 87
Chicago, Ill., attractions for
children, 54–62
Chicago Academy of Sci-
ences, 56
Chicago Children's Museum,
56–57
Chicago Tribune's Freedom
Center, 57–58
Child (magazine), 201–202
"Child Health Guide" (book-
let), 177
Child Is Born, A (Nilsson), 5
Children's Book Shop
(Brookline, Mass.), 49
Children's Book-of-the-
Month Club, 192–193
"Children's Books of the Year"
(booklet), 177
"Children's Choices" (book-
let), 177–178
Children's Hospital of
Columbus, Ohio, 34
The Children's Literature
Web Guide (website), 220
Children's Medical Center of
Dallas, 31–32
Children's Museum (Boston),
50
Children's Museum (Denver),
65

Children's Museum (Indianapolis), 69

Children's Museum (Portland, Ore.), 95

Children's Museum (Seattle), 102

Children's Museum of Manhattan, 87–88

Children's Museum of the Arts (New York City), 88

Children's Theatre Company (Minneapolis), 78

ChildsWork/ChildsPlay (catalog), 19

Chinaberry (catalog), 19–20

Choice Hotels International, 152

Christa McAuliffe Planetarium (Concord, N.H.), 112

Christian Parenting Today (magazine), 202

Christian Parenting Today Club (book club), 193

City Park (New Orleans), 83–84

Club Med, 152–153

Collins, Lynn, 182–183

Colorado State History Museum, 65–66

Como Park (St. Paul, Minn.), 78–79

Computer Museum (Boston), 51

Computer Museum Network (website), 214

Conner Prairie (living-history settlement, Fishers, Ind.), 69–70

Conservation Summits, 140–141

Constructive Playthings (catalog), 20

Consumer Information Catalog, 178

Consumer Product Safety Commission's Hot Line, 237

Country Dance and Song Society Family Weeks (Northampton, Mass.), 141–142

CPR Prompt Home Learning System, 30

Crayola Factory at Two Rivers Landing (Easton, Pa.), 113

Crayola Kids (magazine), 196

Creative Kids (magazine), 196–197

Cricket (magazine), 197

Crossings for Kids (book club), 193–194

Crow Canyon Archaeological Center Family Week (Cortez, Colo.), 142–144

Crown Plaza Resort (Hilton Head Island, S.C.), 124–125

Cuisenaire (catalog), 20

Cumberland Museum and Science Center (Nashville), 81

D

Dallas, Tex., attractions for children, 62–64

Dallas Museum of Natural History, 62–63

Dallas World Aquarium, 63

Dallas Zoo, 63

Days Inn Family Vacation Club, 153

Denver, Colo., attractions for children, 64–68

Denver Art Museum, 66

Denver Firefighters Museum, 66–67

Denver Public Library's Children's Library and Story Pavilion, 67

Directory of National Information Sources on Disabilities, 187

Disabilities, children with, 187–194

Discovery Museums (Acton, Mass.), 51–52

Dragonfly Toy Company, The (website), 220–221

Drinking and alcoholism, 29–30

Dutch Boy Paints, 4

E

Earth's Best Family Program, 4–5

Education Today (newsletter), 207

Egleston Children's Health Care System, 35

Egleston Children's Hospital, 29

Enfamil Family Beginnings, 5–6

Exploratorium (San Francisco), 99–100

Explorer Camps, 159–160

F

Fairchild Tropical Garden (Miami), 75

Family Adirondack Weekend (Raquette Lake, N.Y.), 144

Family adventure vacations, 139–149

Family Education Network (website), 221

Family PC (magazine), 203

Family Planet (website), 221

"The Family Travel Guides Catalogue," 178

The Family Web Home Page (website), 221

Family Week at Great Camp Sagamore (Raquette Lake, N.Y.), 144–145

FamilyFun (magazine), 202

Family/Professional Resource Center (support organization), 226

F.A.O. Schwarz (toy store), 88–89

Father Times (newsletter), 207

Federal Bureau of Investigation (Washington, D.C.), 106

F.E.M.A.L.E. (Formerly Employed Mothers at the Leading Edge, support organization), 226–227

Fernbank Museum of Natural History (Decatur, Ga.), 40

Fernbank Science Center (Decatur, Ga.), 40–41

Field Museum (website), 214–215

First aid chart, 179

Fisher-Price Family Registry, 6

Food allergies, 187–188

Food Allergy Network (support organization), 227

Formulas (baby), 5–6

Fort Worth Zoo, 63–64

Franklin Institute Science Museum (Philadelphia), 91

Franklin Park Zoo (Boston), 52

French Lick Springs Resort (French Lick, Ind.), 125–126

Full-Time Dads (newsletter), 207–208

G

Gas Appliance Manufacturers Association (GAMA), 31

Geographica (Washington, D.C.), 106

Geowhiz Day Camps, 160

Gerber Hot Lines, 237

"Getting Started with Food Allergies: A Guide for Parents" (booklet), 187–188

Ginsburg, Charles, 31

Girls' Life (magazine), 197

GrandParenting and Other Great Adventures (magazine), 204

Grandparents & Grandchildren's Camp (Raquette Lake, N.Y.), 163–164

Grandparents and grandchildren, vacations for, 163–167

GRANDTRAVEL, 164–165

Great Camp Sagamore (Raquette Lake, N.Y.), 144–145

Griffith Park (Los Angeles), 72

Grolier Books (book clubs), 194

Growing Child (newsletter), 208–209

Growing Parent (newsletter), 208–209

Growth chart, 172

"A Guide to Children's Literature and Disability" (booklet), 188

"A Guide to Your Children's Hearing" (booklet), 179

"Guidelines to Help Protect Abused and Neglected Children" (booklet), 179–180

Gymboree, 12–14

H

Hallmark Visitors Center (Kansas City, Mo.), 113

Hand in Hand (catalog), 21

Hayden Planetarium (New York City), 89

Headaches Hot Line, 237–238

Healthtex Immunization Chart, 6

Healthtouch (database), 180

Healthy Kids (magazine), 204

Healthy Mothers: Babies Best Start program (Atlanta), 180

Heard Museum (Phoenix), 93

Hearing problems, 179

HearthSong (catalog), 21

Heinz Baby Food Miracle Labels for Kids Program, 6–7

Herman Goelitz Candy Co. (Fairfield, Calif.), 114

Hertzberg Circus Museum (San Antonio), 97

High Sierra Family Vacation Camp (Los Altos, Calif.), 145–146

Holiday Inn SunSpree Resort

Lake Buena Vista (Fla.), 126–127

Holiday Inn SunSpree Resorts, 153–154

Holiday Inn Worldwide, 154–155

"Home Team Learning Activities," 180–181

Hook's American Drug Store Museum (Indianapolis), 70

Hot lines, 235–240

Houghton Mifflin Education Place (website), 215

Huggies, 7

I

Immunization schedules, 6

Indianapolis, Ind., attractions for children, 69–71

Indianapolis Motor Speedway Hall of Fame Museum, 70

Indianapolis Zoo, 70–71

Internet sites
for children, 214–219
for parents, 219–224

J

Jackson Square (New Orleans), 84

Job Survival Hot Line, 238

K

Keener, Patricia, 32–33

Kennesaw Civil War Museum (Kennesaw, Ga.), 41

Keshner, Judy, 185
Kid City (magazine), 197–198
Kid Pub (website), 215
KidNews (website), 216
Kids Com (website), 215
Kids Craft (website), 216
Kids Ink Children's Bookstore (Indianapolis), 71
Kids Ski Free/Stay Free Program (Red River Valley, N.M.), 146
KidSlope (Denver), 67–68
Kidspace (Los Angeles), 72–73
KidVantage Program, 8
Kohl Children's Museum (Wilmette, Ill.), 59
Kraft Kids Concerts at Ravinia (Highland Park, Ill.), 58–59

L
La Leche League Hot Line, 238
La Mansión del Rio (resort, San Antonio), 127–128
La Villita (San Antonio), 97
Ladybug (magazine), 198
Lambs Farm (Libertyville, Ill.), 59
Lands' End Kids' Catalog, 21–23
Le Petit Theatre du Vieux Carre (New Orleans), 84
Learn & Play (catalog), 23
Learning Disabilities Association of America (LDA), 188–189, 227–228
"Let's Talk About It" booklets, 181
Libraries, 115
Lincoln Park Zoo (Chicago), 59–60
Lite Board (website), 216
Lombard Street (San Francisco), 100
Los Angeles, Calif., attractions for children, 71–74
Los Angeles Children's Museum, 73
Los Angeles Zoo, 73
Louisiana Children's Museum (New Orleans), 84–85

M
Magazines, donating old, 203
Magic House (St. Louis), 114–116
Manic Moms (newsletter), 209
Marriott's Marco Island Resort, 128–129
Maryland Science Center and Planetarium, 44
McDonald's Museum (Des Plaines, Ill.), 60
McGruff (crime dog), 34–35
Mead Johnson Nutritionals, 5
Med Access (website), 222
Medela, Inc. (support organization), 228–229
Metro Washington Park Zoo (Portland, Ore.), 95–96

Metropolitan Museum of Art (New York City), 89–90

Metrozoo (Miami), 75–76

Miami, Fla., attractions for children, 75–78

Miami Seaquarium, 76

Miami Youth Museum, 76–77

Minneapolis–St. Paul, Minn., attractions for children, 78–80

Minnesota Children's Museum (St. Paul), 79

Minnesota Zoo, Apple Valley, Minn., 79–80

Minor Trips, 146–147

MOMS Club (support organization), 229

Monkey Jungle (Miami), 77

Monterey Bay Aquarium (Monterey, Ca.), 116–117

MOSI (science museum, Tampa, Fla.), 117–118

Mothering (magazine), 204

Mothers at Home (MAH, support organization), 229–230

Mothers of Preschoolers (MOPS, support organization), 230

Museum of Children's Art (San Francisco), 100–101

Museum of Flying (Los Angeles), 74

Museum of Modern Art (New York City), 90

Museum of Science (Boston), 52–53

Museum of Science and Industry (Chicago), 60–61

Museum of Science and Space Transit Planetarium (Miami), 77

My Word Book, 172–173

N

NASA (website), 216

Nashville, Tenn., attractions for children, 80–82

Nashville Toy Museum, 81

Nashville Zoo (Joelton, Tenn.), 81–82

National AIDS Hot Line, 238–239

National Aquarium (Baltimore, Md), 47

National Association for Gifted Children (NAGC, support organization), 230

National Association for Parents of the Visually Impaired, Inc. (NAPVI), 191, 230–231

National Black Child Development Institute (NBCDI), 231

National Braille Press, 189

National Center for Missing & Exploited Children, 231–232

National Immunization Information Hot Line, 239
National Information Center for Children and Youth with Disabilities (NICHCY), 189–190, 232
National Multiple Sclerosis Society (hot line), 239
National Organization of Single Mothers, Inc. (NOSM), 232–234
National Resource Center on Child Abuse and Neglect, 234
Natural History Museum of Los Angeles County (Los Angeles), 74
Navy Pier (Chicago), 61
Neglected children, 179–180
New England Aquarium (Boston), 53
New Orleans, La., attractions for children, 82–85
New Orleans Streetcar, 85
New York City, N.Y., attractions for children, 85–91
New York Hall of Science, 90
News Digests (NICHCY), 189
Nilsson, Lennart, 5
Noodle Kidoodle (toy store), 14
The Noodlehead Network (website), 217
Norfolk Waterside Marriott (resort, Norfolk, Va.), 129

O
Oakland (Calif.) Zoo, 101
Obstetricians, 182
Once Upon a Child (store), 14
"100 Most Frequently Asked Questions & Answers About Your Baby" (pamphlet), 174
One Step Ahead (catalog), 23–24, 30
On-line services, 218
Oregon Museum of Science and Industry (OMSI, Portland), 96
Oriental Trading Company, Inc. (catalog), 24
Orlando Science Center, 118
OshKosh B'Gosh Genuine Parents Club, 8
Our Kids (website), 222

P
Pacific Science Center (Seattle), 103
Parent and Preschooler (newsletter), 209
Parent Involvement Handbook, 181–182
Parent Soup (website), 22, 222
Parenting (magazine), 205
Parents' Choice (magazine), 205
Parents Guides (NICHCY), 190

Parents in a Pressure Cooker (Bluestein and Collins), 182–183

Parents Place (website), 222–223

Parrot Jungle and Gardens (Miami), 78

Pediatric Primer (Children's Medical Center of Dallas), 31–32

Perfectly Safe (catalog), 24

Philadelphia, Pa., attractions for children, 91–93

Philadelphia Zoo, 92

Phoenix, Ariz., attractions for children, 93–94

Phoenix Zoo, 94

Pier 39 (San Francisco), 101

Play and pizza joints, 154

Play It Again Sports (sporting-goods store), 14

Playwear Sizer Guide, 6

Please Touch Museum (Philadelphia), 92–93

"Pocket Guide to Federal Help for Individuals with Disabilities," 190–191

Portland, Ore., attractions for children, 95–96

Practical Advice for Parents, 32

Practical Advice for Parents of Teens, 32

Prenatal care pamphlets, 184

Preteen vacations, 159–162

Psych Central (website), 223

Purina Farms (Gray Summit, Mo.), 118–119

Puzzle Archive (website), 217

R

Radisson Hotels, 155–156

Raindrop (website), 217

Ranger Rick (magazine), 198

Rawhide's 1880 Western Town (Scottsdale, Ariz.), 94

"Reading and Your Adolescent" (booklet), 184–185

Resort vacations, 123–137

Right Start, The (catalog), 24–25

Ritz-Carlton Hotels and Resorts, 156

Rocking Horse Ranch (Highland, N.Y.), 131–132

Rockville Creative Learning, Inc. (website), 223

S

"Safe & Sound for Baby" (brochure), 185

Safe Sitter program, 32–34

Safety, and hidden home hazards, 30–31

Safety pamphlets, 34

Safety tips, child, 28–29

San Antonio, Tex., attractions for children, 97–98

San Antonio Zoo, 97–98

San Francisco, Calif., attractions for children, 98–102

San Francisco Zoo, 101–102

Sanvita lactation program, 228–229

Scholastic Place (website), 217

Science Museum of Minnesota (St. Paul), 80

The Science Place (Fair Park, Tex.), 64

SCITREK (playground, Atlanta), 42

Scottish Rite Children's Medical Center, 29

Scottish Rite Children's Resource Line, 239

Scrapbooks, travel, 165

Scruff (crime dog), 34–35

Scruff Beats the Scary Streets Comic-Activity Book, 34–35

Sealed with a Kiss (SWAK) travel kits, 130

Sears, Roebuck and Co., 8

Seattle, Wash., attractions for children, 102–105

Seattle Aquarium, 103–104

Seattle Children's Theatre, 104

Second-hand stores, 13

Sesame Street Magazine, 198–199

Shedd Acquarium (Chicago), 61–62

The Sierra Club, 165–166

Single Mothers by Choice (newsletter), 210–211

SingleMother (newsletter), 210

Ski NH Family Pass (N.H.), 147

The Small Street Journal, 35

Smithsonian Institution (Washington, D.C), 106–108

Smugglers' Notch (resort, Vt.), 132–133

Sonesta Beach Resort (Key Biscayne, Fla.), 133–134

Song books, 183

Space Center (Houston, Tex.), 119

Special-needs children resources, 187–194

website for parents of, 222

Spider (magazine), 199

Squaw Valley USA, 147–148

St. Louis Children's Museum, 114–116

St. Paul–Minneapolis, Minn., attractions for children, 78–80

"Starting School: A Parent's Guide to the Kindergarten Year" (Keshner), 185

Staten Island Children's Museum, 91

Stone Mountain Park (Ga.), 42–43

"Story of Money, The" (publication), 173

Stride Rite Progression Fit System, 8–9
Sundial Beach Resort (Sanibel Island, Fla.), 134–135
Support organizations, 225–234
SWAK (Sealed with a Kiss) travel kits, 130
Swissôtel, 156

T
Talking books, 187
Target (store), 15
Teen Adventure, 160–161
Teen vacations, 159–162
"10 Ways to Help Your Children Become Better Readers" (pamphlet), 174
Tennessee State Museum (Nashville), 82
The Pointe Hilton at Squaw Peak (Phoenix, Ariz.), 129–131
Theodore Tugboard On-line Activity Center (website), 218
Thomas H. Kean New Jersey State Aquarium (Camden, N.J.), 93
3-2-1 Contact (magazine), 199
Tide Clothes Line (website), 223–224
Toys, 6
"Toys & Play" (booklet), 185–186
Toys "R" Us (store), 15

Toys to Grow On (catalog), 25
Travel kits, 130
Travel scrapbooks, 165
"Travel with Baby" (booklet), 186
Triaminic Parents Club, 9
Tribesman Resort (Branson, Mo.), 135
Turtle (magazine), 200
TwinLine (hotline), 239–240
The Twins Foundation, 234
Twins Magazine, 206
The Tyler Place (Highgate Springs, Vt.), 135–137

U
U.S. Consumer Product Safety Commission, 173, 186
United States Mint, 68
University of Pennsylvania Cancer Center Resource (website), 224

V
Vermont Teddy Bear Company (Shelburne, Vt.), 120

W
Wacky Pirate Cruise (Chicago), 62
Warren River Expeditions, Inc. (Salmon, Idaho), 166–167

Washington, D.C., attractions for children, 105–108

Waterville Valley adventure vacation (N.H.), 148–149

Weather Machine (Portland, Ore.), 96

The Welcome Addition Club, 9

Welcome Home (newsletter), 211

Westin Hotels, 157

Whitewater Academy (Moab, Utah), 162

Wildlife Camp, 162

"Wishes and Rainbows" comic books, 173

Woodland Park Zoo (Seattle), 104–105

Working Mother (magazine), 206

World of Coca-Cola (Atlanta), 43

Y

Yahooligans (website), 219

YMCA of the USA (hot line), 240

Your Child's Wellness Newsletter (newsletter), 211

The Yuckiest Site on the Internet (website), 219

Z

Zany Brainy (toy store), 16

Zoo Atlanta, 43–44